# Really Dead?

## The Israeli Brain-Death Controversy
## 1967-1986

# Naftali Moses

ISBN 9789659169504

# A Word about Academic Publishing

This book is based upon my doctoral dissertation. I submitted it for review to Bar-Ilan University in 2008 and on its merits received my degree with highest honors. Like many newly-minted PhDs, I felt that the fruits of my academic labor were worthy of sharing with a broader audience. Unfortunately, in terms of publishing economics, my timing was a bit off. Although two different academic publishers offered me contracts for this book, something about signing over my copyright for little more than seeing my name in print (let alone the question of "subventions") sat ill with me. After not little soul-searching, I decided to self-publish my own work.

The question is not one of remuneration, but rather of the effective distribution of knowledge. I am not convinced that in today's digital age the academic need let middlemen (even if they are the most honest of brokers) stand between his work and the public. Those interested in the issue will find much material for consideration in the (rightly) publically available article by Harvard Law School professor Steven Shavell, "Should Copyright of Academic Works Be Abolished?" (http://cyber.law.harvard.edu/sites/cyber.law.harvard.edu/files/Copyright%207-17HLS-2009.pdf).

In the interest of efficiency, in place of a printed index, a searchable PDF file of the book is available for free download at www.tragic-death.com.

After some study of the subject, I also composed the book's interior layout on my own. I chose to set the book in 12 point Palatino Linotype, which made for more pages, but hopefully easier reading. I know that I have left some "orphans" and "widows" behind and may have not created the most esthetically perfect of works. I apologize to those who may be distracted from the content by the occasional breach of typographical convention and wish them a speedy recovery.

# Acknowledgments

My doctoral thesis advisor, under whose tutelage this book's research was conducted and first written, Dr. Noah Efron, is an ideal scholar devoted to truth and good works. He offered critiques that made this work much better than anything I could have produced without them. The fact that he is only a single person is one of the stronger arguments that can be made for the cloning of humans.

The staffs of the Israeli libraries where I researched this work were always helpful. Special appreciation goes to those who work at one of the hidden gems of Judaic research—the library of Yeshivat Har Etzion where I spent many productive months.

My good friend and award-winning photographer Abba Richman designed the book cover for me.

Of course, Leah, my long-suffering wife who has stood behind me for years (often wondering aloud when I would finish my doctorate and finally 'get a real job'), deserves the most thanks of all for her support and love.

Sadly, since I have begun this project, four of its principals have left this world for the next. Rabbis Waldenburg, Shapira, and Eliyahu, three luminaries of the religious world, all passed away. I was fortunate to meet with an aging, but still feisty, Professor Dan Michaeli only months before he died. My beloved teacher, Rabbi Shimon Gershon Rosenberg (Shagar), from whom I absorbed much of the little Torah that I know, also passed away while I was working on this

# Acknowledgements

project. I hope that some of what is contained herein may serve, in a small way, to perpetuate their contributions to Israeli (and Jewish) religious and intellectual life.

# In Memoriam

I have written an historical study of death. As history, by stepping back, this study aims at understanding and explicating its subject. But horribly, the completion of my doctoral work coincided with a death which has indelibly marked the lives of me and family well beyond any intellectual apprehension. My sixteen-year-old son, Avraham David, was cruelly murdered in what has become known as the 'Merkaz HaRav massacre'. He and seven other youths were gunned down by an Arab terrorist for being Jews in a Jewish state wanting to learn Jewish texts.

My son was a budding Torah scholar, already at sixteen dedicated to a life of learning. An intellectually gifted boy, he devoted sixteen hours a day to the study of Bible, Talmud and *halakhah* with the utmost seriousness. The hours and hours we spent learning (and, in the nature of *havrutot*, often arguing) together were one of the joys of my life. Over the summer just before he turned 15, he sat with me for the days it took to canvas twenty years worth of unindexed Israeli medical journals, helping to sort and photocopy. I know that he abided his father's study of the vagaries of history, sociology and philosophy with a degree of equanimity combined with puzzlement as to what I could possibly find interesting (and even worthwhile) in these foreign lands. "Turn it over and over, for all is within it" (*Avot* 5:22). I can picture him still smiling indulgently from above at my stubbornness in seeking knowledge beyond the walls of the *bet-*

# In Memoriam

*midrash*. How, then, can I dedicate the academically-tainted fruits of such study to his memory?

Rather, I offer my hope that increased dialogue between competing camps in the struggle over defining death and transplanting organs may spare others the pain of loss known only to those left behind to mourn the dead that they loved so deeply. In my son's memory, I hope that this book may help, in at least a small way, to bring about this sorely needed dialogue. And with this thought, I'm sure that even he would not argue.

To my dear boy, Avraham David, may your memory be a blessing.

Naftali Moses
Efrat, Israel
nm@tragic-death.com

# Contents

Introduction                                              11

## Section I
## A History of Brain Death in
## Israel
### 1967-1986

1. The First Heart Transplants                            25
2. Determining Death: Early Halakhic
   Responses                                              51
3. Conceptualizing Death                                  75
4. Public Concern Over Death                             101
5. Continued Halakhic Debate                             113
6. The Resuscitated Patient                              135
7. New Halakhic Considerations                           161
8. A Second Heart Transplant                             185
9. A Growing Consensus                                   195
Preliminary Conclusions                                  213

## Section II
## The Israeli Chief Rabbinate
## Decision

10. Approaching the Rabbinate                             217
11. The Rabbinate Decision                                231
12. The Hadassah Protocol                                 253
13. Death as a Status                                     263
14. Reactions to the Rabbinate                            295
15. Really Dead                                           328
Appendix                                                  353
Bibliography                                              359

# Introduction

"Historically, we have assumed that the death of any living thing is a fact we discover, and not a status we confer."[1]

Death, in an age of ever increasingly complex medical intervention, has remained an enigma. With each turn of the biotechnology wheel it has become even more curiously opaque. As the technical possibilities of resuscitation and the transplantation of live organs from dead bodies have become commonplace throughout the West, the complicated ways of understanding the end of life—biologically, socially, religiously and legally—have become themselves all the more complex. Since the mid-1960s, ethical problems associated with the removal of living organs from patients-*cum*-donors have been debated by doctors and lawyers, religious and secular ethics scholars. Already at the dawn of the transplant era, international conferences addressed the questions surrounding the need to declare such patients dead before removing their organs.[2] Early on in the transplant project, new neurologically-based criteria for death were devised in order to allow resuscitated comatose patients to be declared dead and their organs harvested for use in the living.[3]

While the transplantation of organs like eyes and kidneys raised a number of ethical problems, it was the transplantation of the heart itself (first in 1967) which focused the most attention on the problematics of declaring death for these comatose patients. The removal of a still-beating heart from a neurologically "dead" patient presented

# Really Dead?

doctors devoted to organ transplantation with an ethical problem of a different magnitude. How could a *living* heart be harvested when for so long continued cardiac function was emblematic of continued life—even in dying patients? Was the removal of the heart the sacrifice of one life in an attempt to save another?

The introduction of a new criterion for establishing death was meant to solve these ethical problems. "Brain-death," variously understood as actual necrosis of some (or all) of the brain or the loss of some (or all) brain-function, became an integral part of the organ transplantation project. Brain-death enabled doctors to ethically remove organs from the comatose by labeling these patients "dead," despite the presence of viable organs and other signs of life in their bodies. Brain-death became a new way of *conceptualizing* death—as the loss of cerebral neurological activity and not as the necrosis of vital organs or loss of cardio-pulmonary function. In the end its adoption presented doctors with *dead patients* in *living bodies*.

Philosophically, questions arose as to whether this new criterion was a scientific refinement of obsolete older criteria for determining death or just a "convenient" redefinition of death meant to serve the transplant project.[4] The tension over the *meaning* of brain-death opened debate over the meaning of death itself. Was death a biological state, a philosophic concept, a social category or perhaps a synthesis of all three?

The debate over brain-death in the West has played out in any number of philosophical, medical, legal, and religious works, and has even generated second-tier works devoted to examining the history of the struggles over redefining death.[5] This study is devoted to describing the brain-death debate in Israeli society over a critical twenty-year period: from the beginning of the Western heart-transplant project in 1967 until the establishment of the first Israeli heart-transplant unit in 1987. One of the factors that made the Israeli discourse on the ethics of brain-death and the meaning of death itself unique was (and still is) the role that Jewish law (*halakhah*) played. Not only did doctors, lawyers, and legislators contribute to the debates surrounding the new neurological death, but rabbis and halakhic scholars voiced a variety of halakhic opinions on the medical-ethical-religious difficulties which arose out of the need to re-examine death in light of heart transplantation. These halakhic opinions offered diverse views of the ethics of transplantation, the interplay of science and religion, and the understanding of death through the lens of Jewish law.

The voice of the *halakhah* was, in fact, so important that on the eve of initiating the first Israeli heart-transplant program in Jerusalem's Hadassah Medical Center, both the Center's director-general, Professor Shmuel Pinhas, and the director-general of the Israeli Health Ministry, Professor Dan Michaeli, turned to the Israeli Chief Rabbinate seeking halakhic affirmation that brain-death was a Jewishly acceptable method for determining the death of potential heart donors. In years previous, the relationship between the Israeli secular-scientific elite and the rabbinic community had been stormily tense.[6] The fact that those involved in the translant project turned to the Rabbinate was more than the offer of an olive branch. It represented a unique opportunity to mend fences and join forces in a cutting edge mission to save lives. It quickly became, though, an opportunity lost. The promise of medical-rabbinic cooperation was quashed when the *qualified* halakhic permission granted by the Chief Rabbinate to undertake heart transplants was taken by the Health Ministry and Hadassah as *carte blanche* halakhic acceptance of brain-death. Pinhas and Michaeli used this as an opportunity for the heart-transplant project to commence as they saw fit.

The Chief Rabbinate's halakhic decision (*psaq halakhah*) serves as a focal point for this study. In the book's second section it is thickly described and analyzed. Yet in order to fully understand this *psaq* and

# Really Dead?

its significance, it is important to examine the Israeli discourse over brain-death which preceded it. This discourse was comprised of the opinions of doctors, legislators, lawyers, judges, academics and rabbis who responded to the challenges, both practical and conceptual, that brain-death presented. Over a period of twenty years these opinions were expressed in "real-time" as part of parliamentary debates over transplants; in articles published in professional journals; as part of academic research; in *pisqe halakhah* and halakhic analysis. All of this crucial backstory is the subject of the book's first section.

The brain-death discourse in Israel over this initial period was marked by great conceptual variety. In debating the ethical challenges presented by organ transplants and brain-dead organ donors, the very *meaning* of death and its implications were understood quite differently by many of its participants. For some, death meant biological fact; for others, it was a medically informed estimate regarding the possibility for the recovery of biological function; yet others saw death—exposed as it was under the lens of live organ harvesting—as a social or religious construct. Lying beneath this conceptual mosaic of opinion were also statements about the boundaries between public policy, law, philosophy and medical practice, the place of ethics in science, and the role of Jewish law in Israel's public sphere.

Each of the diverse documents I discuss and analyze reveals its author's often unique understanding of one or more of these issues; each is connected to understanding the meaning and role of brain-death in modern medical practice; each sought to solve the ethical problems that its author envisioned as stemming from this new death. In Israeli Medical Association (IMA) symposia we find discussions of the legal and halakhic implications of organ transplantation. Their participants presented opposing viewpoints on the ethics of human experimentation and medical progress. Doctors discussed these same issues in testimony before Knesset (the Israeli parliment) committees as well.

# Introduction

Knesset plenum protocols offer an opportunity to see how government officials defended the earliest Israeli heart transplant as ethically sound while misinterpreting the very ethical basis for this claim. In published articles and halakhic responsa, medical practitioners and rabbis presented alternative (and at times competing) conceptualizations of the comatose dying patient. For some, he was a donor-in-waiting — a patient whose ethical mass diminished as he moved closer to final death. For others, this liminal patient continued to exert a consistent moral pull on his care-givers. His unsettled state called for ethical resolution with only him, the immediate patient, in mind. This patient was to be treated as an end in himself — either through healing him or letting him die.

In the rabbinic literature we find diverse understandings of the very same traditional halakhic criteria for the determination of death. The role of respiration — the seeming universally accepted sign of death for the *halakhah* — was alternatively understood as only one part of total somatic collapse; as a once clear sign which modern resuscitative technologies rendered doubtful; or as harbinger of modern neurological death. The ways in which these rabbinic scholars conceptualized traditional halakhic sources influenced the ways in which they related to the modern medical project of heart transplantation and its accompanying new "definition" of death. There were those who endorsed heart transplants as *halakhically* sound life-saving procedures and those who condemned them as little more than medical murder (!).

This multi-voiced discourse, then, was hardly harmonious. Ideas central to the debate over organ transplants (such as the status of dying patients) were so variously conceptualized that despite numerous efforts at dialogue in IMA-sponsored symposia and other venues, little actually took place. The slippery conceptual fluidity surrounding the idea of death in an age of "living cadavers" or "neurologically

# Really Dead?

empty" yet living bodies made it difficult for the participants in this discourse to effectively share their ideas.[7] The Israeli brain-death discourse from this period, in its multifaceted discord, accurately reflected conceptual disarray. Brain-death uprooted accepted understandings of death and of the medical-ethical status of the comatose patient. As Margaret Lock has argued, brain-death created a new, confusing type of patient, one who crossed until-then normal biological-cultural borders.

> The brain-dead patient-cadaver is a particularly complex hybrid, constituted from culture and nature while in transition from life to death; both person and nonperson, entirely dependent on a machine for existence.[8]

It should come as no surprise, then, that the reactions of those who dealt with this new medical reality were themselves complex and, even, at times, confused. As medical practitioners, lawyers, rabbis and academics became more familiar with this "complex hybrid" they offered different interpretations and conceptualizations of him as patient qua ethical subject—at times directly, at times by discussing the meaning and definition of death itself. It was the hybrid nature of the subject which allowed those who concerned themselves with brain-death—whether as politicians, lawyers, judges, doctors, rabbis or academics—to offer such varying and competing approaches to, and conceptions of, these patient cadavers. As a result of these *conceptual* differences (sometimes along with prejudicial attitudes) the discourse over this long period was often disjointed, with little real communication among many of its participants.

Taken together, these varied contributions constitute the totality of the Israeli discourse on brain-death for this period. All of the documents presented in the first section detail some aspect of the cacophonous, discordant discourse surrounding brain-death in Israel since its introduction into Western medical practice, yet before it became a medical-ethical *necessity* here. Only the establishment (long awaited by some, much feared by others) of an Israeli heart transplant unit would bring brain-death into focus as actual death. To remove a beating heart for transplant without first declaring the donor dead — *really* dead — would be a moral impossibility.

The push for establishing this medical program helped to silence all the noisy, multifaceted, multivoiced discourse into something *seemingly* much more monolithic. With the success of the second stage of heart transplantation in the United States and England (afforded primarily by advances in overcoming the rejection of donor organs),[9] the mid-1980s saw brain-death become part of normative medical practice in these countries.[10] Understanding donor death *as* brain-death was a vital part of the transplant project, so those who sought to move forward with transplants needed to consolidate the *public* acceptance of brain-death (for it was only the general public who could provide donor organs).[11] The later documents discussed in the first part of this study attest to the fact that doctors, judges, and public servants were well aware that this was the case and were searching for ways to make this happen. Rather than focus on the diversity of opinion and rich philosophical range of views which had been expressed by those who supported brain-death, it seems that its practical adoption by others in the West was seen as enough to warrant its medical use in Israel as well.

However, some felt that the last hurdle left to gaining *public* support for brain-death and the organ transplant project lay in gaining rabbinic support for each. This was the basic rationale behind the appeal to the Chief Rabbinate. The respective queries of the Health Ministry and Hadassah Medical Center along with the Rabbinate's response are analyzed in the book's second section. Despite the efforts made at reaching a medical-halakhic consensus, none was in fact attained. Instead of fostering cooperation and aiding the quest for organ donation, the handling of the Rabbinate's decision by the Health Ministry and Hadassah resulted in mutual frustration and suspicion. In the end the Rabbinate would even rescind their qualified halakhic permission accepting brain-death and allowing for heart transplants in Israel. The analysis of the decision, including its history, content and repercussions, helps to explain why this occurred.

Aside from certain incidents which fostered mistrust between the medical staff and the Chief Rabbinate, the responsibility for their "missing of the minds" lay in the polysemic nature of death itself which kept bobbing to the surface despite efforts to ignore it. The fundamentaly confusing hybrid nature of the patient-corpse-donor allowed each side to conceptualize death itself quite differently and prevented them from reaching agreement on how to move forward *together* with the heart-transplant project. As I will explain, the Rabbinate viewed death as a *halakhic status*, while Hadassah's medical staff understood it (at least superficially) as a biological *state*.[12]

The conceptual confusion surrounding death did not simply disappear even as the use of brain-death criteria became an accepted medical practice. The essential tension between those who held death to be a biological state and those who claimed it was a cultural/legal/religious status was never undone. The confusing liminal hybrids born of the need for living organs and dead donors had helped to expose the uncertainty of death's meaning in modern medical practice. A simple dismissal of this conceptual uncertainty was impossible—in the end it would out.

This study is devoted to detailing the very complexity of death in the modern world as manifested in the Israeli discourse over brain-death. By focusing both longitudinally on a public discourse that lasted twenty years, as well as examining in depth one specific event—the Chief Rabbinate's *psaq* on heart-transplants—I show just how important *conceptualizations* of seemingly solid facts can be. Brain-death presented medical practitioners and ethicists with complex and confusing puzzles which required them to rethink their seemingly settled concepts of biology, culture, and science—along with the relationships between them.

Because Hadassah's medical team and the Health Ministry endeavored to medicalize death by presenting it as a *biological fact*, in the end they failed to gain full rabbinic support for heart transplants. They wanted to suppress the conceptual problems that brain-death raised. The Rabbinate itself failed to properly articulate its own conceptions of death and mistakenly assumed that they could work together with Hadassah's medical staff without doing so. By attempting to co-opt a stance that privileged a biological understanding of death, the Rabbinate effectively made their own halakhic concerns redundant in the eyes of those who sought to ensure complete medicalization of death. The Rabbinate's religious concerns may have depended upon biological categories and facts, but were far from identical with them. The end result of this *conceptual* mis-match tempered the success of the transplant project by robbing it of much needed cross-cultural support.

While the transplant project has indeed marched on in Israel as it has in other Western countries, this in itself has not served to lessen confusion over the meanings of death. Competing conceptualizations of death seem to have impacted the degree of donor willingness to contribute organs for life-saving transplants. Without addressing the conceptual difficulties surrounding death, I believe that this situation will not improve. The question of what it means, in our technologically advanced age, to be *really* dead is still worthy of consideration. Once one of life's only two certainties, death has made a comeback. It

# Really Dead?

is again something of the mystery it once was. This historical study affords a view of how this happened in Israel.

---

[1] Ben Rich, *Strange Bedfellows: How Medical Jurisprudence Has Influenced Medical Ethics and Medical Practice* (New York: Kluwer Academic 2001), 119.

[2] See G. E. W. Wolstenholme and Maeve O'Connor, eds., *Ethics in Medical Progress: With Special Attention to Transplantation 1966 (Ciba Foundation Symposium)* (Boston: Little, Brown and Company, 1966); V. Fattorusso, ed., *Heart Transplantation* (Liege, Belgium: Desoer Publishers, 1968).

[3] The most famous and influential of these were those which came to be known as the "Harvard criteria". They were published by The Ad-Hoc Committee of the Harvard Medical School to Examine the Definition of Death Ad-Hoc, "A Definition of Irreversible Coma," *JAMA* 205, no. 6 (1968). See Belkin, "Death before Dying " (PhD. Thesis, Harvard University, 2000) for an in-depth historical study of their development and use. Belkin's article, "Brain Death and the Historical Understanding of Bioethics," *Journal of the History of Medicine* 58 (2003), distills his thesis.

[4] Belkin argued that brain-death was part of a search for ethical care of patients, but Giacomini and others argued that the latter was the case. (Mita Giacomini, "A Change of Heart and a Change of Mind? Technology and the Redefinition of Death in 1968," *Social Science and Medicine* 44, no. 10 ([1997]).

[5] See the bibliography for many of the former. The latter include, among others, Margaret Lock, *Twice Dead* (Berkley: University of California Press, 2001), Belkin's study and Giacomini's article.

[6] This query came after years of tension between Israeli secularists and Jewish religious groups over the proper place of Jewish law in Israeli society in general and in medical practice in particular. The Israeli Medical Association and the Health Ministry on the one side and groups of concerned religious Jews and rabbis on the other had been struggling since the early days of the State over the proper post-mortem treatment of Jewish bodies—each accusing the other of abandoning ethics in the pursuit of their own narrow interests. (This long confrontation even led to physical violence against doctors who at times required police protection to carry out what in their opinion were medically necessary autopsies.) See section II, chapter 1 for a discussion of the reasons that these medical bodies appealed to the Rabbinate.

[7] Belkin used the phrase "neurologically empty bodies" to describe the brain-dead (Belkin, "Death before Dying ", 146), and noted how the Harvard criteria themselves could not fully focus on one fixed meaning of death (142).

[8] Lock, *Twice Dead*, 40.

[9] See R.C. and J.P. Swazey Fox, *Spare Parts* (New York: Oxford University Press, 1992), 3.

[10] Despite this, the conceptual understanding of death was still not settled. See the often cited Stuart J. Youngner, C. Seth Landefeld, Claudia J. Coulton, M. Juknialis, and Mark Leary, "Brain Death and Organ Retrieval: A Cross-Sectional Survey of Knowledge and Concepts among Heath Professionals," *JAMA* 261, no. 15 (1989). Even more recently, the literature shows that the controversy over the meaning of death is far from settled. See Stuart J. Youngner, Robert M. Arnold and Renie Schapiro eds., *The Definition of Death: Contemporary Controversies* (Baltimore: Johns Hopkins University Press, 1999); Alexander Morgan Capron, "Brain Death—Well Settled yet Still Unresolved," *The New England Journal of Medicine* 344, no. 16 (2001); Lock, *Twice Dead* ; D.A. Shewmon and Elisabeth Seitz Shewmon, "The Semiotics of Death and Its Medical Implications," in *Brain Death and Disorders of Consciousness*, eds. Calixto Machado and D. Alan Shewmon (New York: Kluwer Academic Publishers, 2004); Kunin, "Brain Death: Revisiting the Rabbinic Opinions in Light of Current Medical Knowledge," *Tradition* 38, no. 4 (2004); Winston Chiong, "Brain Death without Definitions," *The Hastings Center Report* 35, no. 6 (2005).

[11] Of course, other options were theoretically available – like removing organs from prisoners, actually suggested by the early, influential transplant surgeon Thomas Starzl (see Lock, *Twice Dead*, 92) and actually practiced in China. A 2001 NY Times article reported: "Executed prisoners are China's primary source of transplantable organs, though few of the condemned, if any, consent to having their organs removed, people involved with the process say. Some of the unwitting donors may even be innocent, having been executed as part of a surge of executions propelled by accelerated trials and confessions that sometimes were extracted through                         torture" (http://query.nytimes.com/gst/fullpage.html?sec=health&res=9500EED71538F932A2 5752C1A9679C8).

[12] The actual consequences of this conceptual disconnect are discussed in Section II.

# Section I
## A History of Brain Death in Israel
## 1967-1986

# 1

# 1967-1968
# The First Heart Transplants

On December 5th 1968, Professor Morris Levy, chief thoracic surgeon in Tel Aviv's Beilinson Medical Center, performed the first heart transplant in Israel. His patient, Yitshaq Sulam, was a 41-year old father of four who worked as an elevator operator. The next day's headlines trumpeted Levy's operation and the media closely followed Sulam's progress in the following weeks. Unfortunately, Sulam died two weeks after the operation was proclaimed a medical milestone for the young Jewish state. This operation joined the many early heart transplants performed in the Western world soon after Christian Barnard's efforts the previous year in South Africa catapulted the surgeon and his achievement into the public eye.[1] While Barnard became an overnight celebrity[2], Levy's turn in the limelight was tainted with public ambivalence. After the initial flush of national pride at his achievement, his operation became the focus of harsh public criticism.

The Sephardic Chief Rabbi, R. Yitshaq Nissim, for example, was quoted as declaring the operation an act of "fame and glory for Israel's doctors". Soon after, though, he withdrew his support, claiming that it was based on misinformation. The Ashkenazi Chief Rabbi, R. Yehudah Unterman, expressed his doubts over the procedure due to

# Really Dead?

the risks involved for the patients undergoing such an operation.[3] The hospital staff tried to guard the donor's identity, but in the small Jewish state it took only a few days to narrow the options down to two trauma victims. Each had died the day before the transplant was performed. Their families both expressed anger and dismay that the heart of their loved one may have been taken without their consent; one threatened both legal action and to "organize a sit-it on the steps of the Health Ministry."[4] Unlike in South Africa some months earlier, heart transplants in Israel would not be eagerly welcomed by all. The idea of organ transplantation was quite culturally loaded—especially for more religiously traditional Israelis who constituted the majority of the country's population.[5]

In the Knesset, the issue of post-mortem operations in general had been hotly debated for over a decade and would continue, for years to come, to be a cause of serious conflict between representatives of religious and secular parties. (These operations pose a variety of *halakhic* problems regarding proper respect for the dead and proper burial of all body parts. The Religious-Zionist and *Haredi* (non-Zionist ultra-orthodox) political parties in Israel have spent much time and energy seeking to insure that autopsies would be performed in accordance with *halakhah*.)[6] Just three weeks previously, hospital directors had been accused by Knesset Member Shmuel Lawrence (*Agudat Yisrael*) of meeting secretly to discuss ways of circumventing Health Ministry regulations which required family consent for post-mortem operations.[7] One week after Sulam died, the entire heart-transplant procedure was debated by the Knesset plenum and the general issue was moved to the Public Services Committee for further discussion.[8] As I will explain, a large part of the debate would focus on how donor death should be established.

Levy continued a successful surgical career, but he would attempt only one more heart transplant, ten years hence in 1978. His second patient, a 23-year-old Israeli Arab, died a month after receiving his new heart. This operation was greeted by a nearly unanimous chorus of criticism. Even the Israel Medical Association questioned Levy's decision to perform the transplant.[9] The initial bloom of excitement over heart transplantation had by then long passed. Most of the medical establishment throughout Israel (and the world) concurred that immunological difficulties needed to be solved before heart transplants could become normative medical procedure.[10]

In the intervening years, however, brain-death criteria had been quietly formulated and accepted by both the Health Ministry and the IMA. Although periodically in the public eye, it was not until the mid-Eighties that the debate over determination of death reappeared more distinctly in public debate. Then too it was in connection to heart transplantation. Like elsewhere, in Israel too, brain-death was closely tied to organ transplants, both theoretically and practically. Public concern with determination of death in Israel would center nearly exclusively on heart transplants.

This chapter traces the development of the earliest Israeli discourse on brain-death. It focuses on a number of responses to the introduction of neurologically measured death in these very first attention-getting heart-transplant procedures. The commentaries of several Israel doctors and politicians on this new medical concept and its ethical challenges are discussed. These early reactions provide us with a template for much of the Israeli discourse in the ensuing twenty years: On the one hand, there was lively debate encompassing medical, ethical, and *halakhic* opinion. On the other hand, divergent conceptions of brain death did not lead to concilatory attempts at cooperation by the concerned parties. These early medical procedures raised not a few problems; those who attempted to answer them came up with quite different solutions.

# Really Dead?

Some nine months before his historic operation, Levy had taken part in an Israeli Medical Association sponsored symposium on heart transplants. The symposium dealt with the myriad problems raised by such procedures – paying close attention to the legal and *halakhic* questions involved. Unusually, the full proceedings were published in the IMA's newsletter a short time later.[11] This was one of the first published responses by the Israeli medical establishment to brain-death.[12]

The symposium included presentations by a number of medical specialists including Levy himself, as well as by Rabbi Baruch Rabinowitz (then the municipal rabbi of Holon—a small coastal town) and Aaron Polonski, a professor of law at Tel Aviv University. Interestingly, the participants spent most of the evening discussing the *halakhic* implications of the procedure.[13] The first presentation was given by a cardiologist. He felt that heart replacement could indeed become a viable method of treatment for those facing heart failure. The first question posed to him by the panel's moderator pertained to the problem of defining death. His answer referenced the CIOMS Conference of 1966 where neurological criteria for death of organ donors had been advanced for the first time.

> Professor [H.] Neufeld (cardiologist): This is a difficult medical-philosophical-legal question, more than a therapeutic matter. We train the young generation and also ourselves to make every effort at keeping the patient and his heart resuscitated using all the methods at our disposal ... without any concern for other outcomes. I believe that practically, only after we have spent a long time at our efforts, we have tried to resuscitate the heart, and have failed, only then can we declare the patient dead.[14]

Neufeld went on to question whether the use of a flat EEG as a clinical indicator of death was actually sufficient. (He cited a reported case where such an indication had been proven wrong).[15]

The next speaker, the Chief of Surgery from Rambam Hospital in Haifa, Professor David Erlik, continued to discuss the problem of pronouncing death. He claimed that if the EEG (referred to by Neufeld) had indeed been flat there was no chance that such a patient could have lived beyond a few days.

> … a [truly] decerebrate patient can only be kept alive through artificial means for perhaps a few more hours, maybe another day or two, but he is decerebrate. He is sentenced to death.[16]

He argued that such a patient was not really alive. The resuscitation machinery attached to such a comatose patient suffering from severe brain trauma only presented a picture of, in Erlik's words, "imaginary life. The machine is alive. Not the patient."[17]

Professor Levy continued the discussion and agreed that the loss of both heart UU_and_ brain function were needed to indicate the actual death of a patient.

> If we check the readings of the ECG and the EEG, both of them show us a flat line.[18]

Curiously, only a few months before performing the first Israeli heart transplant, he also expressed his opinion that the solution for terminal loss of heart function lay in the direction of artificial heart development and not transplantation.

# Really Dead?

Rabbi Rabinowitz was the next speaker. He introduced the relevant *halakhic* categories used to describe the injured and dying. When discussing the state of the *gosses*[19], he stressed that while it was absolutely forbidden to hasten the death of such an individual, there may not be an obligation to lengthen the life of such a patient.

> If we extend the life of one who is already in his death throes (*gosses*) when there is no longer any chance for him to live through the artificial means of machinery, is this something permitted?[20]

R. Rabinowitz felt that Jewish law needed to find the "dividing line" between life and death. He alluded to two different Talmudic opinions as to what that was: cessation of breathing or cessation of heart function.[21] While he suggested that the *halakhah* had traditionally preferred the latter, he stressed that this could no longer serve as a modern indicator of death as advances in medical technology had allowed for resuscitation of those who had lost either function. Therefore, he turned to the medical professionals and asked them how they would define the border between life and death, suggesting that their answer could serve the *halakhah* as well.[22]

In response to the continuing discussion, he described a case where he felt that Jewish law would permit the removal of organs from a patient. If a patient had lost one or more organs necessary for life (the entire brain or both lungs) and was being artificially resuscitated, he felt that

> After all this has occurred, and the individual has ceased to live, and there is only the option to keep him alive through the use of machinery, then I would be able to say that we can stop the machinery, and after the

heart has stopped beating, I would say that it is permissible to see this individual as dead [implying that organs can now be removed].[23]

The symposium ended with Levy vigorously defending the role of
clinical experimentation against the protestations of the lone lawyer
on the panel. For Levy it represented the very motor of medical
progress. In his view Barnard's procedure had been experimental. He
estimated that many other experiments of this sort would of necessity
follow—despite the fact that they tread upon patient rights and as
such were sure to be legally problematic. Levy suggested that antiquated laws only stood in the way of medical progress.

Is it permitted for the law to define what constitutes an
experiment? It is best to leave such matters in the hands
of doctors.... Many of the operations which we perform
today are experimental. ... Without such experiments
we cannot attain the progress which we have lately
reached, and not just recently. There has always been a
conflict between the law and science, for regarding this,
the law is static while science is dynamic.[24]

The record of this early symposium is a wonderful window into
the thoughts of influential medical practitioners of the time. On the
one hand, we have both Neufeld and Levy identifying death with the
classic cardio-respiratory criteria. The representative of the *halakhah*
agrees. Neufeld, however, stressed that *defining* death was not a
"therapeutic" task. That is, from the clinician's point of view, the
death of a patient becomes that moment when further treatment
cannot return normal cardio-respiratory function to the patient.
Medical futility is the *functional* definition of death for the doctor.

# Really Dead?

Philosophical matters, Neufeld implied, cannot alter this functional definition. R. Rabinowitz also asserted that medical futility plays a role in determining death, but in a different fashion. In his understanding of the *halakhah*, the inability to improve the condition of a patient about to die (the *gosses*) opens the door for cessation of medical treatment. This would mean that the patient is *allowed* to die.[25] Of these assembled experts, all of whom adhered to traditional criteria of death, only Neufeld pointed out the difference between death understood ontologically (a medical-philosophical-legal task) and its actual clinical determination.

On the other hand, Erlik argued that the loss of brain function, as measured by an isoeletric EEG was equivalent, by *definition*, to the death of that patient. For him, logically, any life-like signs that this patient evidenced were mere artifacts of the resuscitation apparatus. A patient discovered to be decerebrate could not be alive.

The first discussion of brain-death, then, shows just how heterogeneous the opinions of some of the medical and rabbinic elite were regarding the understanding of death, transplantation and medical ethics. A clear dichotomy can be drawn between Erlik's essentialist stance and Neufeld's functionalist position. Erlik saw death (when viewed through the prism of neurology) as one clearly definable moment; Neufeld (although aware of philosophic complexity) saw it clearly as a function of (changing) medical capability and its inverse — medical futility. Levy presented some of the anxieties facing the modern medical practitioner: Caught in the difficult ethical position between individual patient care and the global advancment of medical practice, he chaffed at being hindered by "static" legalities. Aware of the risks of "experiments", he nonetheless saw the benefit of taking just such risks in order to help advance scientific medicine. "Static definitions" may be fine for lawyers, but doctors needed to operate (in both senses of the term) free from such shackles. The ethical tensions surrounding the cutting-edge, experimental nature of heart transplants and brain-death were writ large in this early discussion.

The next public response by the medical establishment regarding death and organ transplantation came in the fall of 1968—9 weeks before Levy's operation. This was an interview granted by the Dean of the then recently-established Tel Aviv Medical School and Chief of Internal Medicine at Beilinson Hospital, Professor A. Depres. While he asserted his desire to see heart transplants performed in Israel (as they represented a new medical technique that should be studied), he emphasized that doing so would involve a number of difficult moral problems.

> [Heart transplants] revive the question of criteria for determining death – something that has never been absolute, but rather always conventional. After all, when we remove an organ for transplant from a patient we see that he had at least one living organ at the time. And if his brain is damaged, why shouldn't we transplant a [new] brain?
>
> There is no agreed upon definition [of death] today.[26]

He listed criteria for establishing death as:

> The loss of certain reflexes; cessation of cardiac activity; cessation of respiration; loss of consciousness; and today a new test has been added – cessation of electrical activity in the brain.[27]

In answer to a question concerning the reliability of these criteria he stated:

# Really Dead?

> The determination is safe – but not certain. The problem is that the body does not die all at once: different organs die at different times. The function of the brain stops first, although the heart is still alive for some time. For this reason it is possible to transplant the heart of a dead individual into a living individual. Of course, we don't bury anyone immediately upon his demise, but we wait for 24 hours until it is clear that he cannot be saved.[28]

Depres stressed the conventional character of death determination. It also appears that he may have understood loss of brain function as an *additional* criterion meant to be used *alongside* traditional ones. For him, the loss of brain function carried no more import than other necessary biological functions—one day non-functioning brains may be replaced! Echoing the argument for understanding death as process and not event, Depres stressed that the *conventional* meaning of death is led by medical *practice*. Only when faced with medical futility[29] ("it is clear that he cannot be saved") does the doctor allow his patient to be *treated* as dead. The history of medical technique and technologies, then, is the practical history of death. As medical abilities improved so too did the medical definition of death change. Once certain prognoses of death may become treatable conditions. The convention-based boundary between life and death flows with the doctor's capabilities to keep the patient alive. Death, then, becomes that hopeless prognosis when nothing more can be done to restore the health of a dying patient.[30] Again we see that for the practicing physician death was not a fixed point, but a fluid product of medical technology and his own skills.

Once Levy had performed the first heart transplant, the discussions over life and death moved from the realm of the theoretical to the practical. Only days after Levy's operation two parliamentary queries concerning the religious-*halakhic* aspect of the operation had already been presented to the Minister of Religion, R. Zerach Varhaftig of the National Religious Party. The first, from MK Uri Avneri (*Mahaneh Smol Leyisrael* – the Leftist Camp of Israel) simply asked whether the Chief Rabbinate had been asked to formulate *halakhic* guidelines for future transplants (yes);[31] the second was an attack on the minister based on a report stating that the minister (an Orthodox Jew) had lobbied for the inclusion of both doctors *and* rabbis in any team determining the death of organ donors.[32] The tenor and content of the latter query typified the view that determining death was and will always be a ***factual*** medical matter alone.

MK Gideon Hausner (*Liberalim Atzmaiim*- Independent Liberals) asked:

> In the twenty years of the State of Israel's existence who has determined the *fact* of an individual's death? [my emphasis]
>
> How many instances are known to the minister of cases wherein doctors had determined the *fact* of an individual's death and rabbis had questioned this decision? [my emphasis]
>
> Are rabbis capable of questioning a decision made by doctors concerning a life-threatening condition of a terminally ill individual whose only hope in their opinion lies in a heart transplant?[33]

In insisting upon death as a medical fact, the MK's position was much closer to the surgeon Erlik's minority view than to the opinions of the other IMA physicians who were not as quick to so characterize death.

# Really Dead?

On December 25, the first full plenum debate on this issue was held in the Knesset.[34] The debate on heart transplants was instigated by MK Shlomo Rozen, a member of the socialist United Workers Party (*Mifleget Hapoalim Hameuhedet – Mapam*). Most of his floor time was devoted to commenting on the historical significance of the operation and congratulating the country and its doctors on their medical prowess. He called attention to the universal agreement among all Jews regarding the importance of saving lives. Finally, he made sure to address the question of determining death. He described the EEG (mistakenly as a measurement of oxygenation in the brain) as an important technological innovation that would enable "medical-scientific objective" determination of death. He suggested that the Knesset should adopt these "new scientific criteria" of brain-death and use them as the basis for new organ transplant legislation. He emphasized that these criteria would be determined by "doctors and not by rabbis".[35]

The next speaker was from the religiously conservative Poalei Agudat Yisrael. MK Rabbi Shmuel Lawrence presented a multi-pointed argument against heart transplantation in general and raised a number of questions as to the legality and morality of Levy's operation in particular. He stressed that his critique was not based on any *halakhic* considerations, but rather on the legal and moral standing of what he feared might degenerate into a "dictatorship of doctors" whose actions would go unchecked by the public unless the important issues raised by the operation were subject to public review and oversight.[36]

Lawrence's critique was answered by the Health Minister, Yisrael Barzeli, who defended the actions of Levy and the Beilinson Hospital staff. First, he underscored the experimental nature of clinical progress in medicine (citing the steep learning curve of heart valve surgery whose initial success rate was only 5%, but with time rose to

60%). Second, he insisted that everything (especially the removal of the donor heart) was done in accordance with Israeli law and international medical policy.[37] He underscored this latter point by quoting from the Statement of the CIOMS (Council for International Organizations of Medical Sciences) Round Table conference on Heart Transplantation held in Geneva in June of 1968. Barzeli pointed to what he claimed were the clear accepted guidelines for determining the death of a potential heart donor.[38]

He also noted that the Conclusions of the CIOMS conference stressed the need for two separate medical teams–one to test for the above criteria and the other to perform the actual transplant. He noted with ethical satisfaction that two teams were used "in the case of Yitshaq Sulam, of blessed memory...."[39] However, he added an interesting note not found anywhere in the CIOMS Statement. Barzeli stated that all of the 17 countries where heart transplants were being undertaken had accepted the Statement's recommendations, thus

> ...adopting, fundamentally, the criterion [sic] that a flat EEG and the cessation of respiration for a number of minutes is what determines the death of the brain, and that *the death of the brain is the death of the person* [emphasis added].[40]

However, this latter point had been, in fact, debated at the session on "Definition of Death" during the Conference itself. Only one of the five speakers at the session, Professor E. Zander of Switzerland, had argued along these lines. Three others had emphasized that the equation "dead brain equals dead person" was not at all clear. Both French[41] and Russian[42] researchers pointed out problems with relying on the EEG, while a representative of the World Medical Association stressed that the question of defining death was not simple. Before

# Really Dead?

detailing a number of competing criteria for what counted as the death of the brain, the WMA's Dr. J. Jonchéres asked, "…is neurological life the only true form of life?"[43] He ended his presentation with more questions than answers.[44]

While Zander had indeed argued that brain-death was the death of the individual[45], it is difficult to know whether his lone opinion was actually adopted by the conference. The language of the summary Statement suggests that it was not. Nowhere is such a determination mentioned. In place of ever mentioning the "death of the patient/donor," only the more exact "cessation of cerebral function" is used. This is especially noticeable where the Statement advises the use of two separate medical teams.

> One [team] should be responsible for deciding whether all medical or other treatment has become useless because cerebral function has totally and irreversibly ceased; the other should be responsible for all aspects of the transplantation itself.[46]

The logic of this statement is that brain-death has to do with loss of brain function. This, when determined to be irreversible, means that any other treatment is futile. For *this* reason, the patient can become an organ donor – for there is nothing else that can be done for him. Competing patient *interests* is the ethical problem which yields the requirment for two teams. Once there is no longer competition (for the patient has no medical interests anymore, as his treatment is futile) the second team may begin their work. The loss of brain function is not equated with actual death of the patient. Such an unequivocal statement may have been specifically left out in a measure of compromise (as is often the result of committee work).[47]

Barzeli, then, made a logical leap in assuming that what was specifically *not* said in the CIOMS Statement should be understood as its actual meaning. In fact, he stressed that the requirement for the use of two distinct medical teams (as quoted above) was a matter of ethical *stringency* seeing that the patient is most certainly dead. He thus reversed the very logic implicit in the Statement's language. As the Knesset plenum debate continued, he responded to a comment that the issues surrounding donor death were complex by stating that that was certainly not *his* opinion. The debate ended with the entire issue being referred to committee – a victory for those who did view the matter as complicated and in need of further debate.

It is important to note the loose conceptual grasp on this new type of death. The Health Minister quickly read into the CIOMS Statement intent and meaning that was simply not there. As I have already noted, most of the Israeli doctors who had publicly commented on brain-death prior to Barzeli's statement (and prior to an actual Israeli heart transplant) did not draw his same firm conclusions which equated brain-death with the "death of the person." The Health Minister was mistaken about the logic of the CIOMS document which he cited. In fact, its meaning was closer to that found in the majority of the published Israeli medical opinions. Death was conceived as part of a more complicated moral calculus connected to larger questions of futility and experimentation.

We may wonder if the post-facto nature of Barzeli's presentation affected his argument. Did he think that as a defense of one of "his" doctors, brain-death needed to be presented to the public as an unqualified actual equivalent of death? Did he fear that the introduction of the ambivalence already expressed in Israeli medical journals would paint Levy's operation as distressingly questionable or even unethical? The presentation of brain-death as an unfailing, scientifically-measured medical fact may have seemed to be a politically

# Really Dead?

prudent move: a wise defense of heart transplantation as a "measurably" sound moral medical practice. However, it was not an easy claim to make in light of competing medical opinions about the meaning of brain-death. The moral calculus of the competing medical obligations owed to two patients that was in fact behind the CIOMS Statement would remain a major trope throughout discussions concerning brain-death. Death was most often presented as a matter of adjudicating competing ethical claims, and not just reading scientifically produced records of neurological activity.

The committee hearing on Levy's historic operation (decided upon on December 25th) would not take place for over six months. (This lead to accusations of purposeful postponement).[48] In the interim, the Health Minister had taken two specific actions. First, he had sent a Ministerial Order to all hospitals instructing them to adopt the recommendations of the CIOMS that he had outlined for the Knesset. Second, he turned to the IMA's Scientific Advisory Council seeking recommendations concerning the appropriateness of performing further heart transplants in Israel. He wanted their opinion on these guidelines—especially their suitability for Israeli medical practice.[49]

The IMA's Scientific Advisory Council's answer was published in the spring of 1969. Its members wrote:

> In the medical world today, it is generally accepted to equate the death of the individual with the death of his brain.[50]

> The Council has appointed a special committee comprising an expert in cardiology, one in neurology and one in anesthesiology in order to determine the exact criteria for determining "death."[51]

They noted, however, that it was not appropriate to consider as binding any internationally accepted criteria at present, for individual countries each had different sets of criteria for organ retrieval. France was noted as an example where the influence of the Catholic Church had allowed for a more liberal approach. There, "artificial life-support" was not viewed as real life "given by the Creator" – thus allowing those suffering from brain-death to be considered actually dead "for all purposes".[52]

The IMA's response signaled a more nuanced approach than that espoused by the Ministry.[53] It acknowledged some degree of conventionalism as inherent in the determination of death (enclosing *death* in scare quotes). They picked the French case as an example of how how non-medical factors (like religion) could influence that determination. Interestingly, their final recommendation was to advocate the transplant of a heart to an end-stage cardiac patient only if in addition to having the proper hospital staff and equipment, there was concurrently "a compatible donor"

> who was *soon* [my emphasis] to die, from, for example, a malignant brain tumor, which has been diagnosed beyond suspicion.[54]

The IMA, then, recommended transplant so long as the donor evidenced a *prognosis* of compellingly certain death. They were not sure which criteria to use to assure that the donor was *actually* dead. It seems that this was the case because they too understood death as a conventional idea, well tested by different societally-acceptable criteria. Brain-death, essentially a fatal prognosis, was one of them.

To summarize, the initial reactions to the bioethical questions raised by Levy's historic procedure were not monolithic. Anti-religious MKs, like Rozen and Hausner, along with the Health Minis-

# Really Dead?

ter Barzeli, sought to minimize the more open-ended moral dimension inherent in declaring the death of heart donors. By presenting the issue more as a matter of medical fact than ethical dilemma, they attempted to staunch open public debate over brain-death. (Other medical practioners would later take this same tack.) If there was an ethical dimension to the entire heart transplant issue, it had to do with holding back medical progress and letting a potential heart recipient die for want of a donor heart. Levy himself voiced his overriding concern with the ethical cost of discouraging medical advancement.

Opposing this approach, however, were those who felt that equating brain-death with the death of the patient was not merely a scientific assertion, but a moral one as well. The IMA's Scientific Advisory Council's members pointed to the social aspect of death. Others viewed neurologically based donor death as an issue that demanded ethical attention. For a practicing cardiologist like Neufeld, biology took a back seat to philosophy in determining the death of these donors. As he noted, "This is a difficult medical-philosophical-legal question, more than a therapeutic matter." The surgeon Erlik also emphasized the tension between actual death and the medical understanding of the patient as dead. For him, the brain-dead patient was "sentenced to death." For religious MKs, the determination of donor death inherent in heart transplants was yet another affront to general moral values perpetrated by irresponsible doctors at the public's expense. The matter of heart-transplants, and consequently of determining death, was a matter of *public policy*. As such, both needed to be discussed by the public's representatives – the Knesset – and not left only in the hands of doctors who, in the eyes of these MKs (embattled over autopsy procedure for some time), were willing to privilege narrower medical interests over broader public concerns.

If death was understood as a medical fact, logically there was less room for debate over its declaration for organ donors. A patient was either dead or not. Presenting death as a philosophic question or as a medical decision made regarding futility, however, opened up the floor to moral questioning concerning the status of organ donors.[55]

---

[1] Lock reported that in the 15 months following Barnard's operation, "118 heart transplants had been performed in eighteen different countries." 88% died within 6 months of receiving their new hearts (Margaret Lock, *Twice Dead*, 81.) By the early 1970s, the fervor had died down and there existed a 'semi-moratorium' on such operations throughout the West. Only with the introduction of better immune-suppressants in the mid-1980s did heart transplantation again become an accepted medical practice. See R.C. Fox and J. P. Swazey, *Spare Parts* (New York: Oxford University Press, 1992), 8.

[2] He appeared on magazine covers, in television interviews and was the subject of a quickly produced biography, by Peter Hawthshorne *The Transplanted Heart: The Incredible Story of the Epic Heart Transplant Operations by Christian Barnard and his Team* (Johannesburg: Hugh Keartland, 1968) which portrayed him as a daring hero of the twentieth century and ignored any of the ethical questions which surrounded his actions. *Cf.* Lock, *Twice Dead*, 82-87. She notes that not all of the media coverage was positive and that the ethical problems inherent in the transplantation process were being discussed fairly quickly afterwards.

[3] Namir, "*Haqalah qalah halah halilah*," **Yediot Ahronot**, Dec. 8, 1968.

[4] Namir, "*Lilah shaqet avar al Yitshaq Sulam*," **Yediot Ahronot**, Dec. 9, 1968.

[5] The Guttman Report of 1997 showed that a large majority of Israelis could not be fit into either of the two more extreme and opposed categories of "religious" or "secular". In an insightful analysis of this comprehensive report on Jewish identity and behavior of Israelis, Leibman and Sussman wrote: "There is a third public and a third culture–encompassing the majority, perhaps as much as 70 percent of Israeli Jews–that is neither religiously observant in a rigorous way, nor yet secular in the sense of eschewing all religious practice, much less wishing to dissociate the state of Israel from the Jewish tradition. This very disjointed, intellectually incoherent and motley public selectively observes religious rites without being concerned with their theological import.... Jewishness is fundamental to their identity-perceptions and the idea of disengaging Israel from the Jewish people and its history is, for them, unthinkable. .... Major life events are overwhelmingly observed within the Jewish context." This includes 90% who observe mourning rites in "a traditionally Jewish fashion" – second only to the 92% who circumcise their male children in a religious

# Really Dead?

ceremony. (Bernard Susser and Charles Leibman, "The Forgotten Center: Traditional Jewishness in Israel," *Modern Judaism* 17 [1997]: 214, 18.). While they were discussing Israel in the 1990s, their description is all the more true during the time-period discussed in this thesis. It was this Jewishly-oriented majority that would need to be courted as potential organ donors. As I will detail later, even avowed secularists like MK Shulamit Aloni acknowledged this.

[6] As recently as the spring of 2006, ultra-orthodox groups rioted and eventually stole the cadaver of an infant in order to bury it rather than let the Israel Pathology Institute perform a court ordered autopsy. See Aviad Hakohen, "*Mishpat Verefuah Bemedinah Yehudit Vedemokratit': Ben Anatomiah shel Hok Lepatologiah shel Yehase Dat Vemedinah,*" **Shaare Mishpat** 2:2 (2000), 189-221 for a historical review of the conflicts surrounding the ways that the handling of cadavers was dealt with through legislative policy. Hakohen's article focuses primarily on parliamentary and judiciary activity using the Anatomy and Pathology Law of 1953 as a focal point for discussing the relationship between religion and state in modern Israel. He carefully noted how political expediencies influenced this law both in its original inception (196 nt. 34) and in later modifications (199 and 205). For him, it seems that the law (and in turn the actual treatment of cadavers in accord with it) is a reflection of political power balancing between competing *political* camps – the religious and the non-religious. He did not, however, attend to the *moral* significance that the at times violent struggle represented. That is, what each side in this political conflict felt was at stake on the moral plane. (See for example, the work of sociologist Robert Wuthnow on the moral element in political struggles: *Meaning and Moral Order* [Berkley: University of California Press, 1987] esp. chapter 3).

Beyond the religious-secular dichotomy, the Israel Pathology Institute and its long-time director Yehudah Hiss, have been investigated time and again for mishandling bodies and even for organ theft. I believe that a deeper examination of the historical tensions surrounding autopsies in Israel would reveal more than just the *political* conflict described by Hakohen.

[7] Knesset Protocols, November 13, 1968. According to Lawrence, these hospital administrators had advised their staffs to perform post-mortems immediately upon declaring death – even before notifying the deceased's family.

[8] Ibid., December 25, 1968.

[9] B. Amos, "*Hazarah leyemi habenyim,*" **Yediot Ahronot**, March 5, 1978, 9.

[10] See Fox and Swazey, *Spare Parts*, 7.

[11] Anonymous, *"Hashtalat Levavot," **Mikhtav Lehaver*** (Adar 10, 5728), 10-27 [hereafter **ML**]. The symposium had taken place on the 20th of *Shvat* – about three weeks earlier. Interestingly, after looking over hundreds of issues, I found that this was one of the longest articles ever published in the newsletter. The transcript of the symposium was presented in full, headlined in a large font and also included pictures of the participants – the latter two features both extremely rare occurrences for this publication. It appears that the issue at hand was understood by the IMA as being one of extreme importance.

[12] A brief article by one of the participants had appeared a few days earlier: Morris Levy, *"Shtilat Lev," **Harefuah*** (February 15, 1968): 145.

[13]*"Hashtalat Levavot,"* 17. This is noted in a summary of the symposium published along with the actual proceedings written by one of the moderators, Shaul Zolod. In general, only such summaries were published.

[14] Ibid., 12.

[15] Ibid.

[16] Ibid., 13.

[17] Ibid., 14.

[18] Ibid.

[19] This is a *halakhic* category describing a dying individual who is gasping his last breath. The exact meaning and the actual characteristics of this state have been the subject of sustained debate, as I will describe below.

[20] Ibid., 20.

[21] Ibid. This is a reference to the *gemara* in tractate *Yoma* which describes the religious imperative to search for survivors under rubble on Shabbat. The understanding of this talmudic source will play an important role in further *halakhic* discussions as I will explain.

[22] Ibid.

[23] Ibid., 25.

[24] Ibid., 26. Levy seems to have personified this medical philosophy in his own practice. Not only would he perform the first heart transplant, but he had earlier performed the first kidney transplant in Israel as well. In an interview on January 23, 2003, he described in detail how he did this with no prior transplantation experience after studying a few journal articles and consulting by phone with an experienced surgeon in America.

[25] This will be a central trope in a number of *halakhic* discussions of death and transplants.

# Really Dead?

---

26 A. Depres, "*Efshar Vetsarikh Lishtol*," **ML** Tishrei 3 (5769), 20.

27 Ibid.

28 Ibid.

29 For an overview of the various aspects and understandings of medical futility see Benjamin Phillips, "The Concept of Futility in Medical Care" (PhD. Diss., SUNY at Buffalo, 1997). Here I mean a prognosis of death where nothing further can be done medically for a dying patient. Such a situation is obviously fluid, dependent upon time and place.

30 This is what Belkin, in his study of the Harvard Criteria, called "death before dying". Belkin argued that the Harvard Committee members were not so much seeking to redefine death itself, but to acknowledge that technology had interrupted the normal course of dying. They wanted to insert a logical (if somewhat artificial) "death" into this new medically exacerbated dying projectory–a "death before dying," in order to solve a number of ethical problems (Belkin, "Death before Dying" 56, 147, 194).

The argument for the conventional aspect of death was one side of one of the earliest debates over death touched off by brain-death. In the 1971 issue of the prestigious journal, *Science*, Robert Morrison argued that death itself was essentially a social convention. Leon Kass countered that death was an ontological, biological fact not dependent upon human norms–but perhaps difficult to discover. See Robert Morrison, "Death: Process or Event," *Science* 173 (1971): 694-7 and Leon Kass, "Death as an Event: A Commentary on Robert Morrison," *Science* 173 (1971): 698-702.

31 *Knesset Protocols*, December 10, 1968.

32 The minister answered that the report was false. He had suggested that death be determined by a team of three doctors not connected to the transplant procedure and that family permission be obtained to remove the donor's organs. He had additionally suggested that a special committee including medical doctors, rabbis, and representatives of the public be established to study all the relevant moral and legal concerns connected to heart transplants (*Knesset Protocols*, December 17, 1968).

33 The actual content of Hausner's caustic query had, interestingly enough, already been answered by three of the leading *poskim* who had addressed the question of heart transplants within months of Barnard's historic operation. These will be discussed below.

34 As I noted above, there had been much discussion and discord surrounding the medical/experimental use of cadavers. For instance, on November 11th, 1968, MK

Uri Avneri (known for his anti-religious, anti-establishment views) asked whether there was truth to a claim made in a newspaper article that the Israeli Society of Surgery felt that "religious sentiments were an impediment to organ transplants." His query was answered by the Health Minister in the negative. (*Knesset Protocols,* November 11, 1968).

[35] *Knesset Protocols*, December 25, 1968.

[36] Ibid.

[37] His main argument was that Israeli law did not require the permission of the donor or his family for the removal of any organ by medical staff if it was to be used for transplantation purposes. As noted above, the Autopsy and Pathology Law-1953, was the subject of great debate over many years. It was exactly this point–the ability to remove organs without consent that was the epicenter of the fight. The claim of the government and medical establishment could be summarized by quoting Barzeli here: "If the patient is terminal and his days are limited and the heart of the dead [donor] is a rare mercy that fate has offered him – and his salvation could be prevented by the refusal of the [donor's] family – is this not irresponsible abandonment of the chance to save a life!?" (Ibid.)

Interestingly, although Barzeli explicitly rejected the need to follow Jewish law, insisting that only civil law was of import 'in this house', he went out of his way to quote from the remarks made by Rav Rabinowitz at the IMA symposium regarding extending the life of a *gosses.*

[38] Barzeli quoted the actual text from the conclusions of the conference as published in an accurate Hebrew translation. The criteria as published and cited by Barzeli included:

Complete and irreversible cessation of cerebral function.
>The criteria for cessation of cerebral function are as follows:
>(a) Loss of all response to the environment.
>(b) Complete abolition of reflexes and loss of muscle tone.
>(c) Cessation of spontaneous respiration.
>(d) Abrupt fall in arterial blood-pressure once it is not artificially maintained.
>(e) An absolutely linear electro-encephalographic tracing (even with stimulation of the brain) recorded under well defined technical conditions.
>(V. Fattorusso, ed., *Heart Transplantation,* 51).

[39] *Knesset Protocols*, December 25, 1968.

[40] Ibid. This contradiction was noted by Y. Levi, *"Me'emati Mutar Lehotsi Ever Lehashtalah,"* **Hama'ayan** 10:1 (Tishrei, 5730), 10.

[41] Fattorusso, *Heart Transplantation,* 44-46.

[42] Ibid., 46-47.

[43] Ibid., 42.

[44] Ibid., 44.

[45] Ibid., 47-49.

[46] Ibid., 51.

[47] I know of no study that has examined the protocols of the working group meetings that developed this Statement. For that matter, I do not know if such protocols are to found, but their study would obviously help in determining the meaning of the Statement.

[48] See *Public Service Committee Protocols,* July 1, 1969. The meeting was chaired by MK S. Rozen (*Mapam*). He opened the session dealing with heart transplants by noting that he had received a letter from MK Kalman Kahana (*Poale Agudat Yisrael*) a week earlier, which the latter had also read in the Knesset plenum, accusing him of postponing the discussion. His reply was that the entire committee was responsible for determining its schedule. As *Poale Agudat Yisrael* had representatives on the committee, Rozen argued, they should have and could have moved up the discussion.

[49] See *Knesset Protocols,* March 25, 1969. This included the use of two separate medical teams and the brain-death criteria of the CIOMS Statement. From a comparison of the dates, it appears that he had received the IMA council's somewhat tentative first answer. (The council wanted to further study the entire issue via a special committee). He sent out in his directive, however, the criteria contained in the CIOMS Statement.

[50] They may have seen the Harvard report and based their statement on that paper, not merely on the CIOMS Statement, which, as noted, does not seem to equate the two.

[51] Israel Medical Association Scientific Advisory Council, *"El Sar Habriut,"* **ML** (Adar 26, 5729): 18.

[52] Ibid.

[53] This may be understandable as Barzeli was of necessity defending a failed operation post facto, while the IMA was debating future policy.

[54] Ibid.

[55] From what we have seen here it is impossible to know whether some doctors' desire to stifle debate over transplant for fear of hobbling scientific progress led them to take a particular stance concerning death that made debate less likely. Many have, however, described brain-death as an attempt to create a new medical "fact" merely in order to allow organ transplantation to continue. See Mita Giacomini, "A Change of Heart and a Change of Mind? Technology and the Redefinition of Death in 1968," *Social Science and Medicine* 44:10 (1997): 1465-1482 and Lock, *Twice Dead.* Belkin in "Death before Dying" argues against these views.

# 2

# 1967-1968
# Determining Death:
# Early Halakhic Responses

As I have already noted, the Israeli discourse on brain-death took place not only in medical journals and the political arena, but also in numerous halakhic discussions on organ transplantation. In fact, the halakhic aspect of Israeli discourse is what has made it unique among the debates held in many different countries over brain-death. As we saw in the previous chapter, the very first IMA-sponsored symposium on heart transplantation included rabbinic representation. Much of the discussion was directed to the way that these procedures could be understood halakhically. Additionally, the Knesset debate held after Levy's transplant procedure was, in large part, framed around halakhic concerns: Secular MKs worried about the intrusion of rabbinic control (recall MK Shlomo Rozen's comment insisting that death be determined by "doctors and not by rabbis"). Those who contested the morality of Levy's actions and insisted upon further public debate were all representatives of religious parties. The tension (and perhaps paradoxical attitude) surrounding the halakhic stance on the conjoined issues of brain-death/heart transplantation was evident in the Health Minister's remarks as well. Even as Barzeli insisted that only

# Really Dead?

secular law mattered in the Knesset, he took care to point out R. Rabinowitz's published comments on treatment withdrawl. Secular Israelis, for whom Jewish law was not seen as personally obligatory, understood it as an integral part of the Israeli public discourse.[1]

Just about the time that the first human hearts were transplanted, four halakhic responsa which discussed the determination of death were written. Three were devoted to discussing the halakhic problems that organ transplants entailed; one discussed the halakhic definition of death. All, however, addressed the traditional ways in which the determination of death should be made in accordance with Jewish law. As will become clear, despite their use of the same talmudic source material, their authors understood the meaning of the very same halakhic criteria quite differently. Additionally, these responsa differed in their ethical focus. For R. Yitshaq Weiss and R. Moshe Feinstein it was important to highlight the problematic morality of the organ transplant project as a whole. Other halakhic authorities, however, dealt more narrowly with technical aspects of determining death. Taken together, these responsa are an important part of the early discourse on the questions raised by brain-death. Not only do they offer a clear picture of how some of the major modern halakhic authorities related to these issues, but they reveal how seemingly common halakhic concepts took on greatly disparate meanings.

The first modern *psaq halakhah*[2] on the determination of death was published by R. Eliezer Waldenburg coincidently just around the time of Barnard's heart transplant. He was a uniquely prolific Jerusalem rabbinic judge who wrote 21 volumes of responsa before his death in 2007. This responsum (undated, but published in 1967) addressed a rumor that diaspora Jews were waiting for periods longer than 24 hours before burying their deceased[3]. Although he did not address the question of brain-death, R. Waldenburg focused on the classic halakhic criteria for determining death. His presentation and understanding of these criteria are important as he was one of the first modern *posqim* to return to these issues in the age of organ transplants. Years later he would become one of the main rabbinic opponents to the Israel heart-transplant project and to the use of brain-death criteria in general.

R. Waldenburg reiterated the famous position against the delay of burial taken by R. Moshe Sofer (see note three), but sought to ground it in primary Talmudic sources. In Tractate Yoma 83a – 85a there is a discussion concerning the extent of the obligation to conduct a search and rescue mission for one who has been buried under a collapsed building on the Sabbath. On the biblicaly ordained day of rest such work (dismantling the wreckage, moving the rubble, etc.) would ordinarily be forbidden as prohibited *melakha* (profane activity).[4] However, saving the life of one buried under the rubble takes precedence over these restrictions and such work is permitted. This is true when there is doubt as to whether those buried are still alive or even if it is not clear that anyone is actually buried under the rubble. The principle expressed is that the prohibitions of the Sabbath are laid aside even when such action *may* save a life, but most likely will not.

The Talmud then raises the question as to the law when even that doubt is dismissed, such that the clearing of the rubble is again prohibited. That is, if it becomes clear that no one is actually beneath the rubble, clearing is stopped as it is now again prohibitted. (For example, if a missing person for whom the search under the rubble was commenced was found elsewhere). This is also the case if no *living* person is discovered under the rubble. The Sabbath prohibitions herein discussed are only suspended to save a *life*—not to recover a *body*. The Talmud therefore seeks to set criteria for determining whether an individual discovered beneath the rubble is alive or dead for cases where this is not clear.[5] This text has served as the classic

# Really Dead?

talmudic expression of the determination of death. It emphasized the critical role of respiration as the primary halakhic indicator of death.[6]

R. Waldenburg offered his own explanation for the Talmud's view of respiration as the determinative sign of death. Citing a 17th-century *poseq*[7], he described the connection between the heart and respiration (albeit in terms of Aristotelian physiology). R. Waldenburg sought to answer the question of why only respiration at the nostrils of a buried individual need be checked before pronouncing death.

> ...all life resides in the heart of any creature, however, sometimes even though the heart is still alive, as it is hidden in the chest, its beat is not noticeable from without, on the chest's surface, because it is weak. But the breath that leaves the heart by way of the lungs is noticeable so long as the heart is still alive.[8]

> ...from this we learn that respiration serves the heart and if there is no heart, there is no breath....[9]

Leaving the actual physiology aside, it is clear that R. Waldenburg stressed that respiratory criteria for death *necessarily* included cardiac criteria. His argument was that respiration ends only when cardiac function ceases, for it is a *part* of the greater cardiac process. Since respiratory activity at the nose is more readily observed than a weakened, buried heart-beat, once its lack is observed, it follows that cardiac function has also ended. So for this reason, the *gemara* in *Yoma*, by focusing on only one indication of life, was not permissively lenient in excluding the need to check cardiac activity when determining death. Respiration was evidence of cardio-pulmanary function as a whole. Its more-easily-detected lack indicated larger systemic failure.

# Early Halakhic Responses

As a leading twentieth-century halakhic-medical authority, well acquainted with modern medicine, it can be safely assumed that R. Waldenburg understood modern cardio-pulmonary physiology. He wanted to stress here that respiration is part of a complex multi-organ based function.[10] That he did this by citing classic halakhic works, even though antiquated in their biology, tells us something of his understanding of the need for authoritative precedent in *halakhah*, however.

In accordance with this understanding, he also interpreted R. Sofer's responsum as dealing with the ordinary case where respiratory loss follows cardiac failure. R. Moshe Sofer wrote:

> Anyone who is lying like an unmoving stone and has no pulse and if afterwards stops breathing, we have naught but the words of our holy Torah that he is dead and his burial should not be delayed.[11]

Thus, "*afterwards* stops breathing" describes both a temporal as well as teleological state of affairs: Cardiac activity (and also all movement or neurological activity) has ceased – thus ending the *need* for respiration. R. Waldenburg explained, though, that extraordinary cases may also occur.

> However, if we note any pulse or other movement, we should suspect that we have an exceptional case. …we cannot, then, rely merely on a test of respiration as this is an extraordinary case – also [we cannot rely only on this sign] if he has suddenly died for in sudden death it is common that this is some type of seizure.[12]

# Really Dead?

This means that respiration may have ended, as in a seizure, only temporarily and so may return of its own accord, or with modern resuscitation, be restored. And, so long as we can detect some movement or pulse, the teleological function of respiration is still pertinent and so the inclusive nature of its cessation cannot be assumed. As R. Waldenburg's interest here was in arguing against a rumored problem of delaying burial and not with medical problems per se, he did not mention resuscitation or go into detail as to what is to be done in these exceptional cases. He was content to note the importance of retaining the traditional half-hour or so waiting period before proceeding with burial preparations.[13]

To summarize, R. Waldenburg, insisting on the most traditional authoritative texts, has used them to subtly reconstruct the *meaning* of respiration as the definitive sign of death. Respiration is not merely "breath observed at the nose," but rather an indication of a complex biological system at work. Its absence, then, does not *define* death, but only points to the collapse of that system. So long as we may observe other indications of the system's integrity intact – this sign loses its unique *practical* authoritative standing in the *halakhah* without, however, losing its *symbolic* import as the primary potential signifier: "As it is written, 'all that the breath of life is in his nose'."

In 1968, a few months before Levy operated, three significant responsa on heart transplantation and the determination of death were written. The first was contained in a letter written in the spring by Rabbi Shlomo Zalman Auerbach. He wrote in response to a number of questions concerning organ transplants put to him by a leading Jerusalem religious internist, Dr. Avraham Avraham.[14]

R. Auerbach began by insisting that he was writing not *psaq halakhah*, but rather in order to enlighten Dr. Avraham who should feel free to adopt or reject his interpretations.[15] He ended his responsum by noting that all that he had written was applicable only when dealing with two "Israelis"–the donor and recipient of any organ transplant. (This suggests that his opinion may be different when dealing with transplants undertaken in other countries or with non-Jews.) [16] The body of his answer began by noting that the removal of an organ from a cadaver in order to save the life of another is a halakhically required action. However, he added that this does not entitle either the dying patient or another party to steal an organ. (This seems to be a comment on the then-current controversy surrounding cadavers and the use of cadaveric organs in general as well as a reference to the well known halakhic topic of self-preservation through theft of another's property). [17]

Most of his answer, though, was devoted to explaining that cessation of respiration (as found in Tractate *Yoma* and R. Moshe Sofer's responsum) was not a *definition* of death. Rather, with modern medical methods, it had become a *condition* that must be treated.

> It is clear, in my humble opinion, that in our day it is impossible to determine that an individual has already died without using the newest technologies that determine the border between life and death. Heaven forefend that we would only rely upon signs of respiration and the like and ignore other indicators. This would mean teaching that in the case of one buried under rubble on Shabbat who he has ceased to breathe and whose heart is no longer beating he should be abandoned! Or that we should hurriedly inter one who is no longer breathing, when we now know how to save him with resuscitation! Therefore, as long as according to medical knowledge there is some doubt as to whether an individual can be revived, we treat the case as one of suspected seizure.[18]

# Really Dead?

Unlike the subtle placement of respiration in a broader body-wide context undertaken by R. Waldenburg, R. Auerbach claimed that modern resuscitation has (at least seemingly) displaced the primacy of repiratory cessation as a sign of death for the *halakhah*. It has done so by expanding the role of doubt around which the *gemara* in Yoma itself is based. As noted above, rescue work is carried out so long as doubt regarding the survival of the victim still exists. Such doubt only ends when the victim's death can be determined. The modern ability to resuscitate those who are not breathing has expanded the area of doubt to include even those who may be uncovered with no respiratory function at all.

R. Auerbach continued, advancing an interesting claim: if resuscitation is unsuccessful, the individual's time of death is marked as the end of respiration and not from the later time afer resuscitative efforts have failed. He argued that cessation of respiration had *always* been considered an unclear symptom. In the past, when resuscitative techniques were unknown, it could signal either some type of seizure that untreated would inevitably lead to death *or* the onset of death itself. Traditionally, some short waiting period was necessary in order make sure that the individual had not just suffered a seizure, but was indeed dead before treating him as such. [19] Today, he argued, the only difference is that the length of this waiting period has increased to allow for resuscitation attempts. [20]

The logic behind R. Auerbach's claim is connected to his understanding of causation and his differentiation between prognosis and actual death. In any case where respiration ceases, this may *lead* to death (just as massive bleeding may, for example), but is not death itself. In some cases, medical care can treat a potentially deadly condition, in some cases it cannot. A decision concerning the futility of treatment can have definite consequences – we may classify a patient as terminal.[21] But here we have something different. Traditionally, in a *pre-modern-resuscitation world*, the meaning of the loss of respiration was automatically realized by the passage of the short time between this loss and its final outcome. If the patient did not revive on his own, his original cessation of repsiration could not be understood as a mere seizure.[22] However, with respect to respiration today, *our* efforts at resuscitation clarify the *meaning* of the loss of this function. If we succeed, we know that the loss was symptomatic of, or caused by, some 'seizure' or other reversible event. If not, our understanding is that it signaled the end of life.

> We do not say that at first the individual had suffered a seizure and then [when he cannot be resuscitated] died. Rather, we view him as having died from that time when his respiration ceased.

This reveals something important about the *meaning* of respiratory loss in R. Auerbach's view. The halakhah stipulated a time between cessation of respiration and treating the patient as dead (regardless of whether we are attempting resuscitation or not). This was not mandated in order to allow for certainty of death by ensuring that lack of oxygen would bring death to the brain, for instance, but rather to ascertain whether cessation of respiration *signaled* death or not. By waiting for a period of time after initial loss of respiratory function, we *discover* whether this loss was actually the moment of the individual's death or (if he recovers) whether it was merely a seizure. (R. Auerbach admits that this raises a difficult question as to the time of death for one who ceases to breathe and could have been resuscitated, but was not. In this case it would seem that we *know* that the original cessation of respiration was only a seizure without having proved this by attempting actual resuscitation.)[23]

# Really Dead?

Rabbi Auerbach's responsum lays open the conceptual differentiation between medical prognosis and actual death. This contrasts the CIOMS Statement which showed that there the two were conceptually and practically related. In the CIOMS Statement, neurological criteria pointed to the futility of further treatment which in turn allowed for organ removal. R. Auerbach's approach, however, insists that such prognosis is an interpretive tool. It allows us to understand the traditional, unimpeachable sign of respiratory failure which had become, with the advent of resuscitative techniques, complicatedly polysemic. The loss of breath is no longer the loss of life: it demands interpretation, it demands explanation. Perhaps it points to death; perhaps to the need for medical intervention. Modern resuscitative technology itself is the hermeneutic tool which provides our exegesis.[24]

The summer of 1968 saw two other *posqim* write on the question of heart transplants. The first was a responsum written by the *Av Beit Din* (Chief Justice) of the Manchester, England Rabbinical Court, Rabbi Yitshaq Weiss. R. Weiss wrote in answer to a query from the Chief Rabbi of the British Commonwealth, R. Immanuel Yakobovits.[25] The British Chief Rabbi had been invited to a conference on transplants sponsored by the British Health Ministry. He wanted to consult on this issue with the acknowledged top halakhic expert then resident in Britain before participating.[26] R. Weiss used a technically dense discussion of a number of earlier halakhic works to offer a radically different interpretation of the medical imperative regarding resuscitated patients than that argued for by transplant doctors. It was his understanding that transplant surgeons had suggested that these patients be kept 'alive' until transplantation could be arranged. R. Rabinowitz from Holon had expressed his opinion that Jewish law viewed such patients as *gossesim*. Therefore, one was not obligated to treat them, but could let them die.[27] R. Weiss, however, constructed the halakhic obligation towards such a patient very differently.

# Early Halakhic Responses

He began by drawing attention to two different halakhic sources – the first, from Tractate Yoma 85b as discussed above. According to this source, even in the case of finding a survivor who is *doubtfully alive*, the Sabbath is transgressed in order to save him.[28] That is, a Jew is instructed to violate the Sabbath even to minimally extend the life of a severely injured survivor who may not live too much longer. The second source concerns the *gosses*. The Tractate *Smakhot* opens with a number of halakhic directives all of which aim at asserting that the *gosses* is still among the living. As such, neither may any of the actions ordinarily performed on a corpse (ritual cleansing and the like) be performed upon him nor may he even be moved lest this hasten his death.[29]

Now, basing himself on an 18th-century collection of responsa, the *Shvut Yaakov*[30], R. Weiss aimed at collapsing the distance between the case detailed in *Yoma* and the general halakhic obligation to continue medical care for those who are severely ill or injured. The *Shvut Yaakov* insisted that this first source obligates any and all medical care, even if it involves desecration of the Sabbath, for anyone who is still living – regardless of their condition and regardless of the amount of improvement such care might offer. He did not differentiate between the *gemara* in Yoma and the case of the *gosses* individual.[31] In either case care is mandatory both on the Sabbath and during the week. The majority of later *posqim*, most importantly, R. Yisrael Kagen in the *Mishnah Brura* and *Biur Halakhah*, also agreed with this position.[32]

Drawing from these sources, R. Weiss portrayed the brain-dead patient on resuscitative equipment as one who is due, at best, proper medical care, and at worst, the chance to die peacefully. In quite harsh language, he called the harvesting of their still living organs after being kept alive ("they have some life in them still") only for this purpose, simply "murder". He expressed his doubts as to the ability of medical personnel to accurately predict the futility of further treatment, citing a case where doctors had already given up but the patient recovered. He further argued that even in a truly hopeless case the patient should be allowed to die. The medical care these resuscitated patients-*cum*-donors received was obviously not meant to do *them* any good.

R. Weiss discussed concerns over medical futility beyond which no reasonable hope for recovery was held. The *establishment* of such a point was halakhically acceptable for R. Weiss. The legal-ethical obligation of treatment would end once an understanding that further treatment would be futile is reached. However, just in this case the very process of dying needed to be carefully observed so that it not be pointlessly prolonged. Only discontinuation of futile treatment would be warranted in such a case – not its extension in order to use these patients as sources of organs for others.[33]

R. Weiss sent his responsum for review to another of the day's major *posqim*, Rabbi Moshe Feinstein. R. Feinstein eventually published four responsa on the subject of brain death,[34] and together these would stand at the center of an often acrimonious debate regarding his actual position towards heart transplants. The first and longest was his response to R. Weiss written in the summer of 1968. He began by asserting categorically that heart transplants are:

> ...the actual murder of two people, for the donor whose heart is removed is alive, not only according to the Torah's laws in which the definition of death has been passed on to us, but also, according to those doctors who tell the truth, he is still alive. However, in their wickedness they do not take any account of his [the donor's] life which is only temporary, a matter of hours or perhaps even days.[35]

He continued to claim that the recipient's life is also shortened considerably through the transplant as "most of those suffering from heart ailments live many days and years," yet after the transplant they all die much sooner.

R. Feinstein stressed that there was no need for lengthy debate over the matter, as that would only serve to confuse the issue. Rather, he asked that only the clear negation of the legitimacy of these operations be publicized. However, after these two short paragraphs he continued for a number of pages to analyze the halakhic issues of death determination at length.

His first point introduced another basic source on death determination found in a *mishnah* which details the onset of ritual defilement or impurity upon death.[36] Ritual defilement is a complex halakhic category (most of the Oral Law, the Mishnah, is devoted to understanding it). It is enough to know, however, that only the actually dead can become primary sources of impurity (*tuma*) capable of defiling their surroundings. This *mishnah* teaches that despite certain movements which can give the appearance of life, a *beheaded* individual is dead. Any vestigial movements are likened to the twitching of a lizard's tail once detached from its body. R. Feinstein contrasted this source with a *gemara* found in Tractate Gittin which states that even an individual whose throat has been completely cut through and will momentarily expire is still alive and any bodily movement of his testifies to that life. [37]

R. Feinstein then explained that the first mishnaic source describes an individual whose spine and most of the flesh surrounding it has been severed, even though his trachea and esophagus are still intact. The second talmudic souce, then, teaches that even one whose throat is cut such that he will momentarily die is not yet dead. The *mishnah* teaches that one who has been beheaded is considered *by definition* dead – even if we observe movements of the body or head. For such

# Really Dead?

an individual, R. Feinstein asserted, there is absolutely no obligation to render medical care, "even if there was a way of reattaching the head to the body" (!) thus restoring his life. This obligation pertains only to the still living (even if they are dying), but not to the dead (*de jure*, even if they evince signs of life).

The next point raised concerned respiration. R. Feinstein wrote that cessation of respiration for "even a few moments" is that which causes certain death.

> ...even one who has suffered a seizure must breathe, for it is impossible to live without breathing for more than a few moments. All the time that one is alive, even if he is gravely ill, he retains the ability to breathe continuously and this is noticeable at his nose. When he stops breathing, this may be because he has died, but it is possible that his illness has strengthened so that he lacks the ability to breathe—this is the seizure which we suspect—but because he lacks the ability to breathe he cannot live for more than a short time, a few minutes. So after waiting this amount of time he is certainly dead.

Traditionally some time was needed between the cessation of breathing and the pronouncement of death (as discussed above in R. Auerbach's *psaq*). R. Feinstein argued that this was to ensure that respiration had indeed ceased long enough for the individual to have expired from anoxia. Now, those individuals who have lost the ability to breathe may begin to breathe again on their own before they die from lack of oxygen. There may even be some period of intermittent respiration. Therefore, care must be taken to ascertain that respiration has *continuously* failed for long enough for anoxia induced death to have occured. As constant attention to respiration is difficult, the waiting period between first noting its cessation and declaring death may have to be lengthened to exclude the possibility of intermittent, unnoticed respiratory activity.

R. Feinstein's description of the role of respiration differed drastically from that of R. Auerbach. For R. Auerbach, respiratory failure was essentially a *sign* that death had occurred (once any alternatives were ruled out). For R. Feinstein, however, it functioned not just in a semiotic fashion, but primarily physically as a *cause* of death.

The third point in the responsum dealt with the obligations that R. Weiss had detailed regarding care due to the resuscitated patient. R. Feinstein also forbade prolongation of a patient's life when not for his own benefit as it would cause unnecessary suffering. This pain is of a spiritual nature, for it is the result of keeing the soul from departing the body. As such it is not measurable by medical technology. Nonetheless, R. Feinstein held it to be very real and so argued that it was unconscionable to subject the patient to such suffering even in order to help save another's life. On the other hand, however, hastening the death of a patient, even if he is in physical pain, also remains forbidden.

To underline this tension, R. Feinstein quoted a pertinent Talmudic story. During the time of Roman persecutions after the destruction of the Second Temple a rabbi, R. Hanyna b. Tardyon, was being burned at the stake. The Romans had placed wet sponges against his chest so that his death might be slower and more painful. The dying rabbi refused his gathered students' suggestion that he remove the sponges so that he may die more quickly. He did however allow one of the Gentile Roman guards to do so. R. Feinstein suggested that this story may point to a difference between the obligations of a Jew and a Gentile with respect to the hastening of death. While such an act is strictly forbidden to a Jew, some indirect causation of death to allevi-

# Really Dead?

ate suffering may be allowed to a Gentile. (We will return to this suggested difference in moral obligation later on.)

He concluded this responsum by indicating that organ transplantation from a *cadaver* is permitted and, in fact, can be considered a meritorious act. However R. Feinstein unequivably argued that a heart-beating "donor" is a *patient* whose plight obligates us in many ways. He is not dead and he is not to be harmed for another's sake.[38]

These two early *pisqe halakhah*, written by R. Weiss and R. Feinstein, focused, then, both on the technical definition of death in the *halakhah* and on the nature of the religious-moral obligation due that patient who in the eyes of the transplant surgeons had become the ideal heart donor. Continued cardiac function was understood by all of these commentators on the *halakhah* as a sure sign of life. We can detect, though, some evolution in the understanding of what was owed these patients. R. Rabinowitz had noted that Jewish law did not require the extension of life-saving medical care to the *gosses*. In his view, this lack of obligation did not bring with it any other positive obligations (due the patient qua prospective donor). Therefore, artificial extension of cardiac activity until such time that it could be "profitably" stopped (so as to allow for transplant) was not seen as problematic. However, both R. Feinstein and R. Weiss evinced a sense of moral disgust at such a prospect. They saw that these patients were being used as mere means and not medically treated for their own good.[39]

As opposed to the logic of medical futility inherent in the CIOMS criteria, these *posqim* objected to weighing the needs or value of the dying patient against those of another who could benefit from their death. Here, then, is an example of how the halakhic view of the ethics of brain-death differed greatly from that presented by the Israeli medical establishment. Whereas for the IMA and the Health Ministry the ethical imperative of saving one patient's life enabled the use of another (so long as this donor could not himself be saved), R. Weiss and R. Feinstein rejected this calculus. Prognosis alone was not enough to end the ethical commitment to a potential donor. [40]

Additionally, respiration, or its cessation as the primary signifier of death, was variously interpreted in these early *pisqe halakhah*. For R. Waldenburg it was a stand-in for a more complex whole group of the body's essential biological functions. For both Rabbis Auerbach and Feinstein, however, the halakhic endorsement of a waiting period after the cessation of respiration was indicitive of a problem with the simple equation of breath and life. Did the cessation of respiration equal death or was it merely a prognostic? For R. Feinstein death may be signaled by the end of breathing, but it actually arrives through its anoxic effects on the body. The position of R. Auerbach, though, held that loss of respiration was an undeciphered sign, awaiting our ability to decode it. For all of these *posqim*, however, certainty of death, which resuscitative technologies had clouded, was needed before the dying patient could be abandoned or made into the means of saving another's life. The responses of secular Israeli doctors so far discussed, though, pointed towards *prognostic* certainty, visible through the end of brain function, as sufficient.

---

[1] The reasons for secular interest in *halakhic* opinion may be linked to "secular" Israelis' *Jewish* identity (see chapter 1, note 5) and their understanding that the rulings of Jewish law reflect this identity. Even if one would argue that such interest was merely politically motivated and utilitarian in its aim at ensuring that the transplant project could move forward, one could still not deny that the *halakhic* debates over brain-death were indeed an important part of the Israeli cultural discourse.

[2] In the system of *halakhah*, based on a complex system of many-tiered precedent, complicated causative logic as well as on the public position and communal authority of the individual adjudicator, a *psaq halakhah* is an opinion on a question of Jewish law given by one who has been accepted by a given community as an expert whose judicial-like opinions are considered authoritative for that community. Even

# Really Dead?

essentially secular institutions, like the IMA, made certain to include halakhic experts in their discussions. The *halakhic* validity of medical decisions was important both for the IMA and the Knesset, and as will become clear, for the Israeli public-at-large who identify as secular Jews. In general, such validity is to a great degree dependent not merely on the proper application of halakhic jurisprudence, but also on the personal authority of the individual who espouses a particular position. That is, it may matter more who said what, than what was said.

The acceptance of a particular scholar as an authentic *poseq* by a given community is dependent upon a large number of variables. For an exploration of some of these issues see Jonathan Sacks, "Creativity and Innovation," in *Halakha, Rabbinic Authority and Personal Autonomy*, ed. Moshe Sokol (New Jersey: Jason Aronson, 1992). See Moshe Koppel, *Meta-halakhah: Logic, Intuition and the Unfolding of Jewish Law* (New Jersey: Jason Aronson, 1997) for a well-argued philosophical exploration of the halakhic process.

[3] R. Eliezer Waldenburg, *Tsits Eliezer*, 9:46. (Unless otherwise noted, all responsa, Jewish codes and rabbinic material quoted is found on the Bar-Ilan University Responsa–Global Jewish Data Base CD. Reference, therefore, is usually not to printed versions.) This same problem of late burial had sparked a major polemic between Reform and Orthodox European Jewry in the 19th-century. This battle had been settled (at least for the adherents of the *halakhah*) by a *psaq* written by R. Moshe Sofer (the Hatam Sofer) in which the accepted halakhic criteria for establishing death had been laid out some 130 years previously (*Responsa Hatam Sofer*, YD:348). It had been written as part of two larger battles: the fight in Europe against the Reform Movement and the struggle against premature burial which had swept through Europe at the same time. (See Pernick, "Brain Death in Cultural Context," in *The Definition of Death: Contemporary Controversies*, eds. Younger, Arnold and Schapiro, 3-33 [Baltimore: Johns Hopkins University Press, 1999] and "Back from the Grave: Recurring Controversies over Defining and Diagnosing Death in History," in *Death: Beyond Whole-Brain Criteria*, ed. Richard Zaner, 16-60 [Dordrecht: Kluwer Academic Publishers, 1988] for more on this struggle).

The history of the former fight is the subject of a wide-ranging literature. For a brief synopsis of the specific background of this responsum see Avraham Steinberg, "*Kviat Regah Hamavet,*" **Noam** 19 (1976):210-38, 210-212. R. Moshe Sofer had been interested in ending a 50-year-old Jewish European custom of waiting for three or more days (until signs of putrification were evident as proof of death) before burying the dead. He argued that this was not *halakhically* necessary and that it was, in fact, a transgression of the religious obligation to speedily bury the dead (see Deuteronomy 21:23). He famously summarized:

> Anyone who is lying like an unmoving stone and has no pulse and if afterwards stops breathing, we have naught but the words of our holy Torah that he is dead and his burial should not be delayed.

4 See *m. Shabbat*, 7:2.

5 The *mishnah* states:

> If he is found alive, we remove the rubble. If he is found dead, we leave him.

The *gemara* then continues:

> Until where must we check [the victim for signs of life]? Until his nose. There are those who say, 'Until his heart'. ... Rav Pappa explained, this disagreement is only when checking from lower to upper extremities [that is, the victim is unearthed feet-first], but when starting to check from the upper extremities all agree that once his nose is checked that is sufficient. As it is written, "all that the breath of life is in his nose" (Genesis 7:22).

6 It is this text upon which R. Moshe Sofer based his claim that the cessation of respiration was the traditional basis for determining that death had occurred. He argued that just as the lack of respiration allows us to abandon the victim and end any rescue attempts, so too can this loss of function be understood as allowing for the general declaration that the victim has indeed died, with no further indications [such as signs of cellular necrosis] being needed. That the text is speaking of some general determination, and not merely about ending rescue efforts may be inferred by its concluding with its own proof text intending to show that all of life is indeed dependent upon respiration – the biblical "breath of life".

7 *Responsa Hakham Tsvi, 77.* This responsum was a detailed discussion of the role of the heart in respiration occasioned by a question pertaining to a chicken that had been slaughtered and found to have no heart. Was such a chicken still kosher? According to Aristotelian physiology, the heart pumped hot air throughout the body and cool air from outside the body was inhaled in order to cool it.

8 R. Eliezer Waldenburg, *Tsits Eliezer* 9:46, quoting the *Hakham Tsvi*.

9 Ibid.

# Really Dead?

[10] He did this without any reference to the death of the brain, as this was not yet an issue. It is obvious however, that such an understanding of respiration will have implications for those who will describe it as a function of the brain. Another way of understanding his referencing out-dated physiology was that he wanted to read the talmudic text in its own physiological context—in the same way that its author would have understood respiratory and cardiac function. For an explanation of talmudic-era physiology see Edward Reichman, "The Halachic Definition of Death in Light of Medical History," in *The Torah and Madda Journal*, ed. J. Schacter (New York: Yeshiva University Press, 1993).

[11] *Responsa Hatam Sofer*, YD:348.

[12] Ibid. This is his summary of another classic authority – *Responsa Marasham*, 6:91.

[13] See Maimonides, **Mishne Torah**: *Avel* 4:5.

[14] Noted in Avraham S. Avraham, *Nishmat Avraham* (Jerusalem: Machon Schlesinger, 1984), 242. Avraham would become an important figure in the world of Israeli medical *halakhah* publishing the first Israeli compendium on *halakhah* and medicine, *Lev Avraham*.

[15] While this language seems sincere, by the time that this responsum was written, R. Auerbach was universally recognized as one of the outstanding *posqim* in the world. In spite of any denial, the comments do carry great weight. The fact that this letter would come to be included in the codex of his responsa shows that irregardless of his intent it came to be treated as a *psaq halakhah*.

[16] The word, *Israelis* can refer to either race/religion or nationality here. In traditional sources, it is used the way *Jew* is today. The question as to whether the determination of death in the eyes of the *halakhah* is a universally applicable category or one meant specifically for Jews will come up again in further discussions and is quite important in analyzing the meaning of criteria for death.

[17] See Aviad Hakohen, "*Mishpat Verefuah Bemedinat Yehudit Vedemokratit: Ben Antonomiah Shel Hok Lepatologiah Shel Yehasei Dat Vemedinah*" for the history of these debates.

[18] *Minhat Shlomo* 86:5.

[19] See Maimonides, **Mishne Torah**, *Avel* 4:5. See also Steinberg's note on this in "*Kviat Regah Hamavet*," 232, note 95.

[20] *Minhat Shlomo*, 86:5

---

21 See Maimonides, **Mishne Torah**, *Rotseah* 2:4 which is brought in this responsum as an example. Such a classification today may also have distinct consequences, such as the type of treatment offered, insurance payment for treatment, etc.

22 R. Auerbach writes that this traditional case is clearer than the modern case.

23 The argument regarding brain hypoxia is advanced to equate this *halakhic* "definition of death" with brain-death elsewhere. In fact, this is part of the argument made by Frank J. Veith, et al, "Brain Death: A Status Report of Medical and Ethical Considerations," *JAMA* 238:15 (Oct 10, 1977): 1651-5 in the section of their article devoted to the Jewish perspective. We can assume that this section was the responsibility of Moshe Tendler – one of the authors—who is also an Orthodox rabbi who lobbied extensively for acceptance of brain-death in the halakhic world.

24 R. Auerbach does not delve into the problem here of whether artificially aided respiration is equivalent to "natural" respiration or not. He does, though, specifically mention continued heart function as one of the signs indicating life and the need for continued medical intervention. From this responsum it is not clear at what point he would advocate withdrawal of treatment. He does not differentiate between the *gosses* and others with respiratory failure as do Rabbis Rabinowitz and Unterman.

25 R. Weiss would eventually become the leader and one of the main *poskim* of the *Edah Haharedit* (an Orthodox, extremely religiously conservative group) in Jerusalem. Here is an example of the titular head of British Jewry asking for a decision from a recognized *poseq*. We see that political position does not necessarily equal with judicial-religious authority. See note 2 above. The responsum is found in *Minhat Yitshaq* 5:7.

26 In the Chief Rabbi's own words he asked that R. Weiss enlighten him "so as to guide me on the true and just path" so that he himself could properly answer the questions of his own congregants.

27 No one suggested that such a patient is *already* dead however, as long as he has a pulse.

28 This is expressed in the *gemara* as a question concerning the language of the *mishnah* which states, "If he is found alive – we [continue] to remove the rubble" (*b. Yoma* 73a). The *gemara* queries:

> Isn't this obvious? [That if he is alive the rescue is continued?] No, [this assertion comes to teach] even if he may only survive for a short time [literally – "possesses only temporary life"] (75b).

71

# Really Dead?

From this source then, it is clear that even short-term survival warrants rescue efforts. This is codified in the *Shulhan Arukh* as follows:

> ...even if he is found crushed such that he can only live for a short time, we continue to uncover him... (*Orah Haim* 329:4).

[29] This is codified in the *Shulhan Arukh, Yoreh Deah* 339:1. The removal of an impediment to the *gosses'* death, though, is permitted. The question of what constitues such an impediment and what constitutes the hastening of death is one discussed in halakhic literature at length. I will turn to it below.

[30] *Responsa Shvut Yaaqov,* 1:13. He discusses a rather gruesome case wherein an attempt was made to deliver by cesarean section the fetus of a beheaded pregnant woman.

[31] He argued against the *Beit Yaaqov* (**Responsa Beit Yaaqov**, 69) who differentiated between a *gosses* and other cases. For the *gosses*, no intervention was permissible except that which could confidently restore a large measure of health or longevity. Because the *gosses* is in the very throes of death, it is not permitted to lengthen the process of his soul's departure (as this causes him great anguish) unless one can be sure of saving him from death. However, elsewhere the *Shvut Yaakov* himself offered a different explanation for differentiating between these two cases– that as the state of the *gosses* is very fragile, non-expert care may be worse than no care at all (3:85).

[32] See the *Biur Halakhah*, end of 329.

[33] Neither R. Auerbach nor R. Weiss spelled out which conditions would justify the withholding or withdrawl of futile medical treatment. R. Weiss also did not offer any definite guidelines for the removal of resuscitative apparatus from a *gosses* patient. In fact, he merely noted that the permitted removal of an impediment to dying from the *gosses* patient needed to be examined further in the case of respiration.

[34] A fifth was written, seemingly lost, and then discovered in the midst of controversy over the proper interpretation of his opinion. It was published posthumously.

[35] R. Moshe Feinstein, *Egrot Moshe*, YD II:174 (hereafter *EM*).

[36] "An individual does not defile until he is dead. Even if he is severely wounded, even if he is breathing his last ... so too a beast or animal does not defile until dead. If they are beheaded, even if they still quiver/move – they defile, for this [movement] is like that of a lizard's tail which quivers" (*Mishnah Ohalot* 1:6).

[37] *b. Git.* 70a. Cutting the throat is the traditional way of ritually slaughtering animals and it is usually assumed that completely severing the trachea and the esophagus will bring quick, certain, painless death.

[38] The rest of the responsum, as well as the lengthy response to his comments by R. Weiss (found in *Minhat Yitshaq,* 8:8), delineates the limits of one Jew's responsibility to save another's life. To what degree must or may he place himself in danger to save the life of his fellow?

[39] For them it was clear that such practices violated what modern secular ethical discourse would term the "rights" of these dying patients. However, as the late Orthodox Jewish bioethicist Benjamin Freedman explained in *Duty and Healing* (NY: Routledge, 1999), the moral system of the *halakhah* revolves not around moral rights, but obligations. Hence the different framing of their claims.

[40] I think that the amount of space in their responsa devoted to delimiting the actual obligation of self-endangerment and risk required by the *halakhah* in order to save another's life (which I did not discuss here) reflects their understanding that this type of moral calculus was used by those in favor of heart transplantation at the time. They both objected to it, refusing to look beyond the dying patient's own good and own care, ie what this particular patient was due, not what he could do for another. Their view was, for some, frustratingly localized on the individual patient to the exclusion of the larger picture. Noam Zohar, for example, critiqued this atomizing tendency of *halakhic* bioethics (*Alternatives in Jewish Bioethics*, Albany: SUNY Press, 1997, 134). But I think that he misses the devotion that these rabbis and others showed to the particular patient—a firm moral stance set against the slippery slope of experimentation and transplantation.

# 3

# 1968
# Conceptualizing Death

Even as the excitement which the first heart transplants brought with them dissipated, interest in the problems presented by brain-death did not. However, this interest (perhaps abetted by the publication of what would come to be known as the Harvard criteria in the summer of 1968) shifted in focus from the practical immediacy inherent in actual transplantation to the more theoretical questions which brain-death raised. Brain-death, many realized, reflected upon the meaning of death itself. How was death to be defined? Did the localization of death in the brain (or solely as a neurological event) represent a change in how death had generally been understood? Did it change the very meaning of death from a broad-based somatic event to one that could be measured in a singular way—despite what we might label "somatic dissonance?"

In Israel, coincidently or not, the first two published articles that looked closely at the meaning of death itself in the brain-death era did so in nearly antithetical fashion.[1] Both were written by practicing Israeli physicians and both were published in respected Israeli journals. However, where one author, H. M. Ashkenazi, presented death as a biological fact waiting to be discovered, the other, Yaaqov Levi, argued that death represented more a social-cultural decision than a

# Really Dead?

medically proven state. Levi claimed that this was the way that the *halakhah*, as a legal-moral system, understood death. Although each author discussed Jewish law and medicine alongside history and biology in their presentations of death, they conceptualized the relationships between these fields, brought together by this new death, in starkly different ways. The dichotomous view of death observable in the conceptual discontinuity between these two articles foreshadows the tensions which would eventually forestall cooperation between the Rabbinate and the Health Ministry nearly 20 years later. The analysis of these articles undertaken in this chapter shows us just how far back the conceptual conflict over the meaning of death reached in the Israeli brain-death discourse.

Dr. Yaaqov Levi, a well-known Jerusalem pediatrician and halakhic scholar,[2] wrote an article which sought to arrive at a technical definition of death according to the *halakhah*. He contrasted his conclusions with those drawn by secular doctors.[3] Critical of secular medical ethics, over the next four years Levi wrote three articles disparaging the organ transplantation project.[4] In this piece, he began by contrasting the moral ideology of scientific medicine with that of *halakhah*. He wrote that the *halakhah's* goal is to "direct the Jew in the proper path," while making use of physical facts only as means towards this end. Medical science, however, he claimed deals first and foremost in facts. When the clinician is confronted with ethical issues, medical science itself cannot supply him with moral guidance. Rather, he looks to his own subjective values for direction. For Levi, the story of organ transplantation was a tale of moral failure.[5] (However, his own critical reading of the story was not in itself free of factual inaccuracies.)

Using the proceedings of the Ciba Symposium from 1966, Levi detailed how transplant surgeons manipulated "facts" to conform with their own agenda. Objective findings in comatose patients, such as falling blood-pressure and flat EEG tracings, were *interpreted* as signs of death. In Levi's opinion, there was no objective reason to lead to such conclusions.

> In my opinion, these are actually signs of life: although blood pressure is falling, there is still pressure, signaling that circulation is still active, the heart is still beating. The peaks of the EEG may be flat, low, but there is still electric activity in the cells.[6]

While such patients were certainly dying, only those acting in accordance with what Levi pejoratively called "doctor's ethics", could possibly equate such "clinical death" with actual death and allow for organ removal.[7]

His indignation, however, was based on what seems to be an odd reading of the materials available from the Ciba Symposium. He himself differentiated between patients who had suffered severe brain trauma and were prognosed as dying and those who were being "artificially" supported by resuscitation equipment. He held that these latter patients could in fact be labeled dead. His accusations were focused on those doctors who would equate the prognosis of death (of the breathing comatose) with death itself. However, while the Ciba proceedings did mention one Swedish case where a kidney was taken from a comatose patient not on life-support,[8] all the discussions centered on cases where potential organ donors lacked respiratory capability and were being resuscitated.[9]

The main target of Levi's ire, a Belgian transplant surgeon, G. P. J. Alexandre, had proclaimed:

> I would like to make it clear that, in my opinion, there has never been and there will never be any question of

# Really Dead?

taking organs from a dying person who has "no reasonable chance of regaining consciousness." The question is of taking organs from a dead person, and the point is that I do not accept the cessation of heart beats as the indication of death. ...but I think irreversible damage to the central nervous system is an indication of physiological death that permits us to take an organ from a body that is already a cadaver.[10]

Levi only quoted this last sentence, and ignored the fact that just one page further on Alexandre makes it clear that all his patients were not breathing independently. [11]

In our nine cases we switched off the respirator immediately after the kidneys were removed. The heart beats of all the patients ceased within two or three minutes. In my opinion it is irrelevant whether a heart-lung preparation goes on for days or even for weeks: it is still a heart-lung preparation.[12]

Ironically, this was similar to Levi's own conclusions regarding these resuscitated patients!

Levi quoted one Israeli author, the already-mentioned surgeon Morris Levy, who, reporting on the developments in heart transplantation nearly a year before his own attempt, wrote that any heart surgeon contemplating the removal of an organ for transplant would need to adopt the new suggestion of the French Academy of Science that:

...practically, an individual is considered dead at the moment that it can be proven that brain function has ceased or ended, even though other organs, including the heart, kidney, liver and others, can continue to live for some length of time.[13]

It is not clear whether Morris Levy actually endorsed this view himself at the time or whether the French decision referred to patients breathing on their own. Levi, however, understood that Morris Levy tended "towards the French point of view".[14]

I am not sure what brought about Levi's confusion, but in line with his opposition to treating *prognosis* as *death* he proceeded to build a halakhic argument that these two were separate halakhic categories – each entailing different obligations and concerns. He described the halakhic sources and historical circumstances surrounding R. Moshe Sofer's codification of the moment of death as an example of the *halakhah utilizing* scientific fact without compromising on "the moral nucleus" that unites the various opinions concerning the determination of death. As noted above, R. Sofer concluded:

> Anyone who is lying like an unmoving stone and has no pulse and if afterwards stops breathing, we have naught but the words of our holy Torah that he is dead and his burial should not be delayed.[15]

Levi (citing R. Waldenburg) noted that the language here referred only to "usual cases" and brought a series of responsa that rounded out the picture to include "exceptional cases" as well.[16] That is, cessation of respiration could only be used as a *final* sign of death after a patient had previously exhibited the other two signs of death: immobility and loss of cardiac activity. If this was not the case, as for those who suddenly collapsed, then the *halakhah* recognized the need for more careful case by case examination. This would also hold true for

# Really Dead?

those who lost the ability to breathe only temporarily, like those patients under the influence of barbiturates or suffering from hypothermia. [17] This is similar to what we have already seen in the comments of other *posqim*.

The next section of his article, though, represented a novel departure. He cited the Talmudic source from *Yoma* concerning rescue operations on the Sabbath. As he described the case he asked why the Talmud and the halakhic codifiers would assume that the lack of respiration alone would suffice for a determination of death, when (he assumed) it was clear that they knew of cases where cardiac activity persisted for some time afterwards. Wouldn't they want to check for cardiac activity as well so as to also exclude these cases? His answer was that this latter type of case was so *exceedingly* rare that the *halakhah*, even though it allowed for Sabbath desecration in instances where there were a number of doubts concerning the chance for survival, did not consider *cases like this*.

> However, according to the *halakhah* it appears that this is only the slimmest of unlikely doubts. For this type of doubt the Sabbath is not desecrated.[18]

But he asked, what would we say if a Gentile were to excavate the trapped person and find that he was actually still living? Here Levi drew a most interesting conclusion.

> [The non-breathing individual trapped under rubble] only is considered dead *de jure* in the eyes of the *halakhah* which instructs us how to act regarding him on the Sabbath.

> Even if the actual facts of the case prove that he was still physically alive, let us not make a mistake and think

that the *halakhah* was not correct. The *halakhah* never claimed that there was physical death here.[19]

As the *halakhah* is only meant to guide our actions and not establish physical facts for us, Levi claimed that the same logic applies to our obligations to save a life during the rest of the week. That is, an individual may be *treated as* dead in accordance with the ever changing means available to save his life. However, this does not reflect upon his actual physical state, only upon the state of available medical care. The criteria for determining death, then, are actually prognostic criteria which, when there is nothing more for us to do, relieve us of the obligation to save this individual.[20] Regarding an obligation to provide care, the victim/patient may be treated as already dead.

Updating R. Sofer's decision, Levi wrote that this *psaq* required three different signs of death in order to allow for internment: "lying like an unmoving stone" corresponds to unconsciousness and the lack of reflexes; "has no pulse" to the lack of cardiac activity; "stops breathing" to cessation of respiration.[21] Levi argued that in clear cases, such as beheaded individuals, the *halakhah* would agree with scientific opinion on the determination of death as these three criteria are obviously fulfilled. There are other cases, however, where medical "clinical death" may be interpreted by doctors as actual death, but the *halakhah* would not support such an interpretation. These cases, such as patients with severe brain trauma, do not describe "death" according to the *halakhah*. Here Levi stressed not only the need to use all three of the criteria found in the *Chatam Sofer*, but also the need to employ the EEG and ECG to be certain that both the brain *and* heart registered no activity whatsoever.[22]

The question that confronted those interested in organ transplants, according to Levi, was whether unconscious resuscitated individuals (the brain-dead) who did not exhibit all these signs, were to be considered *halakhically* dead. They appear to be unclear cases – perhaps alive, perhaps dead. However, "just as [the *halakhah*] does not undertake to determine physical death, so too it need not accept the decision of science concerning death."[23]

Levi argued, then, that *posqim* must determine whether these patients are halakhically dead–that is whether we are freed of the obligation to treat them. Once such a decision is made, resuscitative equipment could be withdrawn. His question was:

> ...can the *halakhah* give up on complete certainty of physical death in order to determine that this patient has died according to the *halakhah*, so that they may dare to attempt to stop the machinery, at least in those cases where this will allow for saving of life (organ transplants)?[24]

If, after such an attempt we see that "life does not return" to the patient, can we be assured that he has died "in every way"?

Levi also claimed that once such a decision is made, even if respiratory support is <u>not</u> withdrawn,

> ...in order to preserve the life of his organs, then such life has no connection to the life of the person...and organs can then be removed.[25]

He did not consider such a decision as one to be taken lightly and understood that it represented a difficult conceptual leap. He wondered whether *posqim* could "dare" to act on such a radical dismissal of the physical in favor of the conceptual. Levi's understanding of *halakhah* posited an essential difference between physical reality and halakhic conceptional categories.[26]

Aside from pointing to this physical-conceptual gap, Levi presented an interesting logical construction of the halakhic conceptualization of death as a function of medical futility. As the role of the *halakhah* is not to determine physical states, but only a Jew's obligations concerning these states, the determination of death in the *halakhah* will necessarily be essentially a determination of obligations towards an individual in a given state. It would appear, then, according to Levi's view, that the real concern of R. Sofer was a determination of when the obligation of burial takes effect. The concern of the Talmudic discussion in Yoma is to delineate the obligation of saving a life and not to make a statement about life itself. Death, for Levi, was a social, not a scientific, category.[27]

Even after describing the interconnection of the different parts of the respiratory system, and concurring that the loss of brain function would bring about death, he nevertheless questioned what bearing this 'scientific' description would have on the social-religious category of death. [28] The *halakhah*, as he noted, "need not accept the decision of science concerning death" for it was primarily concerned with our moral obligations towards the dying rather than with defining death itself.

This view was diametrically opposed in the first scientific-journal report on brain-death published a few months after the IMA responded to the Health Ministry's query. It was written by a well-known cardiac surgeon, H. M. Ashkenazi.[29] The author devoted one-third of his article to an odd social-cultural analysis beginning with a brief historical survey where he described the evolution of criteria for determining death.

> It was once clear to everyone that the meaning of death
> meant the end of the life of the organism as a whole and
> if hair or nails still grew after death, this was treated as

a mere curiosity. Those who were interested in more exactitude determined death according to one particular organ's loss of function, whichever was considered to be the most important.[30]

He mentioned how respiration was chosen in the Jewish tradition (although he did not show how this is the function of one organ) and how the "mystification" of the heart brought some to understand that cardiac activity was tied to the determination of death.

Technological advances, he claimed "...necessarily bring with them recognition of new concepts, better and more modern, with respect to death...."[31] Ashkenazi then went on to explain how societal laws in every generation must change to reflect the "evolutionary changes" that occur in science, religion, and ethics. Such that, "...surely the laws of the Rambam are no longer suitable to our period."[32]

He lamented, however, the fact that most *legal* definitions of death had not kept up with scientific advancement in understanding death. Legally, death was still understood as an event; while modern science knows that it is actually a "gradual process." He complained that "the legal faculties today, in most countries, understand death as one specific, immediate moment, while we know that we are standing before a gradual process."[33] However, this legal lag, Ashkenazi assented, was beginning to show signs of ending. If the law continued to insist on understanding a "moment of death" which an individual doctor had always been competent to pronounce, why then, he wondered, did the law now require that death for transplant purposes be determined by a team of doctors?![34]

Next, Ashkenazi explained why the death of the brain was equivalent to the death of the individual. First, he wrote of the "well-established fact" that the cells of the brain are the most sensitive to anoxia and will die before the cells of other organs which may continue to function. Second, knowledge of the "...central role of the brain, as a factor in governing and regulating the biological processes in the body, points to the unarguable fact that the death of the brain means death of the entire body."[35]

The then recently published Harvard criteria, according to Ashkenazi, were introduced as a means of closing the gap between the dated cardio-vascular legal definition of death and medical science which had utilized neurological criteria (like unresponsiveness, cessation of respiration, etc.) for some time. Science did not allow for the continued functioning of artificially supported organs to distract from the proper conclusion that "death of the brain, practically, means death of the entire body, even if [this occurs] at a different time".[36] He claimed that the criteria published by CIOMS were practically equivalent to those of the Harvard Committee.

This section of his article concluded with a survey of some of the noticed inaccuracies of the EEG in measuring brain-death, while defending its use in principle and hoping that, as in the past, scientific progress would bring better means for "objectively measuring death".[37] Ashkenazi ended with a call to update the legal definition of death to one based solely on brain-death and a plea for medical doctors to lead the way in helping society to accept this difficult conceptual change.

In his brief article, Ashkenazi made use of a number of conceptual assumptions about the medical determination of death.[38] Essentially, he described the *criteria* of death as having undergone a series of historical changes. These changes reflected the attempts of those seeking to pinpoint its arrival (lawyers, rabbis) to arrive at a singular, reductionist definition of death itself. Despite their best efforts, however, better scientific knowledge has brought this "moment of death" thinking to an end. As modern scientific methodology and under-

# Really Dead?

standing has done a better job of locating the precise point of death's arrival—separating the essential from the peripheral—the older, less successful attempts at determining death (recorded in law) need be replaced by the new and better scientific determination. The older attempts are outdated and, in light of newer knowledge, essentially meaningless. Ashkenazi felt that the law should be rewritten in order to accurately reflect the newer scientific facts about death.

Whether it actually matters or not, his short rehearsal of the history of man's search for some singular determinate of death was historically incorrect.[39] Additionally, his interpretation of the meaning of even specific criterion found during this search have not been universally shared.[40] But his main thrust was that the search for criteria of death, always understood as the death of the *individual as a whole*, had also always been the reductionist search for the loss of some central organ function. Mistakenly identifying respiration (which is not a function of one organ, but rather a complex interaction of muscles, organs, tissues, nerves and cellular processes) as one such outmoded attempt and cardiac function as a romantic myth – he believed that this "holy grail" had finally been found in the brain.[41]

Oddly however, Ashkenazi insisted on viewing death as a *process*, while also subscribing to an essentialist view that there must be *one particular point* that *is* Death.[42] His historical introduction to his article presented his understanding of man's search for proper criteria of death as just this type of search for one point at which death could be declared. He wrote that today "we know that we are standing before a gradual process" *while also arguing that* the "…central role of the brain, as a factor in governing and regulating the biological processes in the body, points to the unarguable fact that the death of the brain means death of the entire body." So for Ashkenazi, brain-death represents *both* a continuation of the historical search for a singular criterion of death, as well as recognition of the problematics of such a search.

Brain-death resulted from the need for "an exact determination of death which takes place within a short time-period" in light of new resuscitative abilities and the development of cadaver organ transplantation.[43] That is, it was a solution to the problems associated with life support and transplantation. It was philosophically warranted because modern science knows that death is, in fact, "a gradual process." Yet, on the other hand, it seems to represent a continuation (and an improvement upon) the age-old search for a singular criterion for establishing death.

The philosopher Karen Gervais suggested that death is not one unitary biological fact, but rather a philosophical, moral decision which utilizes biology. For Gervais, determination of death, "…rests on a decision of significance, that is, a decision concerning the features that humans must possess to be regarded as living persons rather than dead persons".[44] Real biological death would require cellular necrosis of the entire body, but death is declared well before that time based on philosophical reflection about which criteria are the most significant for understanding the end of human life. Where once cardio-linked criteria seemed to be the most significant way of declaring death, the technology of organ transplantation created a rupture between biological death and personal death, as living hearts were being removed from dead bodies. For this reason, Gervais supported a *new* decision of significance, brain-death.[45]

I would argue that Ashkenazi might have agreed with this philosophical conception of death. He did portray brain-death as developed in response to the problems of modern medicine. Yet, because he had other interests, he could not simply portray brain-death as a new philosophical decision. Ashkenazi, unlike Gervais, wanted to hold on to an essentialist understanding of death that he claimed had never changed. Brain-death was not a *new* death, but rather a continuation of what death always was–the death of the "organism as a whole". He

# Really Dead?

stressed that "the death of the brain *is the death of the entire body* [my emphasis]".[46] The beating heart, once a measure of "exactitude" became relegated to "a mere curiosity" like the growth of hair and nails.

His creation of a fictional history of death served to explain how this came about. The *body* of our heart donor appears to be very much *alive*–the donor, himself, of course is (must be) *dead*. But by asserting that this was always the case–even if the body's hair and nails were alive, we always considered that the actual person was dead. This is what we always *meant* by death. Rather than just substitute the death of one organ—the heart, for another—the brain, Ashkenazi equates the death of the brain with *death* itself, more readily painting the (still-beating) heart as part of the mist-shrouded quaintness of olden times.

After explaining how Maimonides chose to focus on the cessation of breath as an indicator of death due to its linguistic proximity to the word for soul in Hebrew (*neshima – neshema*), Ashkenazi wrote:

> Just as we have done, also many other peoples have harped on the metaphysical qualities of the heart. In most languages we can find expressions like our "broken heart." ... It is no surprise, then, how they relied upon the end of heart activity in determining death.

Paradoxically, finding one central organ on which to pin death was at once a move forward and a mistake. On the one hand:

> It was once clear to everyone that the meaning of death meant the end of the life of the organism as a whole and if hair or nails still grew after death, this was treated as a mere curiosity. Those who were interested *in more exactitude* [my emphasis], determined death according to

one particular organ's loss of function, whichever was considered to be the most important.

Yet the focus on the heart was also, as I mentioned above, a matter of romanticism ("the broken heart"). The donor's beating "tell-tale heart" needed to be excised not just physically, but hermeneutically as well–turned into the mere continued growth of hair or nails. This is much more easily accomplished when somatic death is dismissed, and brain-death introduced not merely as a *new* philosophic construct, but as a better version of what we always meant when we spoke of death. Brain-death relegated the living heart to the dead body, together with the rest of its meaningless cellular activity.

For the Israeli debate over brain-death, the way that Ashkenazi staked out an extreme position in respect to legal norms and their relation to science, is telling. Arguing against the way that Levi presented the *halakhah*, he insisted upon a strong legal realism: that the law accurately reflect our understanding of reality as revealed by scientific inquiry.[47] As medical science has shown both that the brain is the central controlling organ of the body and that we can know when the brain has ceased to function, Ashkenzi determined that the death of the brain was the death of the person. The laws concerning death are meant to reflect our understanding of what death (of the whole person) is in actuality. This explains Ashkenazi's great discomfiture with the inadequacies of outdated legal definitions and his surety that we must cast off outdated legal systems (like that of the Rambam) – they are essentially meaningless.

Such an approach—based on legal realism—would have important consequences for any discussions with those who hold that legal (or halakhic statements) are not just meant to be disposable reflections of changing reality (which is most accurately described by scientific methodology), but rather, for instance, statements about important

# Really Dead?

societal values. For those who do not see halakhic statements as reflective of a scientifically proven reality, but of timeless ethical obligations—like Dr. Yaaqov Levi—dismissing them in the face of 'scientific progress' is not a logical option. Levi, we saw, preferred to separate the halakhic from the scientific, essentially negating the need for any halakhic change in the face of new scientific evidence. However, we have already seen a different approach—based on negotiating the relationship between halakhic precedent and scientifically driven medical advances.[48]

The strategy employed in the responsum of R. Auerbach can serve as an example of such negotiation between the legal and the scientific. His responsum is based upon legal interpretation and not dismissal. In chapter two I discussed two halakhic assertions that he made. One, loss of respiration as the indicator of death; two, the need to wait between cessation of respiration and pronouncement of death. The first reveals an interesting interplay between medical progress and this halakhically mandated determination of death. The cessation of respiration cannot be dismissed – for it is described as more than just a likely or useful criterion. A biblical verse ("all that have the breath of life in their nostrils" [Genesis 7:22]) is used to anchor the talmudic decision that the lack of respiratory function is enough to declare death. This gives what may have been a mere criterion much more weight. Add to this the declaration by R. Moshe Sofer marking respiration's status as *the* criterion of death handed down the long chain of tradition, and it grows into something that cannot be dismissed. However, when juxtaposed with new resuscitative technologies that seem to unravel its status, cessation of respiration can be *reinterpreted*. As R. Auerbach suggested, the ability to resuscitate allows for the interpretation or defining of the loss of respiration as *either* a medical condition or a sign that life has ended.[49]

Both the reinterpretation by R. Auerbach and the realism of Ashkenazi lie in opposition to the positivism espoused by Levi. For Levi, the *halakhah* works in accordance with its own definitions, able to function independently of scientific discovery. (This view is not the only way to understand the *halakhah* in general, or the determination of death in particular.) The fact that the first two scholarly articles on brain-death to appear in Israel, each written by a medical doctor, present such diametric views of the relation between science and law, foreshadowed some of the tensions that would follow the debate over brain-death and heart transplants in the coming years. The authors' claims concerning the medical-scientific understanding of death did not differ all that much.[50] They even had similar reservations concerning testing and criteria for measuring the indications of death.

What they did disagree about, though, was the *meaning* of neurological death in the transplant field. For Ashkenazi it meant the abandonment of outdated legal forms and wide ranging adaptations to the revolutionary changes wrought by transplantation. Levi, however, insisted the ways which we need to (ethically) treat the dead and dying were laid out for us by immutable *halakhah*. Ironically, even though in the end there may be little practical difference between these two authors' suggestions regarding the use of *resuscitated* brain-dead patients as organ donors, the way in which they staked out their individual claims set up a seemingly unbridgeable gap surrounding the valuation of halakhic-legal norms. For Levi, they were as *meaningful* as anything presented by scientific evidence. For Ashkenazi, they were in essence meaningless–unless reflective of what science described as real.

This conceptual polarization over the *halakhah* (which can be seen as representative of socio-legal norms in general) came to influence the ways that the problem of death were dealt with in Israel. The *halakhah*, as a regulatory legal system, offered its own definition of

# Really Dead?

death. For those who adhered to Jewish law, this trumped those offered by other ways of understanding death, be they scientifically or socially based, and determined how the dying or dead should be treated. The halakhic definition of death, in the eyes of Levi, gave the deceased a particular socio-legal status. That status then informed the ethical obligations of those left to care for his body. It was this status and not a scientifically determined state which needed to be addressed by those wanting to harvest his organs. Continued conflicts over defining death in Israel were to a large degree related to the tensions surrounding the role of law or halakha in science-based medicine. The basic tension between state and status concerning death would not disappear. The dichotomy represented by these two early articles on brain-death would continue to haunt the attempts at dialogue over heart transplants for years to come.

---

[1] In the fall of 1969, the Chief Rabbi, R. Isser Yehuda Unterman, did write a more narrowly focused article on a number of the halakhic problems related to such transplants arguing, like R. Feinstein, that the risk involved for the recipient was too great to warrant consideration of undergoing such surgery. His main focus in this piece was on the "assumption of life" that may be disturbed in the time between the removal of the recipient's own heart and its replacement with that of the donor. Interestingly, he began his article by stating that he was no *poseq*, and called upon those who were to deal with the pressing issue of transplants. (Again this shows that public position is no indication of authoritative status.) With respect to the determination of death, he repeated the assertion made by R. Rabinowitz that the *gosses* is due no medical treatment. He quoted the *psaq* of the Chatam Sofer while explaining that it only applied to the death of a *gosses* or very ill individual. For those who suddenly stopped breathing, there remained an obligation to try to revive them ("*Hashtalat Halev Behalakhah,*" **Noam** 13 [5730], 1-9).

[2] Levi was a well known teacher and pediatrician in the Jerusalem hospital–Bikur Holim. He wrote over 100 medical articles—many dealing with medicine and *halakhah* and was frequently consulted on medical-religious issues. He was considered by many in the Jerusalem community to be an exemplar of the "religious

doctor"–especially in the early days of the State. See Haim Halberstam, *"Dr. Yaaqov Levi—Kavim Ledmuto Ulemifal Hayav,"* **Sefer Assia** 3 (1983): 485-6.

[3] Y. Levi, *"B'inyan Hashtalat Averim Mehamet,"* **Noam** 12 (5729), 291-312. To prevent confusion between Morris Levy and Yaaqov Levi, I have spelled the former with a *y* and the latter with an *i*.

[4] His criticism was directed more at the way in which the moral calculus of transplantation was explained and put into practice, than with actual organ transplantation, which he did not understand as problematic in itself. In this way, he shared the views expressed by Rabbis Feinstein and Auerbach which we discussed in the previous chapter.

[5] Ibid., 290. In an earlier comment (*"Qeviat Hamavet al Yede Rofim,"* **Hama'ayan** 9:1 (5729): 24, 64 and a later article *"Me'emati Mutar Lehotsi Ever Lehashtalah,"* *Hama'ayan* 10, no. 1 (1969), he makes it clear that his discomfort with transplantation stemmed from the ways that the death of the brain was inaccurately measured. Reliance on a "flat EEG", as opposed to better indications of complete necrosis or at least of complete loss of cellular function through angiography, for example, was seen as a terribly lax way to ascertain death of the brain. The same held for the use of the ECG to determine loss of cardiac function—it was not thorough enough. Aside from these technical points, he disagreed with the interpretation of the death of the brain as the death of the individual–as we will see.

[6] Ibid., 292.

[7] The argument that brain-death was manufactured by transplant surgeons in order to insure ethically acceptable supplies of organs has been made since the entire project began. See Lock, *Twice Dead* and Belkin, "Death Before Dying". The argument that this has occurred because medical science or science in general itself is amoral and so needs outside moral guidance (or policing) has also been made in connection with the transplant project since its beginning. See Hans Jonas, "Against the Stream: Comments on the Definition and Redefinition of Death," in *Philosophical Essays: From Ancient Creed to Technological Man* (NJ: Prentice Hall, 1974) for one of the earliest such critiques. Kurt Vonnegut's *Cat's Cradle* (London: Gollancz, 1963) reflects the unease felt by many regarding the divorce of science from ethics. Already in 1969, one of the stated reasons that the IMA gave in wanting to establish guidelines for transplantation was so as not to give outsiders (non-medical doctors) cause to interfere with medical decisions.

[8] Maeve O'Connor and G.E.W. Wolstenholme, *Ethics in Medical Progress*, 92.

# Really Dead?

[9] See the discussion between Starzl and Woodruff in *Ethics in Medical Progress*, 98-99. Also this type of patient was the focus of the responsa of Rabbis Weiss and Feinstein mentioned above.

[10] Ibid., 155.

[11] Levi, *"B'inyan Hashtalat Averim"*, 292.

[12] Wolstenholme, *Ethics in Medical Progress*, 156.

[13] M. Levy, *"Shtilat Lev,"* 145. This was published a few days before he expressed his opinion that the future lay in artificial hearts as noted above.

[14] Y. Levi, *"B'inyan Hashtalat Averim,"* 293.

[15] *Responsa Hatam Sofer*, YD 348.

[16] Y. Levi, *"B'inyan Hashtalat Averim,"* 298-299.

[17] Ibid., 301.

[18] Ibid. The explanation of R. Waldenburg eliminates any need to make such a claim.

[19] Ibid., 302.

[20] Ibid., 303. He acknowledges, however (note 51), that there is a question if the end of the obligation of treatment would correspond to the change of the patient's legal status in other realms. Would his wife be considered a widow, his children inherit, etc. at the time of such a decision?

[21] Ibid., 305.

[22] It was these comatose patients that Levi felt were being wrongfully killed by transplant surgeons. He understood that such patients were unconscious, but could breathe independently. It is not clear from the Ciba Symposium that this was in fact the case.

[23] Ibid., 310. Levi cited the fact that there were divergent opinions regarding the proper scientific-medical criteria for death as another reason the *halakhah* avoided attempting to give actual physically valid answers.

[24] Ibid., 312.

[25] Ibid.

[26] Ibid., 312.

[27] This argument preceded the work of Robert Veatch, one of the early and influential American modern bioethicists, who was one of the major proponents of death as a social category. For Veatch death had more to do with the permissions granted to society with regard to the 'dead' than with biological facts about a particular body. He supported, however, a certain type of brain-death. He pressed the case that defining death was primarily a moral or philosophical question seeking

to establish the proper time for the introduction of "death behaviors"–such as mourning, the payment of life insurance, the end of medical treatment and burial. Far from insisting that there was only one true way of being dead, he outlined different conceptual understandings of what death could mean. However, he drew a clear connection between the biological and the social in asserting that each different concept of death would have its own suitable criteria meant to affirm its presence in a specific bodily locus whose particular loss of life corresponded to that particular concept. As specifically *human* death was what we really should be concerned with, he sought the essential characteristics of human beings, which when lost would allow for this person to be treated as dead. He argued that the essential quality of *humanity* was the "embodied capacity for social interaction". Only the irreversible loss of this capacity was a proper criterion for human death. The bodily locus of such a capacity was in the higher-brain and could be tested through the use of the EEG or other appropriate devices for measuring higher-brain activity. (*Death, Dying and the Biological Revolution: Our Last Quest for Responsibility* [New Haven: Yale University Press, 1976]). Over the years, Veatch has continued to contribute to the brain-death debate in a number of articles, exploring many of the implications that his thesis of death as a social category suggests.

[28] Y. Levi, "*B'inyan Hashtalat Averim,*" 307.

[29] A letter to the editor defending the use of the EEG as *one of several* criteria for establishing death was published a few months previously (Lavi, *Harefuah* 76:2, 82-3). This journal, one of two Hebrew medical journals, was also published by the IMA. Additionally, a few articles detailing kidney transplants had been published in the mid-1960s in the English language *Israel Journal of Medical Science*. None of them discuss any criteria for determining death, but all indicate the use of cadaveric kidneys. One article noted that the protocol for determining death of the donor utilized a team of three doctors (D. Erlik, et al., "Cadaveric Renal Transplantation in Man: First Report from Israel," *Israel Journal of Medical Science* 3:1 [Jan-Feb 1967]: 88-92, 91).

[30] H. M. Ashkenazi, "*Mot Hamoah,*" **Harefuah** 76, no.6 (1969): 252. Pernick has shown quite clearly that this type of reductionism was not historically true.

[31] Ibid.

[32] Ibid.

[33] Ibid.

[34] This is an odd rhetorical question. The simplest answer, to guard against actual or apparent conflicts of interest when this patient is about to become a donor for

another patient, seems obviously not connected to the point that he wants to make here.

[35] Ibid.

[36] Ibid.

[37] Ibid., 253. Interestingly, he uses the phrase, 'objectification of death'. In an interview on Israeli television on June 8th, 1969 he had the following exchange:

> Ashkenazi: The read-out of the brain-waves is not 100% certain. In fact, a youth presented a read-out that evidenced that his brain had died, yet after a while he recovered.
>
> Interviewer: Are we allowed to suspect that among those who were heart donor's there were those whose diagnosis was mistaken and could have been saved? Can such a mistake occur?
>
> After answering in the affirmative, the interviewer exclaimed: That's murder!
>
> A: Yes. (quoted by Levi, "Me'emati," 7.)

This interview seemed to have caused a number of ripples among the public and was cited by those opposed to aspects of the transplant project. However, it is difficult to gauge from a printed transcript the exact intent of Ashkenazi in this interview. Unless the interview was broadcast live and uncut, I would be suspicious of assuming that what was broadcast was the entirety of Ashkenazi's views and not just what an editor thought newsworthy.

[38] I believe that we may assume that it is representative of the views of the IMA and its members on the matter as well. A- It was published in an IMA publication and B - after searching through the issues following its publication I discovered no letters to the editor (a usual feature) on the matter of brain-death. An article by Yaaqov Levi published in another IMA organ, *Member's Letter,* in the Spring of 1970 critical of the use of neurological criteria alone to establish death carried the *unusual* approbation that the views contained in this article were solely those of the author (Levi, "Hashtalat Averim," **ML** Adar 4 [5730]: 12-13).

[39] See Pernick's two articles, "Brain Death in Cultural Context" and "Back From the Grave: Recurring Controversies over Defining and Diagnosing Death in History". He described how the 18th and 19th centuries were rife with worry over the determination of death. Doctors invented quite complicated multi-system inventories of tests to assure that death was accurately established before burial.

40 There are those who understood cardiac criteria as prognostics indicative of the death of the brain – see Julius Korein, "The Problem of Brain Death: Development and History" in *Brain Death: Interrelated Medical And Social Issues*, ed. Julius Korein, 19-38. (New York Academy Of Sciences: Annals of the New York Academy of Sciences, Volume 315, [1978]).

41 A similar essentialist interpretation of death was later championed in Britain by the philosopher David Lamb in his monograph on brain-death, *Death, Brain-Death and Ethics* (Sydney: Croom Helm, 1985). He wrote, "Essential to the concept of brain death is the belief in the existence of a single critical system whose irreversible loss is synonymous with the death of the organism as a whole" (14). He claimed that the brain-stem was this critical piece equated with life. However, Green and Wikler, ("Brain Death and Personal Identity," *Philosophy and Public Affairs* 9 [1980]: 105-33) convincingly argued against this type of reductionism showing how respiration could not be understood as a localized "capacity" residing in the brain. "…the capacity for spontaneous heartbeat and respiration is not lodged in the lower brain. If it were, a functional lower brain would guarantee the presence of [this capacity (noted as S)]…. But it does not. If spontaneous means unassisted by machine, S is a capacity of the body as a whole. Hence brain death is not the same as loss of Capacity S" (109). The fact that polio patients were resuscitated in iron-lungs while alive exemplifies their claim. As we will see below, Lamb's focus on the brain-stem was, even at the time, biologically problematic in other ways as well.

42 Lamb, at least, was more consistent on this point. "It will be maintained here that brain death is a radical reformation of traditional concepts of death rather than a new concept, since there is no new way of being dead, and that it marks an improvement on cardio respiratory formulations since under certain circumstances the latter states may be reversible. It is in this sense that the term brain death can be used as a better formulation of the concept of death. When fully articulated it is not so much a new concept as the formulation of a definition of death where previously none existed" (19). As death never really admitted of any conventional aspects, but was only biological fact, his essentialist claims about brain-death were more consistent.

43 H. M. Ashkenazi, "*Mot Hamoah*," *Harefuah* 76, no. 6 (1969).

44 Karen Gervais, *Redefining Death* (New Haven: Yale University Press, 1986), 5.

45 Gervais felt that modern medicine had actually trumped normal biology, necessitating the creation of a new death, based more on philosophy than biology. "Now that we can tamper with and interrupt nature as we do, … biological discon-

tinuities ... no longer exist in the way they did before. They have become possible stages or interludes, not the end of the story; they may now have an aftermath.... We can no longer consult nature for an answer, because nature is no longer the sole directing force. When nature alone directed events, the biological definition included the conditions under which a person had died. Now the *death of the person* may precede the occurrence of *organic death*.... Now that we direct events through medical intervention, the meaning of a biological approach and definition is largely lost... (59)". Note how brain-death is understood as a construct which replaces biological death – the very opposite of the conceptualization that Lamb had suggested.

[46] Ashkenazi, *"Mot Hamoah"*.

[47] By legal realism (not Legal Realism which is in some ways the converse) I mean the understanding of Law being true by its being a reflection of a distinct 'out-there' reality. A law is true if and only if it *refers* to a true situation. Dennis Patterson describes that understanding a legal statement as true in this fashion, is similar to understanding statements about objects being true (Dennis Patterson, *Law and Truth* [New York: Oxford University Press, 1996], 4). We say that "My car is green" and understand that this statement can be either true or false depending upon the actual state of my actual car. So too, statements of law can be parsed as bivalent (true or false) depending upon whether they accurately reflect an actual state of affairs. So a statement about it being "illegal to cross the street here" would be true in this sense only if one could show that this statement corresponds to an actual reality. Does finding such a statute on the books correspond to finding a green car? If not, what would? This is the important question which Patterson wants to answer. He devotes some time to the case of legally defining death as well (see pages 9-11).

The opposite anti-realist approach would be a legal positivism which would posit a closed structure where the Law constructs its own true definitions. For example, one attains "majority", not for any reasoning about the nature of 18-year-old's mental and physical state, but rather because that is what the Law has stated. Reaching majority grants changes in possibilities and responsibilities, but majority itself is a closed legal category, not necessarily one that is meant to reflect upon the actual state of the major. As the clock strikes twelve and the date changes – majority becomes legal fact. This of course may raise the question of the origins of legal standards. For the legal realist, though, the Law is capable of being false (or meaningless) if it does not reflect upon what we know to be true in the outside world.

[48] The question of the relationship between scientific advances and the *halakhah* is quite complex. I will return to it in section II, chapter 13.

[49] I am not sure if this interpretive strategy is a species of legal positivism. See chapter 2 above concerning the authenticity of *psaq*.

[50] I pointed to the extreme criticisms leveled by Levi at using neurologically impaired, breathing patients as being off target. As I wrote above, nearly all of the patients considered for organ donation were on resuscitative life support.

# 4

# 1969-1970
# Public Concern over Death

As discussion of brain-death continued in various forums, tensions inherent in the attempt to redefine the end of life became increasingly apparent. Was this something best left to medical experts? Was there any role for the general public in this discussion? How could the public be assured that the entire transplant project was being conducted ethically if they were shut out of the most essential ethical question – the determination of death? This chapter examines how these questions were debated by doctors and representatives of the Israeli public while the memory of Levy's unsuccessful operation was still relatively fresh and heart-transplants were still continuing apace in other Western countries.[1]

In July of 1969, the Knesset Committee on Public Services held two meetings devoted to heart-transplant issues.[2] The first addressed little of substance, but the second featured an in-depth discussion of the issues.[3] This session opened with a short presentation by the chairman of the IMA's Scientific Advisory Council, Professor Melvitsky. His focus was primarily on the question of establishing death. He reported that the IMA three-man expert committee had just drafted their report.[4] In summarizing its basic conclusions he asserted, as Ashkenazi had, that death should be viewed as a process, with the death of the brain being equivilant to the death of the individual.[5] Surprised, and even annoyed, at being called to testify before the committee, he stated: "I agree that there is a medical difference of opinion here, but I do not think that this debate needs to be held in a non-medical forum."[6]

Melvitsky's concern was pragmatic. He felt that public debate would tie the hands of medical doctors who needed a free hand to do what they were trained to do – save human lives. The session evolved into a fascinating debate on the ethics of clinical experimentation. Heart surgeon Melvitsky defended the need for medicine to advance clinically by way of trial and error.

His line of reasoning offers an interesting pragmatic view of the determination of death debate. The desire by doctors to keep this debate from spilling over into the public sphere may not have had as much to do with the philosophic meanings of death as it did with the attending problems that such a public debate could generate for new, cutting-edge surgical techniques and procedures. Were such better described as experimental or therapeutic? Heart transplantation was, of course, a prime example of this type of borderline medical care. As Morris Levy had worried earlier and Melvitsky complained here, medical science could only progress through clinical experimentation. They both argued that questionable, new therapeutic techniques, just those with the capacity to most advance medical practice, would be impeded by non-clinicians who wanted to focus attention on the experimental aspect of these procedures and insist on more careful oversight. Melvitsky asked the committee whether doctors who had performed early unsuccessful surgical heart procedures with known low survival rates should be labeled "murderers" – especially since such procedures had since become standard and had attained good success rates.[7]

The Committee member at whose request the issue had reached the Committee, Kalman Kahana (*Poalei Agudat Yisrael*), argued for public involvement in "medical" decisions:

> At the least, this Committee needs to assert that for those individuals for whom doubts [concerning methods of determining death] do exist, they can live their lives and die as they like—and not as doctors would decide for them.[8]

Here he was referring not only to the religious, but to those who disagreed with the *way* that brain death was being determined – even if they accepted that *proper* determination would be satisfactory for the declaration of death.[9] Kahana's response may also have been a reaction to the questions raised by Yaaqov Levi concerning the efficacy of testing for brain non-function and by Ashkenazi's television appearance only one month previous to this committee meeting.

This discussion offers us some insight into the way that differing conceptions of death were discussed. Presenting death as a scientific/medical *fact* made deliberations surrounding its determination or definition solely a medical matter beyond the purview of the general public.[10] Melvitsky feared that moving this question into the public realm would create untenable interference in normal clinical procedure that of necessity proceded (in his view ethically) by trial and error. On the other hand, Kahana expressed a concern for patient autonomy unusual in an era of paternalistic medicine. As Kahana was aware of medical disagreement regarding the measurement of death, he claimed that the patient should at the least be able to choose between *competing* medical options and opinions.[11]

The Committee session ended with no substantive recommendations and the public-political ripples created by Morris Levy's transplant calmed.[12] The next Knesset debate on brain-death did not occur until 1978 when Levy again transplanted a heart. By then, however, much attention, in the medical, legal and halachic fields, was focused on the problems raised by transplants in general and the determination of death in particular.

A few months after this discusssion, the first of three articles that discussed public perceptions of organ transplants appeared in the IMA's publications.[13] The first, written by a noted neurologist, Professor Amos Korchin, was an editorial that argued for the IMA to assume a regulatory role. This, in order to insure that public interest would not at some future date be translated into "*non-medical* regulation" of organ transplants.[14] Korchin worried that the public would suspect conflicts of interest between hospitals competing for the prestige that cutting edge medical procedures brought. Even the use of separate medical teams—one to determine donor death and one to actually transplant organs—would not eleviate supiscion. A higher, neutral, medical authority in a supervisory role–the IMA – could curtail such worries. Most importantly, such self-regulation would keep others from attempting to regulate this complicated medical practice.

Korchin's view is a classic example of the "gate-keeping" phenomenon.[15] Clearly, he was concerned about guarding doctors' power. However, two pieces of this editorial show that his concerns went beyond merely protecting doctors' professional interests. First, he acknowledged that the need for supervision was needed not only to provide a "smoke-screen" for doctors to do as they wish, but because organ transplantation presented actual difficulties—complicated ethical problems that required extraordinary care.[16] These, he felt, ranged from unreasonable familial pressure on living donors to the establishment and enforcement of uniform criteria of death. The fact that he listed criteria of death as one of the issues, even after the IMA sub-committee had reached its conclusions, showed that he was concerned with actual implementation and enforcement of uniform standards. He argued that it was not enough to "assume that standards are enforced," they needed to "be guaranteed."[17] While the Health Ministry had turned to the IMA for recommendations, it was not clear which, if any, particular body was responsible for overseeing their actual implementation.[18]

The second indication of his broader concerns, and telling of his perception regarding the difficulties of organ transplantation in Israel, was the way in which he opened his editorial:

> In our country, the problem of organ transplantation is complicated by the interests of conservative religious factors who fight against post-mortem operations in nearly every case. It is easy, and of course convenient, to take the opposing stance which denies their criticisms as primitive, non-rational and even immoral. Such an opinion, however, frustrates any attempt at serious discussion of the issues raised by organ transplants.[19]

For Korchin, the ethical problems of the transplantation project were real, and not just the result of accusations from an opposing camp. As such, they needed to be addressed. The almost automatic dismissive reaction of the secular medical community towards these criticisms from those concerned with *halakha* prevented this. The reductionist instinct which saw criticism from "conservative religious factors" as merely some type of "primitive" backlash against medical progress was perhaps "convenient," but avoided dealing with the actual content of their critique. [20] (As mentioned above, the Public Comptroller had already taken note that civil law was not being followed by doctors in their treatment of corpses.)

# Really Dead?

This "convenient" argument against the religious in time became part of the debate surrounding brain-death and transplantation. The opposition of some halakhic authorities to harvesting organs from brain-dead donors *was* one of the problems that needed to be addressed by the doctors and others who wanted to move forward with heart transplants. However, I think that some of these individuals began to believe that overcoming such opposition was all that was required in order to successfully proceed. Later continued frustrations at lack of available donors and organs for transplants show that this was not the case—other ethical issues regarding the transplantation project were ignored with resultant problems in public participation.[21]

Dr. Yaaqov Levi responded to Korchin in an article published a few months later.[22] He repeated his arguments concerning the need for better testing to measure actual loss of brain function, asserting that the EEG alone was not sufficient. He also objected to equating the death of the brain with the death of the individual in cases where the patients were *not* being respirated using what he called "mechanical aids." Levi argued that such an equation treated "vegetative life as naught," although this was clearly a value laden decision liable to provide logical support for the denial of proper treatment to the comatose. For Levi, it was impossible to ignore these cardio-respiratory indications of life in the determination of death. He applauded the fact that kidney transplants in the Rambam Hospital were undertaken only upon establishment of the cessation of both neuro-logical and cardiac function in the donor. Directly addressing Korchin's introductory remarks in his article, Levi wrote that Korchin need not fear religious opposition so long as it was clear that no option other than a transplant was available to the recipient and that the death of the donor had been established according to "all opinions."

Finally, in the summer of 1970, Ashkenazi published a second article on brain-death. He hoped that the slow down in actual heart-transplants would allow for a more considered and less emotional discussion of its criteria.[23] The majority of his article was devoted to discussing a Danish study of 72 cases where patients had presented isoelectric EEG readings. His conclusion was that this study showed conclusively that EEG readings alone could not be depended upon for establishing death as they admitted of too many exceptions. Ashkenazi argued that the EEG was a prognostic tool and as such was based upon the statistical likelihood that certain readings corresponded to certain clinical states. Clinical experience, however, showed that there may always be exceptions to prognoses.[24] The search for more accurate brain-death tests was problematic in that the most likely candidates (like angiography) were unethical. They were invasive, sometimes-dangerous procedures that did not serve the patient himself.

He concluded his article by (again) stressing the need for society to update its legal system in terms of scientific advancement. Death, in his view, was a unitary concept that should not depend upon whether it was being declared for potential organ donors or others. If legal norms would reflect this it would

> …certainly bring about much more public understanding of the transplant issue, as it would serve to remove some of the emotional elements which act in a negative direction.[25]

Better objective testing would be a part of gaining the public's trust.

All of these articles, each written by medical doctors, focused attention on the way in which public perceptions of what doctors were doing could influence the advance of the transplant project. All of

# Really Dead?

their authors argued that the determination of donor death was the major "public relations" problem that needed to be addressed if this project was to successfully continue. Both Korchin and Ashkenazi felt that the public demanded a tightening of death criteria: Korchin claimed that proper supervision could provide this, while for Ashkenazi the solution lay in the development of more "objective" testing for brain-death.[26] Levi's piece, while critical of some aspects of, and tests for, brain-death, essentially sought to present the medical establishment with what he felt would be the key to reaching broader public agreement on these issues.

---

[1] For a brief summary of the surge in these operations following Barnard's most famous first, followed by their abrupt drop-off in most countries as low survival rates and ethical problems were increasingly noted, see Margaret Lock, *Twice Dead*, 96-7.

[2] Then the Knesset Committee responsible for the health system.

[3] On July 1, 1969 the members complained both about the time that had elapsed between the original Knesset debate and the Committee meeting as well as the little time left for them to offer any substantive feedback to the plenum. Parliamentary elections were held in October 1969 and this was one of the last meetings of the Committee before the Knesset disbanded.

[4] This sub-committee had been established as part of the IMA's recommendations to the Health Ministry discussed above.

[5] Public Services Committee Protocol, July 13, 1969. I have not been successful in locating the actual report in the archives of the IMA. To my knowledge it was not published.

[6] Ibid.

[7] He seems to be referring to reported accusations by opponents to heart transplants who characterized these operations as murder. The ethical question that he raised is a fascinating one deserving of attention, but beyond the scope of this history. For arguments on this issue from the same era see Francis Moore, "The Doctors' Dilemmas" in *Give and Take, the Development of Tissue Transplantation* (Philadelphia: Saunders, 1964) and Henry Beecher, *Research and the Individual* (Boston: Little and Brown Publishing Co., 1970). For a fascinating depiction of Moore himself, one of the leaders in organ transplantation, who would eventually

end his own life by shooting himself at home rather than die in a hospital, see Atul Gawande, "Desperate Measures," *The New Yorker* May 5 (2003): 70-81. Also noteworthy is the extent to which the 1966 Ciba Symposium was devoted to discussing the difficult demarcation between the experimental and the therapeutic.

[8] Public Services Committee Protocol, July 13, 1969.

[9] This is an early plea for allowing patient choice between multiple definitions of death. Such 'conscience clauses' would be part of the declaration of death debate in the heavily Jewish states of New York and New Jersey in the 1980s and would be part of the Israeli Yachad Council's recommendations on end-of-life issues in 2003. For a general analysis of the question see Veatch, "The Conscience Clause: How Much Individual Choice in Defining Death Can Our Society Tolerate?," in *The Definition of Death: Contemporary Controversies*.

[10] I will discuss this question of border disputes in chapter 15.

[11] This call may be thought of as all the more radical for it was made in a time and place where the average patient could not even pick his own doctor, but was subject to the whims of the extremely powerful Health Collectives. See Yehudit Shuval and Ofra Anson, *Ha'iqar Habriut* (Jerusalem: Magnes Press, 1991), especially chapter 5 for a historical description of the HMO-heavy Israeli health-care system.

[12] Questions of consent over autopsies along with the handling of cadavers and human remains still generated a great deal of tension. The report of the National Comptroller in 1968 had cited a number of irregularities and illegalities in the way that hospitals handled cadavers and their parts. See also Elqanah Qafir, *Sefer Hilhot Nituhe Holim Vemetim* (Jerusalem, 1969). As may be expected, the issue of attacks (both verbal and physical) on doctors received a lot of attention in the early to mid-1970s in the IMA's Member's Letter.

[13] The next discussion to appear in print was an article written by an eminent halakhic scholar, R. Menahem Kasher in the fall of 1969, "*Be'ayat Hashtalat Halev*," *Noam* 13 (5730): 10-20. However, I will depart from chronology here and discuss it in the next chapter which is devoted to continued halakhic discussion of death.

[14] Amos Korchin, "*Mi Shotel Lemi*," ML (*Heshvan* 14, 5730): 13-14.

[15] Gate-keeping, the selective admittance by a hegemonic group to a status, privilege or position often done in order retain professional control, was first described by Talcot Parsons regarding the medical profession in *The Social System* (Glencoe, IL: Free Press, 1951). Since then, this phenomenon has been analyzed across a wide variety of subjects from studies of government policy to sexual politics.

---

[16] He did note that the Israeli medical establishment enjoyed near-unlimited freedom of action.

[17] Amos Korchin, "*Mi Shotel Lemi,*" 14.

[18] Melvitsky, Chairman of the Scientific Advisory Committee of the IMA, had argued only months earlier before the Knesset Committee against any such role for the Health Ministry itself. The Israeli medical establishment had consistently fought against any outside supervision of its activities and for the most part was successful. Individual hospitals operated quite autonomously, drafting their own criteria for any number of procedures, including transplants. This piece by Korchin is an instance of the unease that some felt over this state of affairs.

[19] Ibid.

[20] I believe that such reactions are part and parcel of many of the debates surrounding a variety of crucial issues in Israeli society. The religious community (especially the Haredi ultra-orthodox, non-Zionist community) is painted as obstructing whatever enlightened national project is under discussion and steps are taken by the state's powers-that-be to ensure that they will not succeed. This reaction makes recognition of actual problems more difficult. For an exploration of this phenomenon in the Israeli judiciary, see Barzilai, "Religious Fundamentalism and Law" in *Communities and Law* (Ann Arbor: University of Michigan Press, 2003). For an excellent overview of the many tensions between liberal democracy and Jewish tradition see Gavison, "*Medina Yehudit Vedemokratit*" in **Rav Tarbutiut Bemedinah Demokratit Veyehudit**, eds. Menachem Mautner, Avi Sagi and Ronen Shamir (Tel Aviv: Ramot, 1998).

[21] The issue of organ shortages has been addressed time and again in a number of ways by different public authorities—including the Knesset—but to little avail. The entire project constantly faces a shortage of donor organs. Suggestions concerning ways to increase the supply of donor organs have ranged from the technical (like easing exchange of information between medical centers) to those which entail radical readjustments of societal norms. These latter have included the lowering of the age of legal consent regarding organ donation, creation of "opt-out" donation systems where any cadaver organs can be legally taken for transplant unless the deceased specifically requested otherwise, the denial of health care to those not willing to agree to cadaveric donation, and allowing for the marketing of human organs. Some have claimed that continual shortage of donor organs in the developed world is an integral part of the moral calculus of the entire project. Lock called

this the "bittersweet outcome of [the] success" of organ transplantation (*Twice Dead*, 5).

The constant and, in the eyes of many, disturbing search for new sources of donor organs has compromised the benefits of transplantation. Two of the closest observers of the history of the transplant project, Fox and Swazey, declared their abject dismay over the ways that in the U.S. and elsewhere, organ transplantation had spun morally out of control. They bemoaned the growth of the project served to "divert attention and human and financial resources away from far more basic and widespread public and individual health care needs" of society. Organ transplantation had grown into "an overly zealous medical and societal commitment to the endless perpetuation of life and to repairing and rebuilding people through organ replacement" while its practitioners ignored the "the human suffering and the social, cultural, and spiritual harm we believe such unexamined excess can, and already has, brought in its wake." (*Spare Parts* [NY: Oxford University Press, 1992], 208, 210.) I will return to this matter in Section II.

[22] Y. Levi, "*Hashtalat Everim Ve'etiqa Refuit*," **ML** (Adar 4, 5730).

[23] H. M. Ashkenazi, "*Haqriterionim Lemot Hamoah*," **Harefuah** 79, no.1 (July 1970): 38.

[24] Ibid., 39.

[25] Ibid.

[26] It is worth noting that some viewed the use of the EEG (which Ashkenazi criticized) primarily as a "public relations" tool. A flat line provided something objective to show a deceased's family. This was perhaps one of the reasons that the Harvard criteria left the EEG as an optional confirmation of death.

# 5

# 1969-1970
# Continued Halakhic Debate

The previous chapter was devoted to describing some of the debate over the weight that public (non-medical) opinion should have in dealing with questions of medical ethics. That is, in what ways was it proper to include the public in making decisions related to brain-death and transplantation. This chapter addresses a different piece of the Israeli discourse which took place separately but concurrently among leading halakhic scholars of the day. As discussed in chapters two and three, the scholars who approached the question of determining death did so with a number of different interpretive approaches. The traditional source texts for determining death were variously read so as to make sense of the ancient in light of the modern. R. Waldenberg explained the Talmud's focus on respiratory function by treating it as a general, body-wide function beyond the sign of breath at the nose. R. Auerbach read the cessation of respiration as a doubtful sign whose true meaning could only be fathomed after resuscitative efforts were made. R. Weiss focused on the ethical obligations due to the dying patient, insisting that he be either treated or let to die in peace. R. Feinstein understood the cessation of respiratory function as the cause, not harbinger, of death. Common to all of these approaches was the rereading of ancient texts in light of modern medical practice.

# Really Dead?

As halakhic scholars continued to examine brain-death through the prism of the halakhic problems which it engendered, several began to more directly address the broader question of how physical death itself is understood halakhically. This chapter will focus on two articles and one *psaq halakhah* in which their respective authors each portrayed "halakhic" death quite differently. Each employed different interpretative strategies to assemble the pieces of traditional text out of which he constructed his understanding of death; each privileged different aspects of the multi-tiered proof texts regarding death; each understood the connection between traditional halakhic categories and modern science differently. These stark differences reflect the heterogeneity of the halakhic portion of the Israeli discourse over brain-death. They also offer a glimpse into the wide range of halakhic opinion which stood before the Chief Rabbinate when they eventually came to debate the halakhic permissibility of heart transplants in Israel. This in itself sharpens the questions concerning the Rabbinate's particular choice at that time.

Over the same year that the IMA journals were publishing calls for greater transparency and "objectification" of the declaration of death, an eminent halakhic scholar, R. Menachem Kasher, wrote an article which espoused a different conception of what the declaration of death entailed.[1] By contrasting two separate halakhic sources, he sought to determine whether the absence of the heart (perhaps also the loss of its function) was equivalent *by definition* to the death of the individual. The question for the case of modern medical care was whether the removal of an (even barely functioning) heart would render the patient halakhically dead before a new heart could be transplanted in its place.[2] His conclusion was that the status of such a patient would be similar to that of an animal at the moment of its slaughter, but before the slaughter is completed. A description of this status is found in a third source, which R. Kasher quoted: "It is no longer among those considered to be alive, yet not yet among those considered to be dead."[3]

Codified *halakhah* insisted upon a short pre-burial waiting period before a presumptively dead individual may be buried. R. Auerbach explained that this was due to doubt regarding cessation of respiratory activity: did it signal actual death or the onset of a seizure; R. Feinstein understood that this period was meant to 'insure' (if no medical assistance was available) that death through anoxia had actually taken place. Here R. Kasher wanted to suggest that this waiting period reflected more of an ontological and not epistemological doubt. Quoting from another work of his own, he wrote that "...death is not merely the absence of life, but also the [presence of an] *actual reality of death*...."[4]

Death was not, as others had theorized, just an absence—but rather it itself is some quality. R. Kasher understood that traditional sources already were aware of fuzzy situations where one state or status—life—may be gone, but it has not been replaced by another status—death (see note 3). As R. Kasher explained—death, for the halakhah, is the actual departure of the soul.[5] By using these sources which pointed towards halakhically undecided cases—neither dead nor alive, it seems that R. Kasher was not interested in differentiating between 'halakhic' and 'actual' death like Levi did. Rather, he wanted to present the problematics attached to any determination of death in the *halakhah*.[6]

While this article did not discuss brain-death, the points that R. Kasher raised are important to consider when reading other halakhic discussions of brain-death and determinations of death in general (some already discussed and some which will be below). In rejecting a straight-forward life-death dichotomy, I believe that R. Kasher opened another way of conceptualizing modern transplant patients. Modern medicine had not *created* another halakhic-legal category, but rather

# Really Dead?

has provided a new instance of one already familiar: a state of both lifelessness and deathlessness. Additionally, his article called attention to the problematics attached to defining death as the loss of one particular organ or function. If the lack of a heart was understood as equivalent to death, the question of coming back from the dead with a new heart would be raised.[7] R. Kasher felt it less troublesome to use other available halakhic sources to describe the status of these patients, thus avoiding this problem completely. He did not seem to be concerned that certain patients may not fit into categories that would allow us to reach simple decisions concerning their treatment – either as organ donors or recipients. Neither did he mention what the ambiguous position of such individuals would allow in terms of treatment. Citing the *gemara* from *Yoma*, R. Kasher argued that like other doubtfully living persons, such patients are certainly entitled to full care. Ambiguity over life and death was not new for the *halakhah*. In R. Kasher's opinion, it may have been, in fact, the best way of describing newly created bio-medical cases.[8]

A year later, R. Feinstein wrote a long responsum in the summer of 1970 in which he reiterated his fierce opposition to heart transplants even in the case where a donor heart could be obtained ethically, ie after the donor's own death.[9] Of more interest regarding brain-death, though, are a number of statements that he made concerning the relationship between halakhic and scientific criteria for measuring and interpreting reality. Unlike the extreme disassociation between the two championed by Levi, R. Feinstein argued for a different level of interaction between the halakhically constructed world and that revealed by modern scientific knowledge and technology.[10]

The responsum began with a discussion of brain-death repeating the assertion that anoxia is the cause of death as understood by both the *halakhah* and by science. R. Feinstein argued not for two separate deaths, but that medical doctors who wanted to adopt brain-death had confused cause and effect.

> But the definite truth is that it is not the cessation of the brain's functioning which is equivalent to death, for as long as one breathes he is alive. Rather, the end of the brain's functioning is that which causes cessation of respiration. It is possible [in the case of the loss of brain function] that since he is still alive there may be some medical treatment, whether known or still unknown to man that can return brain function....

> ...it is not mentioned in the Talmud or the works of *posqim* that the sign of life resides in the brain, and we cannot reason that nature has changed in this regard, for also in the days of our Sages the brain functioned as it does in our day and it provided all the life of the individual, yet one was not considered dead with cessation of brain function, and this is clearly the case in our time as well.[11]

This first paragraph displayed R. Feinstein's criticism of the use of medical futility as a definition of death. Despite the absence of any possible treatment, loss of brain-function cannot be used to declare death. Only the anoxia which may ensue causes the patient to actually die.

In the next section, R. Feinstein discussed the use of the ECG as an example of a modern technologically-generated fact ostensibly interfering with halakhic conclusions. His questioner had surmised that a positive reading of cardiac activity could be ignored in a non-breathing patient as this patient would be halakhically *defined* as dead.

# Really Dead?

However, R. Feinstein dismissed this as fallacious reasoning. Recalling the discussion in *Yoma*, he noted that another text describes a case where an individual had stopped breathing, yet recovered after being entombed.[12] He explained that the reasoning behind the permission given to abandon one who shows no respiration at his nose even when we may know of a case where an individual who exhibited this same symptom actually did not die, is based on statistical likelihood. One is not required to take extremely rare cases into account when deciding whether to abandon such a victim, but can assume that this victim's symptoms follow the general pattern. The fact of a single case wherein the normal pattern was disrupted does not interfere with reaching more general conclusions. However, if met with an exceptional case — as evidenced by a positive ECG reading — probability is set aside in face of the actual and cannot be ignored.

> Therefore regarding an individual in whom life activity is seen through the use of an electric radiogram [sic]... he is alive even though he is not breathing. This is like the man who was entombed because he stopped breathing, yet lived afterwards for 25 years. Since there is, after all, a real case here, even if it is a unique case – it is still real. Therefore, it would be forbidden to declare such an individual [dead]. On the contrary, we must endeavor to heal him....[13]

Cessation of respiration is not understood as a *definition* of death in the way that one holding a view of the *halakhah* as legal positivism might understand it. There is no "halakhic death" which may not accord with a medical reality. The *gemara* in *Yoma* depends upon statistical suppositions about reality, but does not pretend to create that reality. This obviously contradicts the way that Levi interpreted this *gemara*.[14]

R. Feinstein seems to tread a fine line between halakhic positivism and a commitment to scientifically provable fact. As I wrote above, legal positivism is a theory which understands that legal definitions need not correspond to real-world instances, but rather create legal categories which then have concrete implications.[15] A halakhic positivism would hold that the same is true of halakhic definitions. This was how Levi described the halakhic definition of death. In the case of decapitation, R. Feinstein held that an individual was considered by definition dead, despite what medical science may be able to offer such a patient. The halakhic category of decapitation (and not its physical-medical status) is what renders the individual dead, so that any indications to the contrary carry no meaning. However, it appears that in any other case, scientifically discoverable signs of life are to be taken as such and not dismissed as irrelevant, halakhically or otherwise. As we will see, this fine line will be stretched by R. Feinstein's interpreters who wanted to push for recognition of brain-death for organ transplants.

Two months after this responsum was written, a Chicago-based American rabbi and a New York doctor published the most comprehensive exploration of death determination according to the *halakhah* to date.[16] This Hebrew-language article sought to present a unitary, all-encompassing picture of death by examining all of the relevant halakhic sources and extracting from them a uniform understanding of death. This was also the first time that an argument for brain-death as death in the eyes of the *halakhah* was presented.[17]

The authors held two conceptual assumptions: They believed that the various sources could be distilled, as it were, such that one clear explanatory mechanism which defines death halakhically could be found.[18] Second, they advocated an approach which attempted (as far

# Really Dead?

as possible) to describe halakhic categories as corresponding to medical-scientific ones. Together, these assumptions lead R. Rabinowitz
and Dr. Kenigsberg to declare the key "independent dividing line"
between life and death to be "voluntary movement" which is necessarily dependent upon proper brain-function.[19]

This, they claimed could be inferred from the juxtaposition of the
familiar basic text from *Yoma* and the source from *Ohalot* in which the
quivering of a decapitated individual's body is described as similar to
the fibrillations of the severed tail of a lizard. Quoting from the 11th-
century authoritative commentator R. Shlomo Yitshaqi's (Rashi) gloss
on the text in *Yoma* ("until where must we check") they wrote:

> "...if the victim seems dead, in that he is not moving his
> limbs..." [Rashi's comment]. So Rashi explains that the
> entire discussion concerning the signs of death is not
> relevant unless we have before us a sign of the cessation
> of movement. We see that obviously cessation of respi-
> ration by itself is not an independent dividing line [be-
> tween life and death]; if it was why we would be
> concerned that his [the victim's] movements have
> stopped, he has [already] stopped breathing.[20]

As others before them had done, they called attention to the fact
that cessation of respiration on its own should not be automatically
equated with death. Rather, it is a sign that death may have occurred,
not a definition. They used Rashi's commentary, however, to suggest
that respiration is a *sub-category* of bodily movement and that cessation of all such movement is what defines death for the *halakhah*. (Of
course, physiologically, respiration depends upon a variety of muscu-
lar and organ movement in order to provide oxygen to the body.)
They summarized this as follows:

The conclusion of all this is that bodily movements are the only signs we have regarding the life of an organism, for respiration is nothing but one of the body's movements.[21]

However, this seemed to contradict the conclusion of the *mishna* from *Ohalot*. It taught that certain movements have no relevance for life. The authors' suggestion for solving this dilemma was to differentiate between two types of movements – voluntary and involuntary.

Voluntary movements originate only from one source: the large brain – the upper portion of the brain; however non-voluntary movements are created without the help of the large brain and with no consciousness.[22]

They went on to differentiate between non-voluntary movements that are dependent upon the brain stem and those which originate in the spinal cord. The latter may persist even after decapitation and do not signify life. The reason for this is that they are not "brain-centered movements."[23] That is, only such bodily movement which stems from the brain is considered significant by the *halakhah*. It is only its presence which signifies life and its lack which defines death. They concluded:

Since we hold that the life of the body is dependent upon the capacity for brain-centered movement, we must say that not only when decapitation occurs but also if the brain itself dies, the individual is considered dead, for if there is no life in the brain, from where can come any movement capacity that stems from it?[24]

# Really Dead?

The interpretive logic behind this statement is based upon a mechanistic understanding of decapitation in the *gemara*. A decapitated individual is dead only as a result of the loss of his ability to control his body and not because this loss defines him as such. This differs from the way that R. Feinstein understood decapitation as a halakhic category unto itself which defined its victim as dead.

Also unique, though, is the reductionist interpretation they offered of the text from *Yoma*. I have already discussed how *posqim* like Rabbis Waldenburg, Auerbach and Feinstein all treated the issue of respiration in *Yoma* by moving it from definition to signifier in different ways.[25] None of them, however, read this source as suggesting that there was some other defining state lurking behind respiration. (Only Levi read this source as presenting a respiratory 'definition of death' which ignored actual physiology in favor of a stance based upon a halakhic positivism.) Here, though, the authors assumed that there must be some underlying defining criterion. By making such an assumption and choosing movement, they seem to have purposefully set-up the seeming contradiction with the source in *Ohalot* solely in order to untangle it through the introduction of brain-death. Their argument was slanted so that brain-death would serve as the solution to a puzzle of their own making.

This reading of *Yoma* subsumes it to the *mishnah* in *Ohalot*. It forgoes simpler interpretations which posit the significance of respiration seen at the nose as either one part of the entire respiratory process or as the usually last surviving sign of life processes. These readings do not dismiss (especially in light of R. Moshe Sofer's *psaq*) other essential biological signs of life, subsuming them all under a new physiological concept – brain-controlled movement. The *mishnah* in *Ohalot* was not read by the authors as describing a separate or unusual case, decapitation (loss of the brain-body connection). Rather, it became the template for defining all types of death.

This did not, however, complete their attempt at reaching an inclusive definition of halakhic death. They noted that ritual slaughter, where only the throat of an animal is cut, absolutely kills this animal – even though it has not been beheaded and the brain-body connection is intact.[26] Therefore, they concluded that the *halakhah* recognizes two different definitions of death:

> 1) Physiological death, which occurs upon the death of the brain or decapitation;
> 2) Pre-physiological death which occurs when the body has lost so much vitality that it cannot even twitch and the death of the brain is certain to quickly follow.[27]

In this latter definition they differed from R. Feinstein in that he considered cessation of respiration as responsible for anoxia which then brought death to the entire individual. They, however, considered it (or loss of blood, etc) as responsible for the death of the *brain* which was the central defining feature of halakhic death.[28]

Comparing the definition of death which they derived from traditional sources to the way that modern medical discourse presented the resuscitated patient, Kenigsberg and R. Rabinowitz endorsed the use of criteria for death which focused on discovering whether the brain has stopped functioning. They supported the dismissal of involuntary reflexes as irrelevant to reaching conclusions regarding death—they offered no indication of brain function. This included cardiac activity. With this logic, they also discounted any signs of life exhibited by those patients on life-support technology as meaningless, for:

# Really Dead?

> If you say that non-brain centered reflexes which none-
> theless stem from the body itself are not considered
> signs of life because they do not stem from the brain,
> how much more so would we say this regarding
> movements which stem from artificial machines func-
> tioning from without [the body].[29]

Finally, they discussed the status of an individual in a deep coma, yet still evincing brain-based movement (i.e. respiration). They had already argued that the *halakhah* considered that those who were "close to death" yet had still-functioning brains were already dead. They then claimed that "close to death" was meant not as a temporal, but as a qualitative measure. This meant that even though these comatose patients can be supported and kept alive for a long time – no obligation to do so exists as they are considered to be dead. Rather, "it is permitted to withdraw all medical treatment and food supply."[30] The inability to return this patient to normal health affords him the status of a *gosses* and (as discussed above) non-intervention is a le-gitimate option for the *gosses*.[31] They considered this situation as similar to that described by R. Moshe Isserles wherein the removal of an impediment to actual death from a dying individual is permitted.

This last position, however, seems to betray the fundamental diffi-culty with R. Rabinowitz and Kenigsberg's article as a whole. On the one hand, they attempted to conceptually unify a great deal of source material by reductively describing death for the *halakhah* as an essen-tial break between brain and body. This enabled them to describe the physiological and halakhic as equivalent and served them well in advancing their case for brain-death criteria as something satisfying both the medical and halakhic views. However, the halakhic source material admitted of too many exceptions to this conception. They had to, then, offer another construct—pre-physiological death, a more distinctly halakhic-only category, to cover these cases. This near-death as death, then, seems to circle back upon itself in allowing the definition even of those with *completely intact* brain-body connections (the very signifier of life!) as dying so long as their prognosis does not allow for improvement.

They thus deconstructed the very essentialist foundation of death that they had carefully built. The construct of the live-brained, yet dying patient would seem to acknowledge that other essential vital bodily functions—such as circulation, digestion, etc.—although, separate from the brain, do count as indications of life since it is just their weakening which counts towards death.[32] Either way, however, in arguing for a realistic essentialist halakhic definition of death and then reversing the argument to become more expansive, this article seems to collapse under its own weight leaving only what appears to be apologetics for brain-death.

Their conclusions were critiqued by R. Yaaqov Blidstein in a subsequent article.[33] His main argument was that the conceptual premise of their article was faulty.[34] Conceptually, they identified the halakhic with the physical, arguing that one whom the *halakhah* considered dead was considered so for all purposes – both ritual and physical. R. Blidstein disputed this claim by pointing out that the *halakhah* often treats death as a singular categorical status. Thus, an individual who suffers from a life-threatening wound or illness has the status of a *treifa*. If he would be murdered, his murderer is not fully culpable for his death, for, in the language of the *gemara*, he has "killed a dead man."[35] In terms of the individual's ritual status he is considered to be alive – he does not defile, for instance. However, in terms of his legal-social status – he may be considered already dead.[36] The attempt to arrive at a unified definition of death is not valid because as R. Blidstein wrote:

# Really Dead?

> We find that there are number of stages of halakhic death for different purposes, but each is called 'death' within its own relevant framework. This is so even with respect to decapitation. Therefore, care must be taken not to use a definition suitable in its own framework in another foreign to it unless these fields have been examined and proven to be equivalent.[37]

If R. Blidstein's reading of the halakhic material is correct, the entire argument for creating one template for death, from one halakhic source, as proffered by R. Rabinowitz and Kenigsberg, fails. However even without resolving the larger conceptional argument between these authors, the question remains: why should one particular source and not another get selected as the template by which all other sources are judged? Lacking any other historical-textual based preferences, such as locating one source as historically prior to others, the choice of privileging one text over another seems to remain in the realm of personal preference. The historical import of R. Rabinowitz and Kenigsberg's article may very well lie in that it was the first time that brain-death itself was presented as a valid halakhic category. However, the conceptual problems of their argument seem to point out their own preference for the adoption of brain-death in order to facilitate organ transplantation.

This is noted in another critique of their arguments by Dr. Yaaqov Levi who focused on their comparison of the comatose patient to the *gosses*.[38] The *gosses*, argued Levi, is a dying patient

> ...at the end of the process of dying, his respiration is already nearing its end, there is no further possibility to stave off his death. It is enough to remove the sound of

wood being chopped for the patient to cross the border
to death.

The breathing comatose patient, however, may live for "weeks or months."[39] This patient is not on the verge of death, but must be deprived of essential nourishment in order to perish. Levi, I think correctly, concluded that, essentially, the proposal of R. Rabinowitz and Kenigsberg was to allow this patient to starve to death. His direct attack on their conclusions highlighted the major difference between this resuscitated patient, better classified as a *treifa*, and the actual *gosses*. For the first, the *cause* of death would be the lack of nutrition, while the death of the *gosses* is already in process, yet is somehow being prevented.[40] Levi argued that just as we would not describe normal eating as an act of staving off death by starvation, neither would the supply of nourishment to one incapacitated be thus described. Therefore, we cannot view its interruption as equivalent to the mere removal of some impediment to imminent death.

Over the course of just one year, different halakhic scholars and *posqim* produced very different conceptualizations of brain-death. Each of the articles discussed in this chapter presented a different understanding of the interplay between the halakhic and the scientific. For R. Kasher, it was a distinct possibility that a given scientifically described situation would not necessarily correspond to either of the distinct halakhic (or medical) categories of *living* or *dead*. Ontologically doubtful cases did in fact exist. R. Rabinowitz and Kenisberg, on the other hand, were eager to argue that brain-death was not only a clear and acceptable medical description of actual human death, but corresponded to the halakhic definition of death as well. However, their claims were not without difficulties on both the conceptual and textual levels. Finally, R. Feinstein held that death could be understood both as a physical state and also as a halakhically determined

# Really Dead?

status. Halakhic status could trump medical prognosis-*cum*-definition in the case of decapitation, but was not immune to the influence of scientifically discovered fact.

---

[1] R. Menachem Kasher, *"Be'ayat Hashtalat Lev," Noam* 13 (5730): 10-20.

[2] Ibid., 11-14. He dealt with a question that had originally been raised by R. Unterman: what was the halakhic status of a transplant patient during the time between the removal of his own heart and its replacement with a donor heart. Was such a patient, in the eyes of the *halakhah*, likened to one who had died and then returned to life? As R. Unterman expressed it: has he lost his presumption of life? The first source, discussed by R. Waldenberg, is that of the *Hakham Tsvi* (R. Tsvi Hirsch Ashkenazi, b. 1660) which we have already seen above. If the heart is the telos of respiration and responsible for life, then it follows that the removal of the heart will be, *by definition*, the equivalent of the death of the individual.

The *Hakham Tsvi* wrote: "The law is that upon the removal of the heart the creature dies, if it is a person—then he defiles, if an animal—then it is now impossible to be properly ritually slaughtered. It is possible for it to run and jump about [but] this is [merely] the quivering mentioned in Tractate *Ohalot*."

However, R. Kasher pointed to a *gemara* found in *y. Avoda Zara* 2:3 that discusses a type of ancient idolatry which required the removal of a beating heart from a live animal. The heart was then sacrificed. The *gemara* mentions that the animal can live for a short time after its heart has been removed.

[3] Ibid., 15 citing *b. Hulin* 121b. The case is of an animal whose trachea and esophagus have been cut but not completely severed. This article is a good example of the casuistry inherent in halakhic thought. New cases must be compared to the proper precedent in order to be understood. For an exploration of the workings of casuistry in medical ethics, see Albert Jonsen and Stephen Toulmin, *The Abuse of Casuistry* (Berkley: University of California Press, 1990).

R. Kasher also cited a commentary that suggested that death per se is not what is being considered in these sources. Rather the role of slaughter is to render the animal suitable for consumption—which may be a different category than actual death (p. 16, citing the *Tiferet Yaaqov*). This interestingly corresponds to the opinion of those who consider that what we call 'death' may actually only be a category that allows for the beginning of certain death behaviors. See Veatch, *Death, Dying and the Biological Revolution: Our Last Quest for Responsibility*.

[4] Ibid.

[5] Ibid., 20.

[6] R. Kasher points out his disagreement with Levi near the end of his article (20).

[7] Ibid.

[8] R. Kasher may have been responding to the way that Levi, in an attempt to deal with the new phenomenon of the brain-dead patient, presented a drastically positivistic picture of the *halakhah,* thus sundering it from reality. He specifically mentioned and rejected Levi's position regarding the status of a patient with no heart where oxygen was supplied via a 'heart-lung machine.' Levi claimed that this patient was clearly alive according to medical opinion, yet wondered whether this would be the case halakhically as well (20). R. Kasher, however, questioned whether this was indeed the case and presented the possibility of an unclear case as a means towards uniting the halakha with medical-scientific categories again.

[9] *EM* YD II:146. This was because the removal of the recipient's heart cost him his life. Even when a new heart was successfully transplanted, he argued that the death of the recipient occurred much sooner than it would have if he kept his failing heart. The one year mortality rate around the time of his *responsum* was very high— 70%. (Hastillo, Hess, Richardson, and Lower, "Cardiac Transplantation – 1980," *South Medical Journal* 73:7 [July 1980]: 909-11).

[10] His responsum addressed, in part, a question concerning the differences in the world viewed with the naked eye as opposed to through a microscope. All halakhic authorities had rejected the need for microscopic vision for determining halakhic categories and measures, like the required "squareness"of phylacteries, for example, even though the use of such technology would provide more objective accuracy.

[11] Ibid.

[12] This is based on a Talmudic text from *b. Smahot* 8:1. It describes an individual who was placed in a crypt after ceasing to breath who awoke and lived for another 25 years.

[13] Ibid. The deleted section is a technical sentence which reads "there is no possibility to attribute this to the majority of cases of death or even to a minority". R. Feinstein is referring to a halakhic rule that sometimes allows for unknown cases to be subsumed to an established majority of similar cases.

[14] R. Feinstein also addressed the ruling of the *Hakham Tsvi* that was discussed by R. Waldenburg concerning the heart. He took pains to explain that the *Hakham Tsvi* surely did not intend to use cardiac activity as a positivistic definition of death.

[15] A legal positivist may hold that a legal statement is true if it describes not some external reality correctly, but rather legal conclusions which accord with that

# Really Dead?

statement. So the truth of the claim that it is 'illegal to cross the street here' is checked not against an external reality, but against whether such a law appears in the relevant legal corpus, is regularly enforced, etc. These indications of truth are understood as part of the same closed legal system and not external to it. See Dennis Patterson, *Law and Truth*, 1-21 for more on this subject.

[16] R. Gedaliah Rabinowitz and Mordechai Kenigsberg, "*Hagdarat Hamavet Veqviat Zmano Leor Hahalakhah,*" **Hadarom** 32 (Tishre, 5731): 59-76.

[17] While some, like Levi, had pointed out that mechanically respirated patients could be considered dead, this opinion did not focus on the death of the brain as the defining factor of their death.

[18] This is a conceptual assumption which is open to debate. It reflects an analytic mindset which constantly attempts to look at widely ranging sources as part of a greater unity—the '*halakhah*'—regardless of the historical disparity between them. More academic approaches to the same sources would likely be concerned with differentiation of the sources. Anyone familiar with the classic Lithuanian yeshiva style '*shiur klalli*' would surely recognize it in this article's approach. It attempts to conceptually unite its sources such that any and all apparent inconsistencies between them can be easily explained away through the use of one key concept. Their article was subsequently criticized by R. Yaaqov Blidstein, for this very assumption ("*He'arah B'inyan Qviat Hamavet Behalakhah,*" **Hadarom** 37 [Tishrei, 5733]: 73-5).

[19] Ibid., 61.

[20] Ibid., 60.

[21] Ibid., 61.

[22] Ibid.

[23] They based their distinction on the wording of Maimonides commentary on the *mishna* in *Ohalot* which describes what they call voluntary movement as that which stems from one source. They understood this source to be the brain.

[24] Ibid., 62.

[25] This was done in conjunction with interpreting the *psaq* of R. Moshe Sofer.

[26] Ibid., 63. They went into some detail describing a rather obscure case in order to make this point. The *mishnah* in Tractate *Hulin* (2:6) reads:

> One who slaughters an ill animal – Rabin Shimon ben
> Gamliel says: either its fore or hind legs must quiver [dur-

ing slaughter]. … The Sages say: both fore and hind legs must quiver. …

In what case: only for an animal assumed to be ill; if it assumed to be healthy, even if it displays none of these signs, it is kosher.

The reasoning behind these conditions for the ill animal is that we want to be certain that it is the slaughter itself that kills it and that it does not die from its previous illness. That would render it a *nevelah* – an animal that is forbidden for consumption because it was not properly slaughtered.

Now here they pointed out that quivering signifies life and is not dismissed. That is, because the animal is sick, we are not sure as to whether it will survive (as it were) the slaughtering process or not. If the animal reacts to being slaughtered by quivering this serves as proof that it indeed was living at the time of slaughter. What killed it was having its throat slit, rendering it kosher. (With healthy animals, there is no reason to assume that anything other than the slaughtering process killed it.)

They brought up this exceptional case to make their point when it would have been simpler to merely mention normal ritual slaughter, apparently, because of their focus on movement as the decisive factor in defining death.

[27] Ibid., 64. They described a number of other formidable injuries (such as being split in two) where the *halakhah* considers one who has suffered them to be dead despite the fact that the brain is still alive and connected to the body in the same way—as halakhic, pre-physiological death (66-70). The fact that they needed to point out quite a few of these exceptional cases would seem to detract from their claim that the end of the brain-body connection is the halakhic standard for death against which every case need be measured.

[28] Ibid.

[29] Ibid., 73.

[30] Ibid., 75.

[31] They mention here the same comment by the *Shvut Yaaqov* discussed by R. Weiss above concerning the obligation to save a victim when we cannot restore him to health.

[32] Alternately, they may believe that a lack of consciousness itself, although not a part of their description of death, does play a role in defining the individual as dead (Ibid., 73). They did in fact attempt to utilize a comment by the important early-19th-

century talmudist, R. Akiva Eiger (*Eliyahu Raba, m. Ohalot* 1:6), concerning one who has been severely injured, as a source for the importance of consciousness. However, and I do not write this criticism lightly, they so distorted the meaning of R. Eiger's comment that their conclusion barely admits of being taken for anything other than an attempt to fish for some halakhic loophole to consider the living-brain comatose as as-good-as-dead.

[33] Blidstein, "*He'arah.*"

[34] Additionally, he brings a talmudic source which supports differentiating between decapitation and presumed death (*m. Hulin* 117b). This is a more technical argument that may be debated. If Blidstein is correct, it is difficult for R. Rabinowitz and Kenigsburg to claim that decapitation is the fundamental basis of defining death in the *halakhah*.

[35] Ibid., 74.

[36] It may be possible to claim that this example is faulty in that the question of culpability is one that only devolves upon the killer, but the *gemara* itself ties the murderer's culpability to the status of the victim.

[37] Ibid., 75.

[38] Y. Levi, "*Davar Hame'aqev Yitsiat Hanefesh,*" **Noam** 16 (5733): 53-63, 54. He describes the authors' support of brain-death criteria as blind faith.

[39] Ibid., 56.

[40] The question of what constitutes a cause of death is not simple. Some would claim that it is anoxia of the brain—whether the patient has been shot in the chest or had liver cancer. Others, I think, more cogently, would argue that *cause* is a term used to describe, as Schiffer writes, "a 'notion of causality' [that] in this sense seems to be that of sufficiency, or of the minimal set of conditions sufficient to produce effectively another condition, death" ("The Concept of Death: Causes and Criteria," *The Journal of Medicine and Philosophy* 4, no. 3 [1979]: 227-30, 228).

# 6

# 1971-1975
# The Resuscitated Patient

The early 1970s saw a number of efforts aimed at characterizing the focus of organ transplantion's ethical anxiety, the resuscitated patient. Those interested in medical ethics and practice pondered whether this patient represented a new type which rendered older categorizations obsolete. Perhaps the neurologically dead patient was not a patient at all, but merely a donor in waiting? As Israeli and international medical centers gained more experience with these patients, they debated how to understand them. Differences in grasping who (or what) this patient was necessitated differences in his treatment. The conceptual slipperiness of the comatose brain-dead patient who resided inside of a living body is made clear in the multiplicity of ways that doctors and scholars understood him. This patient was not easily classified. It was not a simple matter to logically and cogently decide how to treat him. Competing ethical claims hovered over his medical status.

In this chapter I discuss a number of documents whose authors all attempted to accurately portray the difficult to grasp brain-dead patient. Some used philosophical and/or halakhic categorizations, while others sought to establish set medical criteria for his treatment. Those who sought to ethically treat these patients were met not just with a single patient, but with a variety of conceptual types which

# Really Dead?

these patients represented. This explains some of the resulting confusion. Additionally, it presents us with a clear picture of the conceptual variety which at one time existed within this discourse (as I also noted regarding the *halakhah* in the previous chapter) which would eventually vanish as Israel moved towards establishing its heart-transplant program.

In the beginning of 1971, the recently established (1966) center for *halakhah* and medicine, the Schlesinger Institute held another public symposium on organ transplants and the determination of death.[1] The symposium presented medical, legal and halakhic views on brain-death. (Unfortunately, the protocols were not preserved in their entirety, and the legal viewpoints presented are not available.) The first medical specialist, a Hadassah Hospital anesthesiologist, Y. Davidson, argued for the adoption of brain-death criteria for death. Echoing a familiar trope, he began by differentiating between the legal-halakhic "moment of death" and the biological understanding of death as a process.[2] The "moment of death" had been displaced, he claimed, because events such as cardiac arrest or cessation of respiration due to head trauma had become treatable conditions. Davidson described the ability to succesfully utilize resuscitative technology for "days or weeks" on certain patients suffering intracranial swelling. (Their impaired brain stem function interfered with respiration). While some of these patients fully recovered, others never did.

> Sometimes after prolonged artificial resuscitation and prolonged heart massage we see that the individual docs not regain consciousness. He is in a coma, unmoving, with no reflexes, no thoughts, no memories, but the heart still beats and the patient is artificially respirated. We describe this pitiful situation as a vegetative state.[3] In this case, is he alive or dead? … At what moment

134

does the individual's status change from patient receiving treatment to potential organ donor?[4]

While his arguments were not new, what is noticeable is his emotive evaluation of the patient-*cum*-organ-donor: He has no 'thoughts'
or 'memories.' Davidson read more into the EEG than was actually
warranted. It was quite a conceptual leap to claim that these diagnostic machines could somehow register thoughts and memories.

The unknown and the unseen had been brought to the surface by
such tools as the EEG. Yet here Davidson had interpreted its readings
as describing an absence of *mind* and not just of brain.[5] The EEG was
not built to record *thought*, only electrical *activity* in the brain. Davidson was quick to add emotional evaluation to basically affect-neutral
findings.[6] His reading of death as process had, it seems, opened the
door for merging the ephemeral with the physical in a way that
allowed for the individual to disappear as patient and reappear as
donor. Lacking any mind, yet certainly not lacking life, these 'beings'
occupied only physical space and lost their hold on what made them
into "patients receiving treatment". Whether "neurologically empty"
as named by Belkin or "heart lung preparations" as referred to in 1966
by the Ciba Conference participants, these patients were both present
and absent at once. For Davidson, what made them physically available as resources seemed to be their spiritual lack—their mindless-
ness. Yet it is questionable, at best, to assert that this is what his tests
for brain-death were actually capable of measuring.

The next speaker was once again R. Rabinowitz from Rehovot. He
too stressed that death came in stages. Arguing that an actual moment
of death had no real medical basis, but existed only from "a legal-
chronological point of view", he again described how it would be
halakhically possible to transplant hearts from non-heart beating
donors. The donor would be a patient who had been kept under

# Really Dead?

mechanical resuscitation until a recipient had been properly prepared. [7] After the recipient was ready, the donor—as a *gosses* at best – could be disconnected from life-support. After his heart stopped beating it would be removed. He ignored the problematics of such an approach—primarily those outlined by R. Weiss who strongly critiqued the prolonging of any 'treatment' when not done for that patient's own good.

According to a critique of his claims written by Dr. Yaakov Levi, he also confused these patients and actual *gossesim*.[8] As we saw above, for Levi, the artificially respirated brain-dead patients are not similar to *gossesim*. He defined them as questionably living because while they do evince cardio-respiratory signs of life—these are dependent upon artificial support. Removal of this support may reveal that they are already dead, but it may also bring about their death if they are actually alive. Levi argued, quite correctly, that a *gosses* is not questionably alive—but certainly alive, yet dying. As such, he is either due proper care or, if impossible, the removal of anything that may disturb or prolong his passing. [9] When something of this nature (such as excessive noise) is removed, it is not, then, the *cause* of his death—the *gosses* is already dying and nearly dead. However, Levi argued, the active removal of life support would, in fact, be the actual cause of death for the respiratory-supported patient if he is still alive.

> The function of the machine is of essential importance for the [life] of all parts of the body. It supplies the needed oxygen—and delivers it—together with nutrition and fluids—to all the cells. The stopping of the machine, therefore, prevents the flow of these essential elements to the body. Preventing nutrition [or oxygen] is the physiological cause of death. This is not the case when stopping a loud noise....[10]

While even the doubtfully living cannot be actively killed, for these patients withholding care is an acceptable halakhic option. Levi's solution, then, lay in not *resupplying* essentials in the case where the supply was necessarily interrupted – such as to change oxygen tanks or the like.[11]

In the same year that the Schlesinger Institute held their interdisciplinary symposium, Amnon Carmi, one of the major Israeli commentators on medicine and law, published the first edition of his book on law and medicine.[12] Carmi, however, was not interested in exploring brain-death in a multi-focal way. His chapter on transplants was for the most part reportage of basic claims already discussed above. He quoted from Ashkenazi at length and presented this view as the dominant one among medical professionals. Following Ashkenazi's stance towards the law, he called for administrative changes in the Pathology Law to allow for formal recognition of brain-death. This statute (in its 1971 formulation) permitted doctors to take any and all organs or tissues from a cadaver for the purposes of saving the life of another patient. Carmi correctly noted that no definition of "cadaver" was given in the law. He argued that the Health Minister, authorized to implement this particular statute, could define cadavers to include the brain-dead by administrative fiat. This, he felt, would solve the legal problem of determining death (at least for organ transplant cases).[13]

His solution to the ethical problems presented by transplants lay in simply renaming the brain-dead. These patients should be called cadavers. Once identified as such, he reasoned, the path to harvesting their organs for transplant would be opened.

Carmi's attitude towards the *halakhah* is also noteworthy. He turned to Jewish law at the end of this chapter where he discussed the determination of death. However, rather than reflecting on the differences of opinion within the *halakhah* as to the determination of death or the actual possibility of heart transplants, he chose to focus only on the then-current storm surrounding the question of autopsies.[14] He noted that there were rabbis who argued against the permissibility of autopsies, even at the cost of progress in medical knowledge and the saving of lives, as well as those who took a more permissive view. A two-paragraph endorsement of medically indicated autopsies by R. Rabinowitz was quoted as an example of the latter.

The solution to the ethical questions of the transplant project was that suggested already by Ashkenazi: the updating of antiquated laws. Carmi's only reference to the *halakhah* came as part of a satellite discussion appended to his primary subject. It served to exemplify the difficulties that faced doctors such as Ashkenazi in their struggle to help society catch up with scientific progress, while offering a glimmer of hope by pointing out that some religious authorities were more lenient and might cooperate with this effort. But interestingly, Carmi omitted any mention of the *halakha* directly connected to transplants or the definition of death. He seemed intent on reducing the (then) current legal situation to one in which religious authorities might chose to either fight against legitimate medical progress or step out of the way. By ignoring the questions raised by rabbis and religious scholars, he seems to have fallen into the very trap warned against by Korchin in his previous year's editorial.

Carmi's attitude reflected an ofttimes found Israeli secularist position towards the *halakhah* – dismissive, unless it can be cited in support of whatever side of the issue is being argued. He felt strongly about removing religiously based impediments to medical-legal progress.[15] This case of cultural elision would not be the last time that those interested in promoting organ transplants would ignore the actual views of those critical of brain-death or promote tactics (like changing the definition of "cadaver") which reflected conceptions about the law which adherents of *Jewish* law would understandably find difficult to follow.

Two years later, the then recently appointed Chief Rabbi, R. Shlomo Goren, published a radical reassessment of the halakhic determination of death. With no mention of other contemporary *posqim* or halakhic positions, R. Goren painted a path towards halakhic acceptance of brain-death in swift, broad strokes. First, he differentiated between the "private" life of an organ and its continued function as part of the general life processes in the human body. He argued that both the brain and the heart could only be considered signifiers of human life so long as they fulfilled their function within the organism.

> Therefore, the moment the brain ceases to function and does not provide reflexes, even if the heart is still beating, but does not bring blood to the brain, its beating has no significance as a sign of life in the individual.[16]

Once organ *function* vis-à-vis the rest of the body has ceased, he argued, there was no need take no note of cellular ('private') activity within the organ. R. Goren pursued a strong anti-essentialist path, going so far as to claim that a heart "which ceases to fulfill its function in the life of the body... is not a heart." Structural essence, then for him, played no role in defining a thing – definition was entirely functionally dependent.[17]

Insisting that according to halakhah, death is not a process, with some individuals languishing between life and death, but rather an all-or-nothing status, R. Goren (with a tone of near-dismissiveness) reviewed the *psaq* of the R. Moshe Sofer. He suggested that the inclusion of the pulse (cardiac function) in the triad of unresponsiveness, cessation of respiration and end of cardiac activity was an innovative

# Really Dead?

deviation from standard halakhic praxis which had always viewed respiration alone as indicative of life. (In his opinion, R. Sofer inserted the need to check for cardiac function only in light of Maimonides' description in the *Guide for the Perplexed* of certain unusual patients who maintained cardiac activity while dying.)[18]

Modern medical technologies and abilities, such as resucitation, R. Goren claimed, had rendered even the basic respiratory criteria of the *halakhah* problematic.

> Does not this great medical advance [resuscitation] necessitate, also from the halakhic point of view, our recognition that cessation of respiration is no longer sufficient to determine the death of an individual....[19]

His solution was not to suggest a wholesale rejection of this classic criterion, but rather to expand the obligation of providing care even to those considered "clinically dead."[20] Thus just as classic medical-halakhic cardio-respiratory criteria of death could no longer serve as as actual criteria for death, neither could they be the end-point for medical treatment.[21]

R. Goren then shifted the resuscitated brain-dead patient into the category of a *gosses* who "will surely die, but whose life can be extended by artificial means."[22] The question, he felt, was whether the novel obligation to care for even the dead extended to this patient. R. Goren answered, like R. Rabinowitz before him (and in terms of suggested actual practice like Levi), that the solution lay in bringing about the withholding of care. This he argued (unlike Levi) was similar to the now familiar removal of an impediment to death.

> In accordance with the ruling of R. Isserles who permitted the removal of salt from the tongue in order to has-

ten the soul's departure, it seems possible to prove that in the case of a difficult end-stage of dying, wherein death is an improvement for the patient, it is permitted to withhold from him oxygen or other treatment that may extend his respiration...[23]

What seems unclear in his argument, however, is how he made the move from an obligation to "save the life" of (or revive) even the clinically dead on the one hand to giving permission to allow certain patients to die on the other. R. Goren stated that function is the defining characteristic of essential organs such as the heart. If one 'heart' is merely replaced by another (ICU apparatus), so long as there is proper function, it seems to me that R. Goren would be hard-pressed to deny that this individual is alive.[24]

R. Goren resolved this difficulty by turning to individual quality of life valuations. For some, life is better than death. For others, however, the opposite is true. As he noted, death may be an "improvement" for some.[25] Extreme suffering may be unbearable and its only end may lie in death. This moral calculus was supported by citing two instances from the Talmud where sickly Rabbinic Sages, suffering in their illnesses, were wished death when it seemed that there was no hope to heal them.[26] (R. Goren's comments are remeniscent of Davidson's concern over the "pitiful" state of the comatose. However, it is difficult to judge whether the comatose patients under discussion actually suffer – even though those who care for them and about them may.)[27]

In 1973 the IMA's journal *Harefua* published a review of the many different criteria then in use to ascertain the death of a brain. The author, J. Ouaknin, echoed the logic of the CIOMS Statement and the Harvard Criteria in treating the death of the brain as what "medically, ethically, and legally allows for the withdrawal of futile and expensive life-support and for the removal of an organ for transplant purposes."[28]

While it might be assumed, nowhere did he explicitly equate the death of the brain with the death of the individual. Rather he portrayed the futility of further treatment as that which turned this patient into a donor. In his article's conclusion Ouaknin deliberated among the many possible tests of brain function in order to find those that seemed to provide the best balance of accuracy and ease of application. The more complicated, such as measuring cerebral oxygen consumption, were considered

> ...neurological research tools and are not conventionally applicable to all cases, however, it may be that in the future they will be used for early detection of potential donors, who are still not in the stage of brain-death, but in whom its development is inevitable.[29]

The path from patient to donor was already being marked in the neurology department, not by the death of the patient, but by the falling curve of his condition and the rising futility of what medicine can offer him.

In 1974, for the first time in Israel, a complete set of criteria for brain-death was published by Hadassah Hospital. These criteria were the result of the deliberations of a seven member panel commissioned in 1972 by Hadassah's Medical Committee to "establish procedures and criteria for the determination of the point of death in organ donors."[30] These findings were accepted in the summer of 1974. They included the following:

> 1) Fixed, dilated pupils that do not respond to light.
> 2) The lack of all central reactions to outside stimulus.

3) Lack of tonus, reflexes and independent movement.

4) Lack of independent respiration for at least four minutes after disconnection of the patient from respiratory apparatus that had functioned for at least one hour and had succeeded in creating full oxygenization of the blood.

5) A sharp fall off in blood pressure when not supported artificially through medication.

6) Complete lack of any electrical activity of the brain according to an EEG test with no suspicions of patient poisoning through medications. This test is to be conducted in a venue free from all electrical interference which may disturb the readout of the EEG. It is essential to repeat this test again over the 12 hour period since the first test.

7) Administration of an arteriograph of the carotid artery that will demonstrate complete lack of blood flow in the vasculatory system of the brain.

Additionally, Hadassah stipulated that:

The point of death will be established according to these criteria by at least three members of a panel chosen for this purpose by the Medical Committee for a two year period. At the end of this term the Medical Committee will appoint a new panel for a similar term.

Upon the determination of the donor's death, the established procedures for organ transplantation from donor to patient will be followed.

# Really Dead?

These criteria, issued by Israel's arguably most-respected medical facility,[31] drew much attention, both medical and forensic. The Director General of Hadassah, Professor K. Man, sent them to the Director General of the Health Ministry with the intent "to receive your authorization to make these procedures mandatory for the state and not [only] on the institutional level."[32] The General Counsel for the Ministry, Shmuel Ne'eman, rejected this request as beyond the legal purview of the Ministry.

> Even though in section 33 of the Order of Public Health, in which the type of directive the Director General is authorized to enforce is recognized as including "general domestic and medical arrangements"… it is not certain that the intention of the Legislator pertains to procedures and criteria of the type suggested by the Medical Committee. I am afraid that [adopting these recommendation as] a directive additional to the Order would grant further authority in these matters.[33]

However, the Counsel did in fact see that these legally non-binding recommendations could serve an important legal purpose. They would provide a "standard of care" against claims of medical malpractice in cases of determining death.[34] Although he did not explain the difference between this set of criteria and those "general domestic and medical arrangements," it may be that these failed the test of generality. That is, they were specifically medical measurements and as such not part of the public-policy sphere within the purview of the Ministry. Ne'eman saw the role of the Ministry as limited; it was not responsible for recommending this suture over that, these criteria over others. Decisions regarding medical technique and practice, even those which attracted public interest such as the determination of death, were beyond the Ministy's purview. (This attitude changed during Dan Michaeli's term as Director General. He brought the introduction of specific criteria under Ministry auspices.)

However, despite his view that the Ministry could not endorse these criteria, Ne'eman felt free to offer his own critique of the recommendations. He noted that the language "point of death," replacing the usual "moment of death" seemed to indicate that Hadassah was interested primarily in "the functional aspect of the event of death" above anything else. By this, he meant the focus was clearly on arriving at a suitable time for the removal of the donor's organs rather than describing the actual death of the donor. He did not give any reason for this reading. Perhaps he felt "moment" would be better understood as the actual time of the donor's own death, while "point" indicated something more abstract. Later on, though, he asked whether Hadassah intended that these criteria would "allow for even heart transplant?"[35] It seems that he had his doubts as to whether Hadassah was interested in arriving at an absolute claim of actual death or a "point" which would ethically allow for the removal of organs.

Ne'eman also noted that two important items were left off of Hadassah's list: One, an explanation that "all efforts at saving the life of the donor had been made—before his death and the decision concerning transplant." Two, no mention was made regarding the policy dictated by the Ministry concerning the use of two separate medical teams for determination of death and the actual transplant.

Ne'eman's commentary drew attention to the admitted focus of these criteria: not so much the determination of death, but the determination of the proper moment for organ harvesting. Worrying about potential problems (like any good lawyer) he noted that this focus could cause problems by ignoring the donor as patient. The criteria contained no indication of this change of status, raising suspicion that

145

this patient may have not received adequate care qua patient. Not even the death of the patient is mentioned – only a 'point' in that process which allows for the harvest of his organs. Hadassah, Ne'eman pointed out, had begun *in medias res* – leaving itself open, perhaps, to a number of claims concerning its care of these donors.

Amos Korchin leveled deeper criticism against Hadassah, finding much to fault with the wording and focus of their criteria.[36] He correctly noted that the criteria were both obtuse and redundant. Korchin found phrases such as *"sharp* drop" and *"central* reaction" overly subjective with no means of inferring what was meant by them. Worse, the need to check *"all* central reactions" both opened the door to an unwieldy never-ending procedure and reflected back upon the specifically mentioned tests of eye dilation and reflexes as linguistically redundant, adding more confusion. Additionally, he argued that the inclusion of an arteriograph, if taken together with all the other criteria, was in itself redundant. If it was to be used, it rendered other tests unnecessary. Another problem concerned the meaning of the phrase "voluntary movement". Korchin questioned whether it included the beating of the heart? If so, these criteria would preclude its transplantation.[37]

The following year, in 1975, David Frankel, who later became the Vice-Counsel of the Health Ministry, completed his doctoral dissertation on the legal aspects of organ transplants.[38] Regarding the question of defining death, he rejected the dichotomy of process versus moment and argued that death needed to be understood as a "state" that in some ways resembled a process, yet in practice, was a moment. Finding this moment devolved upon current medical abilities.

Frankel utilized the then-current American legal discourse surrounding the beginning of life as a template for discussing its end in Israel. In the American debate over abortion the "viability" of the fetus then served as the measure of its legal life. This meant that the rights granted to a living human were granted to a fetus only at that time when current medical practice concurred that this developing human was possessed of the ability to maintain its 'life', even though as unborn it was still not living.[39]

> At the moment of conception the process of pregnancy begins and this process terminates at the end of the act of birth. Only at the conclusion of birth does life begin, yet rights begin already during this process, and the solution to the question as to when do these rights begin, devolves, practically, upon doctors, as it is their task to determine from which moment the fetus is viable.[40]

He argued that this situation was analogous to the process of dying which ends in death.

> When an individual reaches the end of his life, a two staged process begins; *gessisa* and afterwards *gevia*.[41] With the beginning of the death process, comes the moment when the individual no longer has legal rights. From a biological perspective, one dies in stages. … Through the use of special means an effort is made to delay the beginning of the death process for as long as possible, and so to extend life. However, the moment that life ends and the process of death begins, we no longer speak of a living individual. The beginning of the process of death means that from that moment the individual is no longer alive. That is, there is no longer any possibility from the perspective of medical science, at its present stage, to return him to a state in which his or-

gans will continue to regenerate and function, and he
will be conscious or possess any mental capability.[42]

Frankel's argument, then, was two-fold: death was essentially an
ethical category, but one which needed to be determined by medical
means. This was similar to the position espoused by Kass in his
rebuttal to Morrison—yet worked in the opposite direction.[43] Morrison had claimed that no real moment of death existed, but was a
social-moral construct based upon ethical concerns. Kass held that
death was a biological-medical moment with important ethical repercussions. Frankel took Morrison's view of death as a process, thus
making room for the ethical as the key element, but agreed with Kass
that scientific-medical conclusions delineated this process. As such, it
was clear to him that the connection of death to medical capabilities
meant that the delineating line of death would be mobile—along with
medical progress. But, because death was essentially a question of
rights, this was not a problem.

The practical outcome of his approach was that it allowed for the
harvesting of organs from biologically active patients no longer in
possession of any human-legal rights:

> From the moment of the onset of the death process, we
> understand that it is permissible to make use of the in-
> dividual's body or parts of it for the purpose of healing
> another.[44]

Frankel argued that "most doctors" equated irreversible loss of brain-
function with this loss of rights called death. [45]

Death, a concept associated by many just with physical conditions,
was translated into a matter of legal rights. This conceptualization
allowed for the dismissal of still physically apparent "life" once no

legal defense of this life could be mounted. Lacking legal rights, the brain-dead patient ceased, as it were, to legally exist. As such, no legal or ethical boundary stood before utilizing his legally lifeless body as a means to help others whose claim on life was still intact. For Frankel, legal categories trumped physical indications: the former parsed the latter into operative categories. This view stood in opposition to that expressed by Carmi, for whom the law could be easily manipulated in order to make it confer with scientific-medical advances.

Over this five-year period, as clinical familiarity with the comatose resuscitated patient grew, the conceptual categories which this patient occupied diversified. The acceptance of brain-death was, for thinkers as different as Davidson and R. Goren, a solution to the suffering state that this patient inhabited. In R. Goren's view, technological advances had disturbed formerly accepted halakhic categories, necessitating reconsideration of this patient. The brain-dead became a new type of *gosses* being kept unfairly from his final reward. Although Davidson did not use the same typology, he too believed that the brain-dead occupied a moral-medical space that required, as a matter of ethical treatment, that we release him from his suffering. The transfer of this tragic figure, from the ethical space of patient to that of donor, was enabled by the particular conceptualization of his personhood.

Ouaknin's vision of this patient was a reflection of the way that medical technology could be best utilized. As the nearly brain-dead patient was increasingly unable to benefit from "futile and expensive" life-support, he became less patient and more prospective donor. The change was finalized when all benefit ended. Utilization of technology and patient status were linked.[46]

Nowhere was the liminal status of the dying patient shown to be more complexly (and perhaps confusingly) linked to his potential as donor than in the first Hadassah criteria. As described above, Korchin made the confusing nature of this medical directive clear. This I

# Really Dead?

believe reflects on the confused nature of its task. The learned Hadassah panel set-out to arrive at a particular "point of death" for one singular purpose—the transplantation of organs. Yet, this singular particularity somehow grew into an at once over-expansive yet redundant list of criteria. The difficulty in creating a well-focused set of criteria is yet another example of the conceptual and practical slipperiness of death.[47]

Frankel's argument was an interesting addition to the collection of opinions, attitudes and conceptualizations of the brain-dead that would allow for them to become "useful" organ donors. However, the language of rights as a means of setting up proper boundaries between the 'living' and 'dead' never found any mention in the continued discussions over brain-death in the period being studied (aside from its presence in Frankel's unpublished dissertation). [48] Despite the large amount of writing devoted to the questions surrounding brain-death, the wide variety of opinions held, the symposia held and the need for general cooperation that those involved in organ transplantation expressed, there were few instances of actual fruitful dialogue. As we saw above with Carmi's book, even easily available resources were ignored as positive attitudes towards transplantation made consideration of others' more negative opinions difficult to consider. So while many honestly felt the need for public support in using brain-dead people as organ donors, little of the dialogue which may have helped to engender this support was actually taking place. In light of this background, the gesture made by the Health Ministry and Hadassah in approaching the Rabbinate, was perhaps even more radical. Finally, it seemed, some long awaited and hoped for cooperation was going to take place. The final failed result of that one cooperative moment is in a sense, then, all the more tragic.

[1] Anonymous, "*Qeviat Regah Hamavet,*" ***Sefer Assia*** 1 (1976): 183-201. This institute, connected to the religiously-oriented Jerusalem hospital, Shaare Zedek, was established in order to explore questions of medical ethics from a halakhic perspective. It was the first such institute of its kind and continues to function today. Its journal, *Assia,* is one of the main repositories for research on matters of halakhah and medicine. It has also offered extensive in-service training for medical personnel on these matters and sponsored the publication of Prof. Avraham Steinberg's comprehensive encyclopedia on medicine and halakhah. Anonymous, "*Qeviat Regah Hamavet,*" ***Sefer Assia*** 1 (1976): 183-201.

[2] Ibid. 188.

[3] It was not until 1978 that the New York neurologist F. Plum would coin the phrase PVS – for persistent vegetative state.

[4] Ibid.

[5] Pallis similarly inserted emotive content into the readings of medical machinery by suggesting that if resuscitated, unresponsive patients were capable of consciousness, their state would be too awful to imagine. (Christopher Pallis, *ABC of Brain Stem Death* [London: British Medical Journal, 1983.])

[6] See note 7. I will point out in section II how patients who qualified as brain-dead may very well have not lost all capacity for consciousness.

[7] Ibid., 193.

[8] Y. Levi, "*Davar Hame'aqev Yitziat Hanefesh.*"

[9] See the discussion above of R. Weiss and the position of the *Shvut Yaaqov.*

[10] Y. Levi, "*Davar Hame'aqev Yitziat Hanefesh,*" 61.

[11] Ibid., 62. The entire question of treating the *gosses* is important but beyond the scope of this study. After years of deliberation in a wide variety of public settings and a special commission, a law outlining guidelines for the care of the dying patient was passed in the Knesset in 2005 essentially authorizing such withholding of care. See *Hok Haholeh Hanoteh Lamut 2005* (available on the Israeli Health Ministry web-site: www.health.gov.il).

[12] A. Carmi, *Refuah Vemishpat* (Tel Aviv: Sifriat Maariv, 1971). He was a judge, professor of law, and author of hundreds of columns on medicine and law for the IMA. His work is the standard Israeli text and has been periodically updated in various forms, most recently in 2003.

[13] Ibid., 647.

[14] Ibid., 648.

[15] Ibid., 648. Regarding the then-current tumultuous "autopsy wars," Carmi wrote that the medical profession was worthy of, and in need of, both legal and public support in their fight against incitive religious elements—"no matter how manifested." Was he condoning violence against those whom he described as intimidating doctors or merely encouraging legal manipulations?

[16] Goren, "*Hagdarat Hamavet Behalakhah*," **Shanah Beshanah** (Jerusalem: Chief Rabbinate of Israel, 5734): 125-130, 125.

[17] Ibid.

[18] Ibid., 126-8.

[19] Ibid., 128.

[20] He supported this rather unusual position by noting that a medieval commentary on the Talmud (the *Tosphot* on b. *Baba Metziah* 114b) permitted transgressing a first-degree Torah prohibition in order to revive a dead individual. This source is based on the Biblical story where Elijah revived a 'dead' child told in I Kings 17. As Elijah was a Kohen, he would have been prohibited from contact with the dead. The *Tosphot* solves this problem by answering that "as it was certain that he would revive him, it was permitted because of the commandment of saving another's life." The main argument for the permission granted is the claim of certainty. This is not the case in general, however. Additionally, it is a comment on a Biblical story and not a legal ruling. Both of these points were omitted by R. Goren in his expansion of this commandment to include the brain-dead. One might get the impression that he is referring to a clear normative statement of the *halakhah*. He did, however, point out that others do not agree with his new expansive interpretation of this commandment. As detailed above, it is clear that R. Feinstein certainly did not.

[21] This is clear despite R. Goren's claim that the end of respiration remains the nominal defining characteristic of death for the *halakhah*.

[22] This is obviously a particular understanding of what it means to be a *gosses*. It is at odds with that described by Levi above—although the practical consequences are the same.

[23] Ibid., 130.

[24] Such an argument was made by Green and Wikler in their conceptual attack on then current defenses of brain-death. They claimed that increasingly sophisticated ICU equipment would come to replace a variety of somatic functions usually controlled by the brain. So long as somatic function was being supported, they saw no reason to dismiss it as irrelevant. (Green and Wikler, "Brain Death and Personal Identity," *Philosophy and Public Affairs* [1980]: 105-33).

[25] The Hebrew text reads: "where there is something beneficial for the patient in his death".

[26] Ibid., 129. He also stated that he distinguished between praying for someone's death (permitted) and active euthanasia (strictly prohibited).

[27] See Cohen-Almagor, *The Right to Die with Dignity* (New Brunswick, NJ: Rutgers University Press, 2001) for a critique of the meaning of 'dignity' for those who argue that euthanasia would allow "death with dignity" for the dying. His focus on the Dutch model of "euthanasia on request" is one of the most concise critiques of the many issues involved that I have seen.

[28] Ouaknin, "*Mot Hamoah,*" **Harefuah** 84:6 (1973): 328-30.

[29] Ibid., 329.

[30]Letter from K. Y. Man to Prof. Padeh in Ne'eman, "*Havat Daat al Qeviat Nequdat Hamavet,*" **ML** (Tevet 11, 5735): 7-9, 8. These criteria were not published elsewhere and I did not find them in Hadassah's archives. I do not know the identity of the actual authors. The Hebrew in the original reads *nequdat hamavet– point* and not *moment* of death. This usage will draw critical attention, as we will see.

[31] The Hadassah Medical Center had been founded well before the State of Israel and had housed the only medical school until 1964. It was, and continues to be, a prestigious institution, at times leveraging that prestige into an ability to dictate practice to the rest of the medical establishment. The late Professor Dan Michaeli (former Director General of the Health Ministry) told me in an interview that when Hadassah wanted to move ahead with heart transplants in 1986, they did not ask the Ministry for permission, but informed them of their decision. Additionally, according to Michaeli, their location in Jerusalem, the state capital, gave them something of an advantage as a number of their higher-level legal and administrative staff were well connected to powerful government figures (Interview from Nov. 29, 2004).

[32] Ne'eman, "*Havat Daat al Qeviat Nequdat Hamavet,*" 8.

[33] Ibid., 7.

[34] Ibid. This would indeed be the case in a 1982 criminal appeal to the Israeli Supreme Court which analyzed brain-death. The general "standard of care" argument had long been the main measure of legal-judicial acceptability and among the main defenses against medical malpractice in forensic claims. (The American Daubert case of 1993 registered something of a change.)

[35] Ibid.

[36] Amos Korchin, "*Qeviat Nequdat Hamavet,*" **ML** (February 10, 1975): 7. I have listed only his main criticisms – he made several more.

153

---

[37] I think that this last criticism is off target. Most medical professionals would understand cardiac activity as an essentially involuntary bodily activity, regulated, but not under the "voluntary" control of the cerebrum. The fact that the criteria did not include an easily administered ECG or other monitor of cardiac activity seems to confirm that cardiac function was not considered to be relevant regarding a "point of death" for this panel. Therefore, a beating heart could be removed for transplant.

[38] David Frankel, *"Ha'aspectim Hamishpatiim shel Hashtalat Averim,"* (PhD Diss., Hebrew University, 1975).

[39] Ibid., 200.

[40] Ibid., 201.

[41] He understood *gevia* – a Biblical and Modern Hebrew term connected to death – as denoting the actual act of dying. This meaning follows from a number of Biblical verses. It is usually translated as 'expire'. *Gessisa* is a broader term denoting the process of dying which ends with expiration.

[42] Ibid.

[43] See Leon Kass, "Death as an Event: A Commentary on Robert Morrison," *Science* 173 (1971).

[44] Ibid., 202.

[45] Ibid.

[46] One of the ethical arguments often advanced for the recognition of brain-death was that ICU resources were scarce. They were no longer of any benefit to these "dead" patients, but could be used advantageously by others. Such a utilitarian approach segued nicely into a similar argument for harvesting organs being "wasted" on these patients for whom treatment was futile. This was the case with the Harvard criteria. In 1974 Ouaknin published another article on brain-death. He and his fellow author observed ECG changes among a group of brain-dead patients in the hope that they might be able to track such changes already in dying patients as useful criteria *indicative* of a diagnosis of brain-death. While having some success in finding characteristic changes in ECG readings, they did not reach any final conclusions. (G. Ouaknin and Y. Drori, *"Pe'ulat Halev Bematsav shel Mot Hamoah,"* **Harefuah** 86:10 [1974]: 489-93).

[47] While the staff at Hadassah has been quite helpful, they have not succeeded in finding any records of this panel's deliberations in their archives. This is unfortunate, as it would certainly be valuable to understand what transpired among its members as they worked on these recommendations. No response to the various criticisms was recorded in IMA publications and as far as I know, these criteria were

put into actual use by Hadassah. However, the text of a lecture given by Hadassah's Legal Counsel a few months before these criteria were adopted was printed in *ML*. His subject was the legal obligation of doctors to provide care to patients (A. Naor, "*Qriterionim Lematan Tipul Refuie Leholeh*," *ML* [Av 17, 5735]: 7-10.) Naor stressed that no obligation to provide care in Israeli law existed beyond that which was enforceable as part of a private contract which may be undertaken between a doctor and patient. This led him to conclude that doctors were free to decide upon criteria for the granting of medical care to different patients. It would not be unreasonable to assume that this type of legal advice accompanied the creation of Hadassah's criteria. It fit well with an understanding of death as the point where any obligation for care ends.

It may be, at the risk of over-interpreting the criteria produced by Hadassah, that it is possible to read them as depicting an increasingly invasive tracing of a Foucaultian "medical gaze" focused on the suspected dead patient. They start with the easily accessible pupils and move to the gross "central" motor reactions and then on to readily induced and noticed reflexes. Only after this primary list do they move inward to respiration, blood pressure and electrical activity. Last is the actual invasion of the brain with the arteriogram. The doubtful state of the patient is tentatively explored without ever declaring that he is certainly dead. No mention is made of the death of the patient or his brain until the final sentence, "with the determination of the donor's death…" at which point the procedures for harvesting his organs begins.

The patient is as figuratively opened to view as he will be actually afterwards. The list here resembles a list of mounting procedural invasiveness which moves along turning the body from patient to donor. The patient reaches the 'point of death'—that is, his reduction to donor, slowly, uncertainly. This progression is traced by the mounting invasiveness of these criteria—each allowing more and deeper disruption of the patient's status – from checking his eyes, his body, his respiration and actual blood flow – until finally, as donor, he is fully opened and his organs removed. Here then is an order reflective both of the patient's devolving status and the increasing liberties that this reduction offers the medical staff. The ethics surrounding this patient's medical care devolve together with his status— moving from treatment to harvest as he changes from patient to cadaver.

It is no wonder that no mention of the move from patient status to potential do- nor status is explicitly elaborated—it is being revealed in the progression of the criteria themselves. This list, then, presents the "point of death" as the vanishing

# Really Dead?

point on the horizon of the transplantation project where the ethics of medical care bring life and death together. This is similar to the logic of the CIOMS recommendations. No authoritative definition of death is proffered. Death need not be defined — it *is* that 'point' where medical staff are no longer treating a patient, but with the invasive arteriogram (recall Ouaknin's description of them as "neurological research tools") and finally actual dissection — are dealing only with a "heart lung preparation."

[48] With one acceptation: The philosopher Asa Kasher would argue along these lines in an IMA symposium in 1986.

# 7

# 1976

# New Halakhic Considerations

In 1976 two additions to the halakhic discussion of death criteria were published. The first was a comprehensive article on the determination of death by pediatric neurologist Avraham Steinberg.[1] Steinberg was well on his way to becoming recognized as one of the major authorities on questions of *halakhah* and medicine (which he remains to this day), eventually authoring an entire encyclopedia on their interface. In 1976 he argued against the use of brain-death criteria, yet ten years later he became one of their main proponents in the religious establishment. The second piece was a *psaq* written by R. Feinstein which would become the halakhic basis for the Chief Rabbinate's own decision ten years hence. While both of these documents were important contributions to the halakhic discourse on brain-death in their time, analysis of R. Feinstein's *psaq* will be the main focus of this chapter. As I will describe in section II, it stood at the center, not just of the Rabbinate's decision, but of much controversy as well. R. Feinstein's intent and his *psaq's* meaning have been debated for over three decades.

First, however, it is worthwhile to briefly describe Steinberg's contribution to the brain-death debate at this stage. Although he would later serve as one of the medical advisors to the Rabbinate committee

# Really Dead?

which drafted the decision on heart transplants, his stance at this point in time offers a stark contrast to his support of the Rabbinate's decision in 1986. Understanding the basis for his initial opposition to heart-transplants helps contextualize his later endorsement of brain-death. (The Rabbinate's decision must have, in his eyes, properly dealt with the halakhic and ethical problems he had raised here.)

A good portion of Steinberg's article addressed the philosophical aspects of determining death. Like Gervais, Steinberg presented a picture of death as an amorphous process, yet given to more exact determination through the use of

> …rational criteria, although there exist strong differences concerning how they should be chosen. … to a great extent we can say that any system of criteria is artificial, for it comes to define a point and certain stage within a number of advanced states.[2]

He faulted the use of brain function as a criterion for death for several reasons. First, equating the death of the person as a whole to the end of brain function needlessly differentiated between vegetative and intellectual life. He felt this was a classic example of outmoded Cartesian dualism. Second, the ongoing dispute regarding what exactly needed to be measured in order to determine loss of brain function—the neocortex, the brain stem, the whole brain—was symptomatic of this criterion's weakness. Third, he insisted that ethically, any criteria used must be designed only for the good of the patient himself and not to enable others to benefit from his death. In his view, transplant-driven brain-death did not fit this ethical requirement.[3]

After providing an overview of actual brain-death criteria, Steinberg moved on to discuss the halakhic perspective. He covered the now familiar source material from the Talmud through its modern interpreters.[4] Ultimately, his rejection of brain-death was tied to the philosophical problems that it presented. Steinberg argued that somatic life in the body's important organs also counted as life for the *halakhah*. It could not be dismissed as mere twitching of a lizard's tail.[5]

Finally, he found that modern medical practice did make a difference regarding the traditional need to wait for a short time after the determination of death until actual burial.

> …in my opinion, when we are dealing with organ transplants it is possible to ignore this custom of waiting, as death has been determined according to all of the [traditional] criteria and in accordance with the diagnostic tools available to the doctor at a given time.[6]

For Steinberg, technology could be used successfully as an interpretive tool to check and test traditionally valid criteria, but did not affect the criteria themselves.[7] If the cessation of respiration could be ascertained through modern technological means instead of traditional tests (like looking for chest movements) this could enable quicker determination of death possibly aiding in the retrieval of viable organs from dead donors. However, while the fixing of an exact "moment of death" may vary in individual cases according to the available technology, no change in the definition of death is warranted.[8]

The most significant event of the year, however, was a third responsum authored by R. Feinstein (*Egrot Moshe* YD III:132). This responsum would eventually serve as the major linchpin of the *psaq* of the Israeli Rabbinate, yet it would also become the center of much controversy (which continues up to this day). The amount of discussion devoted to its actual meaning is an exception to the usual lack of dialogue that I have described above.

# Really Dead?

The interlocutor to whom this responsum was written was R. Feinstein's son-in-law, R. Moshe Tendler—a well-known American teacher, community rabbi and professor of biology who dealt extensively with medical-halakhic issues (always relying upon his father-in-law's halakhic authority in his decisions).[9] In discussing this most controversial of responsa, I will first carefully unpack the language and meaning of the text and then move on to describe the thirty-year debate over its interpretation.

The responsum begins with R. Feinstein reiterating his earlier position that continuous cessation of respiration is *the* halakhic criterion for the determination of death. However, he then acknowledged that there are three other types of patients who required more complex testing than merely waiting for some time after respiration has ceased. The first was the seriously ill respirated patient. As respiratory assistance does not allow for anoxia, the patient's true status is masked and testing can only be accomplished when the patient is not being respirated. Such testing is no simple matter.

> Through this machine, it is possible that he will breathe even though already dead, for this respiration does not render an individual alive. Now, if no other characteristics of life are noted [in this patient], we see he has no feeling, even no response to [being stuck with] a needle (which is called a coma), as long as the machine is functioning, it is forbidden to remove it from his mouth lest he is living and this action will kill him. However, when the machine stops functioning, due to the emptying of the oxygen tank, it should not be immediately replaced for a short time period -15 minutes – and if he is not alive he will not breathe [independently] and they will know that he is dead....[10]

This apnea test was to be carried out from time to time: any sign of independent respiration would be noted as a sign of life and the respirator must be immediately replaced.[11]

Another group of patients was also exceptional. R. Feinstein argued that trauma victims may have suffered *reversible* nerve damage which has affected their ability to breathe independently. In time, though, this damage may heal and respiratory ability can and may return. He wrote, "...even though they cannot breathe independently and exhibit no other signs of life, it is possible that they are not yet dead."[12]

Obviously, such patients would fail the above apnea test and be permanently disconnected from respiratory support even though not actually dead, but only injured. A solution to this problem was suggested by his son-in-law who described the use of arteriograms.

> ... you [R. Tendler] have said that there is a procedure by which expert physicians can determine through injection of a liquid into the body, into the arteries, whether the connection which exists between the brain and the entire body has been severed. If it [the dye] does not reach the brain, it is clear that the brain no longer has any connection to the body and [the brain] has completely rotted away so that it is as if the head has been virtually removed. If this is the case, we must be stringent with those [patients] who have lost all feeling...and cannot breathe at all without the machine and not decide that they are dead until they administer this test. If they see any connection between the brain and the body, even though he cannot breathe, he must be respirated—even for a lengthy time period. Only when

# Really Dead?

this test reveals no connection of the brain to the body
can the loss of respiration render him dead.[13]

Finally, there was the need to establish that actual *irreversible* cessation of respiration had occurred. Patients suffering from barbiturate poisoning and the like, needed to be carefully examined in order to eliminate possible secondary causes for respiratory failure before disconnection from life-support. A blood test showing no further presence of poison was suggested.[14]

This responsum is clear in distinguishing between assisted breathing and independent respiration. Only loss of the latter holds any halakhic meaning in determining patient status. This, of course, only in the case where the patient shows classic neurological unresponsiveness as well, with no reaction to pain stimulus such as "a needle" pushed into the body.[15] What is not clear, however, is what R. Feinstein meant regarding his instructions for the use of an arteriogram. It was supposed to determine that a patient has been "virtually" decapitated.[16] As the breathing of mechanically respirated patients is hermeneutically neutral, its presence cannot serve as a sign of life. Only testing a patient off-respirator can offer evidence of life or death. It does not seem that any *final* (or irreversible) loss of respiratory capacity can be assumed so long as artificial respiration is continuing. The continually resuscitated trauma patient cannot be adequately tested. But, he can be given an arteriogram. The question is whether R. Feinstein meant to have this test *replace* the usual test needed for independent respiration in order to prove that death had occurred.

Note that the language of the responsum states that, "only when this test [the arteriograph] reveals no connection of the brain to the body *can the loss of respiration render him dead.*" It is not disconnecting the patient which renders him dead, but the cessation of respiration. Which loss of respiration is being referred to here? Is it what can be evidenced only after the patient's artificial respiration is disrupted, as is the case with other patients? If this is so, then, the "stringency" of the test lies in its serving as an additional step before breathing capacity can be tested.[17]

Or by "loss" did R. Feinstein mean the capacity which had already been lost but was being masked by the machinery? This is referred to at the beginning of his discussion of trauma victims, "even though they *cannot breathe independently* and exhibit no other signs of life, it is possible that they are not yet dead." This possibility of continued life exists because the loss may only be temporary. Does this potentially-only-temporary loss get coupled with the severing of the brain-body connection so that it becomes understandable as irreversible, i.e. halakhically meaningful?

If the latter is the case, then, it may appear that R. Feinstein has replaced what he has insisted is the only halakhic criterion for death—continuous cessation of respiration until anoxia—with something different: brain damage which establishes the permanence of a given condition which is responsible for a current loss of respiratory capacity. However, in an earlier responsum he was quite clear that the death of the brain was not equivalent to death.

> But the definite truth is that it is not the cessation of the brain's functioning which is equivalent to death, for as long as one breathes he is alive. Rather, the end of the brain's functioning is that which causes cessation of respiration.[18]

The loss of brain function, though, can secondarily *cause* death through ending respiration.

# Really Dead?

Conversely, in the same earlier responsum, R. Feinstein also contended that the use of an ECG which showed cardiac activity was conclusive proof of life – despite the cessation of respiration.

> Therefore regarding an individual in whom life activity
> is seen through the use of an electric radiogram [sic]...
> he is alive even though he is not breathing.[19]

The trauma patient, even though he is not breathing (he is merely being resuscitated), may also show evidence of life—cerebral blood flow. If this is the case, it seems clear that he should be considered as alive as one whose heart is beating. This explains why the arteriogram is a stringency ("we must be stringent")—it is designed to check for a sign of life in the non-respirating patient who would ordinarily (recall the exceptional entombed character who lived) be considered dead. When such a case presents itself, it cannot be dismissed. However, if no other signs of life are found, cessation of respiration—the usual sign of death—functions as usual. It would appear, then, that once *no* contrary signs of life are found this patient is considered dead.

However, one other factor is also relevant: the status of the decapitated individual. Again, according to his previous responsum, only in this case is death categorically present—regardless, for example, of whether this individual could be saved and regardless of whether other signs of somatic life can be found. The status of this trauma victim seems hermeneutically questionable because R. Feinstein did not clearly classify him as an actual case of decapitation—but only virtually so. If, then, his heart is still beating—is cardiac activity considered a sign of life which "trumps" his loss of respiratory capability such that he is still alive? This would be his conclusion according to *Egrot Moshe* YD II 146. Or, does *virtual* decapitation render him dead regardless of any other signs of life? If this was the case, then, this responsum could logically be understood as allowing for organ transplants from these comatose patients whose hearts were fully functioning. This would render his earlier extremely strong objections to heart transplants moot. Those who argued that R. Feinstein had decided in favor of heart transplants contended that this was the proper interpretation of this 1976 *psaq*.

Many, however, questioned whether he would he have changed course so drastically without making an explicit statement as to this fact.[20] His silence on this matter served to fuel doubts about his true intentions. (Additionally, he would reiterate his objections to heart transplants two years later in a succinct responsum to the Israeli Knesset Member Kalman Kahana.)[21]

In attempting to reach clear conclusions about R. Feinstein's actual intent concerning transplants, attention has been focused on three different aspects of the responsum: its historical context, its understanding by those closest to him and its own the internal logic. Regarding the last point, aside from what I have explained above, R. Mordechai Halperin claimed that if one were to assume that the angiogram (arteriograph) was to be performed as an *additional* confirmatory test on trauma victims this would mean that until brain death could be established:

> … it is forbidden to interrupt the resuscitory apparatus and full treatment must be given…. It is clear that this conclusion is opposed to world-wide standards, we have never heard of an obligation to check cerebral blood flow in all those who have died from traffic accidents….[22]

While R. Halperin felt that the implications of the *psaq* understood a certain way were troubling, I am not sure why this is the case. It

# Really Dead?

may very well be that R. Feinstein wished to include a procedure that was not part of regular medical practice.[23] Additionally, it seems quite reasonable to wait for an indication that possibly temporary nerve damage has become permanent before endangering a patient by depriving him of oxygen at a critical stage of his injury. Apnea testing at this point could in fact become the cause of death and not just a test![24]

Historically, this responsum was written against a background of medical-ethical questions concerning the withdrawal of treatment for the comatose. In 1976 a New York State bill concerning death criteria was under consideration. (R. Feinstein was a New York City resident and R. Tendler resided in Monsey, New York where he served as a community rabbi). The bill included an allowance for brain-death criteria to be used to pronounce death for resuscitated patients. (It is no coincidence that the New York State Assembly was debating this while the celebrated case of Karen Ann Quinlan was being pleaded before the Supreme Court of neighboring New Jersey.)[25] In fact, three weeks after penning his responsum, R. Feinstein wrote a letter to New York Assemblyman Hebert Miller, chairman of the Assembly Committee on Health, detailing his opposition to the bill.[26] In this letter he makes no mention of the exceptional cases of trauma or poison victims, nor of any brain-death criteria. Instead, he only writes that support for respiration cannot be actively withdrawn even from the clinically dead, but only withheld as he spelled out in his *psaq*.

> In a patient presenting the clinical picture of death, i. e., no signs of life such as movement or response to stimuli, the total cessation of independent respiration, is an absolute proof that death had occurred. ...

If such a "clinically dead" patient is on a respirator it is forbidden to interrupt the respirator. However, when the respirator requires servicing, the services may be withheld while the patient is carefully and continuously monitored to detect any signs of independent breathing no matter how feeble. If such breathing motions do not occur, it is a certainty that he is dead.

In the event that these specific requirements will not be incorporated in your bill, I strongly endorse and support the "religious exemption" clause in the Governor's program Bill, a concept which is in keeping with religious rights and social ethics.[27]

For those who opposed the "pro-transplant" reading of R. Feinstein's responsum, the lack of any mention of brain-death determination in his letter has been taken as proof that his intent in his *psaq* was to delineate the steps needed before withholding care and not offer another track, as it were, for establishing death. If R. Feinstein had himself accepted a brain-death determination as valid in some cases why did he not include this recommendation?[28] Thus, many claimed that it made better sense to understand his suggested angiogram as a *pre-condition* to the actual apnea test outlined in his *psaq*.

However, if this is true, why did he not mention the use of the angiogram in his letter? It may be that his intent was to suggest that this was a stringency only incumbent upon Jews. As noted above (*Egrot Moshe* YD II: 174), R. Feinstein did in fact suggest that there may be a difference in the prohibition of hastening the onset of death between Jews and Gentiles. Jews are prohibited from such activities that may hasten the death of the dying, while it may be permissible for Gentiles to save a dying sufferer (even a Jew) from his agony by quickening his passing. Keeping the same Jewish/Gentile differentiation in mind means that the use of the angiogram may have been a stringency only incumbent upon Jewish doctors, but that for New York State law, this *extra* step was not needed.

The family of R. Feinstein, including his son-in-law, R. Tendler, and his grand-daughter's husband, R. Shabtai Rappaport, [29] claimed that their close personal contact with him uniquely positioned them to understand the true intent of his words.[30] They both argued that R. Feinstein accepted brain-death criteria as valid. R. Tendler has been the primary vocal proponent of this view. Writing in JAMA in 1977 he argued that Jewish law was in full agreement with brain-death criteria of death.[31] He and his co-authors defined brain-death criteria as describing "...a condition in which the brain is completely destroyed and in which cessation of function of all other organs is imminent and inevitable."[32]

While brain-death was understood as complete destruction of the brain, the authors did mention that this may not actually occur in all cases.[33] Throughout this article, though, brain-death was continually construed as actual, physical destruction of the brain.[34] It seems to be that this understanding allowed for R. Tendler to link R. Feinstein's understanding of decapitation as by-definition death with brain-death, which could be understood as *virtual* or physiological (if not physical) decapitation. Conversely, it appears that as R. Feinstein's informant on medical and biological science, R. Tendler may very well have explained brain-death to R. Feinstein in terms of actual physical destruction: this was clearly the language used by R. Feinstein himself to describe the severing of any body-brain connection in his *psaq*. This point has led to one of the recurring criticisms of R. Tendler's reading of this *psaq*: the question of whether *only actual physical* destruction of the brain was intended by R. Feinstein as equivilant to this virtual decapitation.[35] If so, perhaps without actual lyses of the brain, R.

Feinstein would not have held that brain-death could be equated with decapitation. This holds regardless of whether this understanding would then allow organ retrieval or only the withdrawal of respiratory support.

R. Tendler has continually asserted that there is no discrepancy between his pro-transplant interpretation of this responsum and R. Feinstein's registered opposition to heart transplants elsewhere. He claimed that the responsa in which such opposition was voiced all referred only to those potential donors who were capable of independent respiration.[36] As I detailed when describing Levi's opposition to the same, however, it is questionable if non-resuscitated patients were ever really considered as potential heart donors. More problematic, though, is the fact that the first responsum (*Egrot Moshe* YD II 174) was written in reply to R. Weiss who directly addressed the problem of *keeping patients resuscitated*. In the third section of his responsum, R. Feinstein agreed with R. Weiss that the use of artificial respiration by transplant surgeons on potential donors only to keep organs viable for transplant was prohibited as it was not done for the donor's benefit. The second responsum (*Egrot Moshe* YD II 146) clearly starts off by discussing patients who "can still breathe," yet in the second section equally clearly moves on to discuss those who lacked the ability to breathe independently and were on resuscitation equipment. Here R. Feinstein concluded that the use of an ECG reading was valid evidence of life for a patient not breathing independently, but being resuscitated artificially.

It is true that R. Feinstein's objection to heart transplants specifically in this second responsa (*Egrot Moshe* YD II 146) devolved upon the lack of the proceedure's success. This is also the case in a later *psaq* from 1978.[37] While this means that his opposition to heart transplants may not be solely dependent upon questions concerning unethical harvesting of the donor heart, I cannot understand how anyone can

# Really Dead?

explain that his position concerning *resuscitated* patients did not change if they read the 1976 responsum under consideration (YD III 132) as R. Tendler did. That is, as allowing for organ removal after brain-death. The question, then, remains – did R. Feinstein reconsider his earlier opinion and in this responsum accept brain-death criteria as sufficient for declaring death? This is a point which has been much debated both by those who were in personal contact with R. Feinstein and other halakhic scholars.[38]

However, R. Tendler has also produced other evidence that aimed at proving that regardless of previous positions taken by R. Feinstein, in the end his father-in-law did permit heart transplants. This evidence was in the form of a previously unknown responsum that was written to a Dr. Bundy in 1984, but only discovered by the Tendler family in 1992 (the story behind this letter and its contents were published in *Assia* 53-54 [VI 4:1-2] Elul 5754: 24-25). The responsum was written regarding a New York State Supreme Court case wherein the Court had accepted brain-death criteria as a legal definition of death.

R. Feinstein wrote:

> Practically: I have heard from my son-in-law, R. Tendler, that the Court only accepted the definition which is also correct according to the *halakhah*, the definition called, "Harvard Criteria" which are equivalent to "decapitation" (Heaven forbid) of the patient in that the brain is already (Heaven forbid) actually dissolved [The Hebrew here reads *n·kl* which literally means digested].

> Now, even though the heart can still pump for a few days, in any case all the time that the patient has no in-

dependent respiratory capacity, he is considered as dead (as I explained in my responsum YD III 132).

The rest of the responsum is devoted to the question of whether a Jewish doctor who is ordered to remove a patient from life support before the brain-death criteria are fulfilled can do so. He suggested that for a gentile patient this may be permissible, but concluded that for a Jewish patient this is certainly forbidden.

R. Tendler felt that with the publication of this letter the entire question of how to interpret the position of his father-in-law would be put to rest.[39] It was clear to him that his interpretation was unassailable.

Others, however, disagreed. Some noted that the letter only concerned the withdrawal of the resuscitation apparatus and did not contain permission to actually remove organs from a brain-dead patient.

R. Shlomo Zalman Auerbach, for example, wrote:

> However, in my humble opinion, even though [R. Feinstein] wrote, "it is correct according to the *halakhah*" and "even though the heart can still pump for a few days," it may be that these expressions only concern his intention to decide that, "it is permitted to remove the patient from the respiratory apparatus." The time that this letter was written was in Kislev 5745 [winter 1984] when the entire Torah world was debating whether these transplants were permitted or prohibited. If his opinion was that the patient was considered actually dead also regarding the matter of organ removal, it is odd that he did not mention that it is a commandment to take organs from this patient in order to save the lives of the

> critically ill. … I therefore believe that he did not want
> to rely on these tests in order to allow for the active re-
> moval of organs.[40]

Despite the best efforts at pushing a pro-transplant interpretation of R. Feinstein's position by many, upon weighing all of the evidence, textual and historical, it is difficult to claim that R. Feinstein's intention in writing his *psaq* was, in fact, to offer halakhic permission for organ transplantation. The meaning of his *psaq* remains, at best, equivocal. However, this ambiguity was ignored by those who promoted its use as the cornerstone of the Rabbinate's decision to endorse heart transplantation. As I will discuss in section II, the equating of brain-death with decapitation, which could then be understood as a by-definition state of death, promised to solve many of the halakhic and ethical problems that organ transplants presented. As noted in the beginning of this chapter, it was one of the main actors in the Israeli field of medical ethics, Professor A. Steinberg, who in the same year that R. Feinstein wrote his *psaq*, had enumerated these difficulties and rejected heart transplantation as an ethically and halakhically unsound practice, who would help to ensure that it was adopted by the Rabbinate. If in 1976 he viewed the still-beating heart of the resuscitated patient as a sign of life and technological medical advances as diagnostic tools with which to check traditional criteria of death, by 1986, he would understand that brain-death had replaced these criteria.

---

[1] Steinberg, "*Qeviat Rega Hamavet,*" **Noam** 19 (5737): 210-38.

[2] Ibid., 214. His use of "advanced" here seems to imply that he understood that a number of different advanced stages of dying may reasonably be interpreted as a moment of death.

[3] Ibid., 215.

[4] He agreed with R. Goren's suggestion that the inclusion of cardiac function in the classic triad of movement, respiration and pulse was novel. But he also argued that as this was included by every *poseq* who dealt with the determination of death, it had become an integral part of the *halakhah* (237).

[5] Ibid. He differentiated between the life of essential organs and the growth of hair and nails which he considered to be inconsequential.

[6] Ibid., 238.

[7] This is in contradistinction to R. Goren's opinion discussed in chapter six.

[8] Ibid. He did note that in "extreme cases," such as decapitation, there is no need to check for other vital signs before declaring death. This exception will come to play an important role in his change of opinion concerning brain-death. Steinberg understood the need to wait in the absence of respiration as understood by R. Auerbach—as an unclear sign of either death or shock, needing time to be resolved. If technology allows us to more quickly decode this halakhic sign, no waiting period is required. This is different than the way in which R. Feinstein understood the waiting period—as the time in which anoxia certainly took place.

[9] R. Tendler would become one of the main voices pushing for halakhic acceptance of brain-death criteria. Taking a quite activist and often polemical position, he vigorously advanced his interpretation of this *psaq*. In some measure, it was his insistent reading of this *psaq* as tantamount to permission for organ transplants from the brain-dead, that allowed the Israeli Rabbinate and others committed to *halakhah* to accept neurological criteria for death. It was to him, in addition to the Israeli Rabbinate, that Hadassah turned to verify the halakhic position on the determination of death.

[10] *EM* YD III 132.

[11] The efficacy and ethics of such a test may be problematic. Recently, serious problems with apnea testing have been observed with results which indicate that "the apnea test is not an innocuous procedure." (Saposnik G, Rizzo G, Vega A, Sabbatiello R, Deluca J.L.; "Problems associated with the apnea test in the diagnosis of brain death," *Neurology India* 52:3 [2004]: 342-5).

[12] *EM* YD III:132.

[13] Ibid.

[14] Ibid.

[15] This point is important as without it, one might confuse death with other states where no independent respiration is possible—patients with punctured lungs or polio, for example.

# Really Dead?

---

[16] The original Hebrew reads *k'hutaz rosho bekoah*. This last word means "potentially" and is often used in opposition to "actual." Here "virtual" captures its meaning more simply.

[17] This is the understanding of Avraham, *Nishmat Avraham*, 344.

[18] *EM* YD II:146—discussed in chapter five above.

[19] Ibid.

[20] See *Nishmat Avraham*, 339:2; Shor, "*B'inyan Simane Mitah*," *Hamaor* 298 (Sivan-Tamuz 5747): 12-19, 12; and note 37 below.

[21] *EM* HM II 72.

[22] Mordechai Halperin, "*Al Da'ato shel HGRM Feinstein*," **Assia** 47-48 (Kislev 5750): 6-13.

[23] This is also the response to this critique by Avraham, "*Hashtalat Lev Beyisrael*," **Assia** 43-44 (1987): 83.

[24] See note 11 above.

[25] Pernick argued that this case served as an impetus for establishing determination of death legislature throughout the United States in Martin Pernick, "Brain Death in Cultural Context," in *The Definition of Death: Contemporary Controversies*, 17.

[26] While this letter is written on his stationary and signed by R. Feinstein, it is not clear that he himself wrote the actual English text as his command of English was somewhat limited.

[27] Letter from R. Feinstein to NYS Assemblyman Miller (May 24, 1976).

[28] This is essentially the argument found in Chaim Dovid Zweible, "A Matter of Life and Death-Revisited," *The Jewish Observer* (October 1991): 11-22, 21.

[29] See Halperin, "*Al Da'ato shel HGRM Feinstein*," 11.

[30] See Shor, "*B'inyan Simane Mitah*." The author details his personal communications with R. Feinstein's son whom he claimed knew nothing about any change in his father's opposition to heart transplants. Also see R. Tendler and F. Rosner, "Brain Death," *Tradition* 28, no. 3 (Summer 1994). In this letter, R. Tendler attempted to marshal a number of different proofs for his own interpretation of R. Feinstein's *psaq* and for the use of brain-death criteria in general. One of these is misreported; some seem suspect. His letter elicited vehement denials from Rabbis Auerbach and Waldenburg, two of the Israeli *posqim* named as seeming supporters of brain-death.

[31] F. J. Veith et al., "Brain Death. I. A Status Report of Medical and Ethical Considerations," *JAMA* 238, no. 15 (1977).

[32] Ibid., 1651.

[33] Ibid., 1652.

[34] The authors strayed from this straightforward understanding at times. In his article in *JAMA*, R. Tendler and his co-authors wrote that these criteria described a brain as "completely destroyed" or "a person whose brain is totally destroyed" (Veith et al., "Brain Death," 1651). The very validity of these criteria "must be founded on the certainty that a person who meets [them]… has had ***actual*** complete destruction of the brain [my emphasis]" (1652). Oddly, though, they admitted that some studies showed that this is not the case.

> In a larger series of autopsy studies, however, the exact nature and distribution of these fatal morphological lesions in the brain were also shown to be dependent on the etiology and on the interval between fulfillment of the Harvard criteria and pathological examination. [This] observation is consistent with the well-known finding in other organs that time must often elapse before morphological evidence of cellular destruction can be detected (1652).

They also wrote that lack of blood flow is "uniformly associated with *subsequent* necrosis and liquefaction of the brain" [my emphasis] (1652). It is unfathomable to me how one can reconcile the call for actual physical destruction with what is clearly the lack of such immediate physical change. Were Veith et al. themselves confused about normal English usage? Were terms that denote actual physical change – destruction – mistakenly used when what they meant was the cessation of function or of certain life processes? They wrote, "complete destruction of the brain, which includes loss of all integrative, regulatory and other functions of the brain." Did they mean that destruction is equivalent to loss of function? Why use the word "destruction" then? Or did they so want to accept the philosophical and practical advantages of declaring those with no brain function dead, that such confusion was an acceptable price?

[35] The language used by R. Feinstein—"rotted" and "dissolved" in his *psaq* (*EM* YD III 132)—clearly denotes the actual physical change of matter – not the loss of function and not future change. As his son-in-law was the clearly named source of his medical information, I can only wonder whether R. Tendler shared with him just his view that brain-death was actually equivalent to what is normally taken to be actual physical destruction. Or did he also mention that this was in fact true only if understood as he subsequently explained in the pages of *JAMA*: as something

# Really Dead?

"associated with subsequent" destruction or that needed the philosophical buttressing of explanatory smokescreens such as consistency with time-lags in morphological changes?

Recently, an Israeli surgeon, Joshua Kunin, cogently argued that it is clear that R. Feinstein's *psaq*, even if interpreted as expansively as possible, was predicated just upon the supposition that the loss of brain function measured by these criteria entailed actual physical destruction of the brain (Kunin, "Brain Death: Revisiting the Rabbinic Opinions in Light of Current Medical Knowledge," *Tradition* 38, no. 4 [Winter 2004]: 48-62). He showed that most recent studies of the actual physical state of the brain show that this is not the case at all. He concluded that brain-death criteria in general have failed since they do not accurately reflect the actual destruction of the brain and complete severing of the brain from the body. Halakhically, then, he argued that one cannot compare brain-dead patients to the decapitated, as their brains are not actually destroyed nor completely disconnected from their bodies.

Now, while this critique is focused on the *current* validity of an earlier *psaq* (which is not our concern here), I have mentioned it because I think that it is also true historically. That is, one cannot deny that R. Feinstein wrote about brain-death criteria as describing actual physical destruction of the brain. In both YD III 132 and his later letter to Bundy (see below note 36) he uses unequivocal language to describe the brain of the brain-dead as physically destroyed and not merely non-functional.

Perhaps aware of the practical consequences of his conclusions, the journal, *Tradition*, which published Kunin's article, saw fit to simultaneously publish a rebuttal written by a New York professor of medicine, Edward Reichman. (Usually rebuttals against opinion's expressed in articles only appear in subsequent letters-to-the editor. Ready inclusion of rebuttals is a rare occurance for this journal.) Reichman argued that even brain-dead patients with physically still-intact brains, have nonetheless lost their capacity for independent respiration. This being the case, it is as if the respiratory function of these brains has been completely severed from the body. As it is the respiratory capability that is essential in determining death for R. Feinstein, he argued that this functional severing is adequate to render a patient equivalent to an actually decapitated individual (Reichman, "Don't Pull the Plug on Brain Death Just Yet," *Tradition* 38, no. 4 [Winter 2004]: 63-69). I am not convinced by his argument; it seems to be primarily an apologetic for keeping faith with those devoted to brain-death. However, as this study is concerned with earlier history, I will not expand upon this point.

36 R. Tendler, "Confusion: Brainstem, Death, Pikuach Nefesh and Halakhic Integrity," *The Jewish Observer* (October 1991): 12-15, 13.

37 *EM* HM II 72.

38 According to the phone logs of the past president of the Agudat Israel of America (a more religiously conservative Orthodox organization than the Rabbinical Conference of America of which R. Tendler was a prominent member), the answer to the above question is "no." R. Feinstein was a famous individual and famously available to hundreds of concerned Jews who turned to him for advice. He had personal contact with many outside of his own family. In a polemic published by Chaim Zweibel of Agudah, he recorded the following transcriptions of phone conversations held between Rabbis Moshe Sherer and Feinstein just after the responsum was written ("A Matter of Life and Death," *The Jewish Observer* [June 1991]: 11-14):

> Phoned R. Feinstein to ask for his meaning of the psaq re: "blood flow" test of Rabbi Tendler. He said:
>
> It is only a stringency, and only in case of an accident. I then asked: What is the "din" [law] if an ordinary sick person on a respirator is breathing and has a heartbeat, but we don't know whether he would continue breathing if the respirator is removed – can we trust the "blood flow" test to determine death?
>
> Rabbi Feinstein's reply:
> Explicitly not. I wrote clearly that with an ordinary sick person one is not permitted to stop the machine if he is breathing – and the test means nothing. It is only a stringency concerning accidents.
>
> May 12, 9:30 A. M. – Rabbi Feinstein phoned … Rabbi Feinstein repeated explicitly what he had said yesterday, that the 'blood flow' test is only a "chumra" [stringency] in accidents. To my question as to whether a "blood flow" test has any sig-

nificance when a patient is breathing only through a respirator, Rabbi Feinstein replied:
Certainly not, as I clearly wrote in the beginning of the *psaq* – and the test should not be performed altogether since the person is after all a *gosses* [in the throes of death] (page 22).

If we are to believe this transcript, it appears that R. Feinstein very clearly intended that the angiogram only be used as an auxiliary test before testing for anoxia. He never intended that it itself be used as an independent test to ascertain the death of the brain and from this alone conclude that the patient himself was dead. According to this transcript, then, his position was not compatible with the pro-brain-death, pro-transplant stance that his son-in-law staked out through the use of his *psaq*. Rather, it seems clear that R. Tendler's stance reflects only his own reasoning and not that of his esteemed father-in-law.

However, R. Tendler has been quite dismissive of those who raised doubts concerning the correctness of brain-death criteria either from a medical or halakhic point of view. See his response to critics of brain-death criteria in *JAMA* 240, no. 2 (1978): 109 and 243, no. 18 (1980): 1808 where he caustically argued that only expertise in both science and Torah can lead one to truth. I have already mentioned that he is a firm believer in death as a unitary natural kind. He also holds a strong belief in scientific realism accompanied by halakhic-legal naturalism.

For example, discussing the natural and halakhic worlds he wrote:

Torah and science share axioms that stamp them both with the Seal of God, the seal of truth. The first of these axioms is the all-encompassing truth that there is order in nature. ...The second axiom that science and Torah share is that the human mind can perceive the order in nature. Faith in a God who is rational and omniscient led to faith in reason. ... There is never a conflict between science and Torah. If there is the appearance of conflict, it is only due to one of three factors: ignorance of Torah principle; ignorance of scientific facts; or most commonly, ignorance of both, (Moshe David Tendler, "Torah and Science : Constructs and Methodology," *Torah u-Madda Journal* 5 [1994]: 170-1).

Interestingly, it appears that his esteemed father-in-law took a different approach to the legal naturalism of the *halakhah*. In his introduction to his collection of responsa, *Egrot Moshe*, he wrote:

> ... regarding the actual *halakhah* [literally *true teaching* in the Hebrew] it has already been stated 'it is not in heaven,' rather it is in accordance with what the decisor [*hakham* in the Hebrew] understands after adequately delving into the matter through the Talmud and accompanying literature according to his ability, with all due seriousness and fear of the Lord. It is this decision that he is obligated to expound – even if it does not accord with the actual objective Truth. Of this it is said that his [mistaken] words are also "words of the living God" for he is convinced of their truth and does not find any inconsistency in them.

Commenting on the famous tale of Moses' viewing G-d affixing crowns to the letters of the Torah (*b. Menuhot* 29) he continued:

> It is as if G-d made the letters of the Torah into kings ["crowning" them with a level of independence] so that a *poseq* can look into them and according to his own understanding of these letters render a decision ... even if this understanding was not the intention of G-d [the author]....

Here we can see more of a legal positivism than the strong naturalism propounded by R. Tendler.

[39] R. Tendler, "*Od Al Da'at HGRM Feinstein*," **Assia** 51-52 (Iyar 5762): 187-188.

[40] His own opinion at this time, in 1993, was that only outside of Israel where the large majority of doctors and donors were gentiles, was a Jew permitted to receive a "cadaver" transplant. See *Minhat Shlomo Tnina*, 86.

# 8

# 1978
# A Second Heart Transplant

A second Israeli attempt at transplanting a heart was made by Morris Levy in 1978. The transplant patient survived only for a few weeks before dying of complications. This operation, like the first transplant, also received much media attention and refocused public attention on the questions surrounding the determination of death. Two years previous, the language used in an Israeli medical journal article on progress in kidney transplants reflected the still unsettled state of thought concerning the definition of death. Its authors noted three classes of kidney donors: "living donors, cadavers with beating hearts and cadavers shortly after death has been declared."[1] In Israeli medical practice declaring death and actual death—becoming a cadaver— were still not necessarily equivalent. This chapter is devoted to describing the somewhat stormy aftermath of that operation. Once again tensions over the ethics of scientific medicine were exposed. Although Israeli doctors were quite aware of the ethical difficulties that organ transplantation presented, they saw brain-death, no matter how conceptualized, as one of the main tools that should be used to move forward with the transplantation project. Others, however, were less willing to skirt over the ethical questions involved.

# Really Dead?

On April 4<sup>th</sup>, two weeks after the death of Levy's second heart transplant patient, a plenum debate was held in the Knesset.[2] The Agudat Israel MK Shlomo Lawrence denounced the transplant as illegal and unethical. He asserted that the necessity of removing the heart from the donor while still beating meant that the donor was not yet actually dead. Even when done with the noble intention of saving another's life, doing so at the expense of the donor's life (even at the last moments of that life) was both unconscionable and forbidden by the *halakhah*. He requested that the matter be referred to committee for further discussion. [3]

Lawrence was answered from the speaker's podium by the Health Minister, Eliezer Shostak (Likud). His response aimed to show that while international and Israeli *medical* opinion agreed that death could be determined without taking cardiac activity into account, no progress had been made in formalizing these medical conclusions into Israeli *law*. He noted that this had been done in other countries and perhaps the time had come for Israel to join them. So while he could not have disagreed more about the reasons, he agreed that further debate in committee was warranted.[4]

Three months later debate began in the Knesset Law Committee. The choice of this forum, rather than the Work and Welfare Committee (which at the time was usually responsible for matters pertaining to public health), was in itself a measure of victory for the Health Minister who was interested in upgrading policy into law. The Committee Chair, David Glass (*Mafdal* – National Religious Party) used his position to turn what could have been a pro forma discussion of one operation into a far-ranging series of meetings devoted to discussing the determination of death from a number of vantage points. The general tenor of the discussion shows that despite the second failure in heart replacement, there was a feeling that the situation would improve—just as it had with other earlier organ transplant procedures. The intuition that general progress in organ transplants was inevitable meant that the discussion was primarily aimed at discussing how such progress could be facilitated, legally and socially.

The first of the committee sessions opened with a presentation on the legal aspects of declaring death for organ donors given by Dr. David Frankel. Frankel (whose doctorate was discussed above in chapter six) was by then the Vice-Counsel for the Health Ministry. Citing then-current Israeli law which permitted the removal of organs from the dead, he made the obvious claim that all agreed that potential donors needed to be legally defined as corpses before organs could legally be removed for the purpose of transplanting them into another patient.[5] The *manner* in which this should be accomplished was the subject of debate. He identified three different approaches that had been adopted by various countries. Among those nations that had passed legislation, some had insisted upon retaining the traditional cardiopulmonary criteria; some had adopted a variation of neurological criteria; and others had decided not to legislate criteria of death, but rather to grant a given group the authority to determine death—medical experts.[6] He devoted much of his presentation to examining the benefits of this last approach.

> OK, we have updated the law to a certain date. Medical science changes from day to day. The day will come when a case will reach the court and the judge or the jury will have no choice but to rule according to the criteria that were established by law. No scientific advancement will affect any case, because the law has fixed the criteria.[7]

For this reason, he stressed, it seemed advantageous to grant physicians the authority to actually determine death while the more

# Really Dead?

'elastic' administrative details could be taken care of through various ministerial directives.[8]

An interesting exchange occurred during his presentation when he briefly mentioned some of the halachic issues concerning translants. As he read from Maimonides' ruling on the irrelevance of bodily quivering in cases of decapitation, he was interrupted by another guest of the Committee, Professor Areyeh Durst, Hadassah's Chief of Surgery. Durst proclaimed:

> Here is a direct implication for our own circumstances. No one relates to decapitation, but the broken neck — most of those who suffer brain trauma do not die immediately, but arrive at the hospital. A broken neck is similar to decapitation, there is a hematoma. It is easy to evaluate that such an individual has no chance to live. How long can he live — this can be a number of hours or even days. We have no ability to treat him, he is declared dead in the emergency room. He doesn't function, he is awaiting his death. Maimonides was right![9]

Here is a fascinating piece of medical philosophy captured, as it were, live. The *mishnah* about decapitation cited by Maimonides could be interpreted in different ways — as offering a template for a prognosis of no possible recovery, as referring to involuntary movement or describing a particular situation as by definition dead. We have seen all of these interpretive approaches. The Israeli surgeon, though, heard this and immediately related it to the modern potential for the displacement of death from the state of the body. If the beating heart can be discarded by Maimonides, then so can the *still living* body be dismissed by medical prognostics. Durst reasoned that a declaration of death, while based on physical circumstances, need not reflect the actual present physical state of affairs. He delivered a quite clear statement of brain-death as prognosis.

The rest of the meeting was devoted to presentations on the medical aspects of heart transplants. There was discussion of the progress that had been made in the field since 1967. This was accompanied by the by-now familiar argument that clinical progress in medicine necessitated a learning curve.[10] Initially low survival rates would improve with practice and accumulation of knowledge and experience. Regarding the determination of death, Durst asserted that the matter was not critical. He was certain that the use of non-heart beating cadavers could eventually become the norm.

> It is not right to say that we need to transplant a beating heart. The heart needs to beat, but even if we are discussing the death of the brain … there is a certain moment of cessation of function in the heart. … After a few minutes we can revive the heart.[11]

For Durst, death was malleable. If need be, it could be based on medical prognosis and the futility of treatment. Nothing further *can* be done. However, if necessary, the very opposite approach could be taken: the requirements of cardiac stoppage could be technically fulfilled. *Let's not* do anything. In either case, Durst felt that the transplantation project could and should continue.[12]

Three days later, at the next meeting of the Committee, the question of what recommendations should be returned to the Knesset was debated. All agreed that the accusations of murder directed at the heart transplant team by MK Lawrence were not the main issue. His call to desist from further organ transplants was dismissed. The committee felt that the main problem was the purview of the Knesset in general, and the Law Committee in particular, regarding medical

# Really Dead?

issues. MK Shulamit Aloni (*Ratz* – Citizens' Rights and Peace Party), one of the more vocal Committee members in this session, argued that questions such as the determination of death were not public matters but rather medical issues best left in the hands of medical authorities. While no one argued that organ transplantation was not primarily a medical issue, some felt that the Knesset, as public representatives, had a duty, at the least, to voice an opinion and at the most, to proactively use their power as legislators to mold public order. [13] The general sense of the Committee, though, was that the doctors involved in the transplant project needed to be sheltered from the shifting vagaries of public opinion.

Professor Gutsman, a cardiologist from Hadassah invited to the meeting, asked quite directly:

> Let's assume that tomorrow I have a candidate for a heart transplant in Hadassah. How does the law protect me so that I can perform a heart transplant like this? … Will a transplant like this lead to another committee, to another meeting?

He stressed that any new legislation must address three different areas of concern: rabbinical permission, hospital standards and legal protection for doctors from the families of both the donor and recipient. Regarding the first concern, he noted that the problem was the disconnection of the patient from respiratory support. [14]

Aloni felt that the public needed to be *reassured* that transplants were being carried out in accordance with modern medical ethics and methods.[15] The committee's conclusions stated that organ transplants in general, and heart transplants in particular, "were critical in saving and lengthening human life and should continue in accordance with accepted criteria…." It also expressed support for legislation which would address the various problems inherent in organ transplanta-tion.[16] No specific mention of what these problems were, nor of which criteria were the accepted ones, were made. After years of debate, the Israeli public's representatives were still divided as to what their role should be vis-à-vis the medical profession in general, and regarding heart transplants in particular.

The vague report that this Committee returned to the Knesset re-flected more than a politically expedient compromise which trans-lated into an abstention from taking action. Rather it was the result of actual uncertainty as to how to proceed in the face of the difficult descriptions concerning the ethics of transplantation to which their invited experts testified. Much of the medical expert testimony they heard had been devoted to describing the risks of medical progress. The doctors' view was that such early-stage risk was an inescapable part of eventual success.[17] In the face of the troubling ethical calculus which seemed to practically sentence early-stage patients to the dire risks of failure, while promising a better future for those who fol-lowed, these non-experts found it difficult to adjudicate between competing claims.[18] Although they were the concerned public's representatives, one can understand the ethical appeal of "leaving it to the experts." Not asserting any public prerogative also meant not taking ethical responsibility for difficult decisions. Left to set their own criteria, doctors found brain-death—whether understood as prognosis (as Durst asserted) or as actual death, a way of ethically moving forward with the transplantation project. What they looked for from the public was *support* for their own ethical calculus and protection from interference. Recall Gutsman's worry. Part of that support had to come from the adjudicators of the *halakhah*, as both Gutsman and Durst explained. In fact, as the first decade of debate over defining death ended, no other heart transplants were to be

# Really Dead?

conducted in Israel until Hadassah had indeed secured the rabbinic permission that Gutsman desired.

---

[1] Yaakov, et al., *"Nitsul Meravi shel Klayot min Hamet,"* **Harefuah** 90, no.12 (June 15, 1976): 552-6. This was the last mention of such issues in the Israeli professional literature prior to the 1978 transplant.

[2] The recipient of the heart was a 23-year-old Israeli Arab, Abdullah Azam.

[3] His speech generated media attention regarding the ethical aspects of the transplant process. An op-ed piece written by B. Amos, a physician, stressed how medical ethics were properly handled by the profession itself and that calls like those of MK Lawrence were a danger to medical progress reminiscent of the "dark ages" (Amos, *"Hazara Leyemei Habenyim?,"* **Yediot Ahronot**, March 3, 1978, 9).

[4] *Knesset Protocols*, April 4, 1978. A single Knesset member, Yaakov Amir (Labor), objected to any discussion of the matter claiming that the entire issue was one best left to medical experts.

[5] I noted this in Carmi's suggestion which was discussed in chapter six.

[6] *Knesset Law Committee Protocols*, July 5, 1978, 4-7.

[7] Ibid., 9.

[8] Ibid. Such directives did not require the long process of legislation. They were essentially the fiat of the acting minister.

[9] Ibid., 8.

[10] For an ode to the heroism of scientific medical advancement through clinical trial and error – especially with respect to heart transplants – see A. Shechner, Y. Ovil, and M. Levy, *"Shtilat Lev-Avar Veatid,"* Harefuah 98, no. 5 (1980).

[11] Ibid., 12.

[12] The final speaker, Professor Meir, reiterated many of the previous points and argued for the necessity of explicitly legalizing organ transplants. The determination of death could be decided in any number of ways, but what was important was moving ahead with transplantation (14).

[13] *Knesset Law Committee Protocols*, July, 10, 1978, 7. The former was the opinion of MK Moshe Amar (Labor); the latter, the opinion of MK Amnon Lin (Likud).

[14] Ibid., 9.

[15] Ibid. Interestingly, Gutsman questioned whether anybody really knew what had transpired at Beilinson Hospital during Levy's second procedure. Durst also insisted that the real problem regarding organ transplants at that stage in Israeli practice (that is excluding the heart) was neither medical nor religious, but had to do

with public perceptions. He claimed that Hadassah's rabbi supported the harvest of cadaver kidneys, for example, and that "really religious" families, upon getting his consent, consented as well. The trouble was with those he labeled "pseudo-religious" who would not grant consent for organ harvest (*Knesset Law Committee Protocols*, July 5, 1978, 13). I will return to this understanding in section II. For those who promoted the heart-transplant project, it played a role in their decision to turn to the Rabbinate.

[16] *Knesset Law Committee Protocols*, July, 12th, 1978, 2.

[17] Gutsman, backed by the other invited experts, had made the explanation of this, accompanied by figures, the centerpiece of his testimony (*Knesset Law Committee Protocols*, July 5, 1978, 10).

[18] A headline which accompanied the obituary of the first Israeli liver transplant patient read, "The Price of Being First" (Anat Tal-Shir, "*Mirah Shicmanter*," **Yediot Ahronot**, November 11, 1986). This operation is discussed in section II.

# 9

## 1980-1986
## A Growing Consensus

In the years leading up to the implementation of the Hadassah heart transplant program, the Israeli discourse on brain-death began to focus primarily on building a consensus that would support organ transplantation. This chapter is devoted to discussing the remaining pieces of this last stage of pre-successful heart-transplant discourse. In the early 1980s a number of articles appeared in Israeli medical journals which helped to pave the way for the implementation of Hadassah's program. Shekhner and Levy wrote a paean to scientific progress in the heart transplant program.[1] They claimed that the polemics over transplants had been too long based on emotional claims by each side.[2] Review of the facts, they claimed, showed that despite a difficult start, these operations were growing more successful with each passing year—saving more lives as doctors gained more experience.

A similar article (also co-authored by Morris Levy) describing the advances in the field appeared a few years later and ended with a call for public support of the heart-translant project. The authors argued that cooperation both in the form of "positive response by the family of the deceased" potential donor as well as "suitable legislation" was necessary for success.[3] What is interesting, however, is that while the conclusion of the article presented these two factors as complementary, the body of the article was clear that they were actually two opposing ways of attaining the same goal—the required number of donors. The authors, Drs. Morris Levy and A. Deveri, bemoaned the legal state of affairs in Israel that conditioned the removal of organs from the deceased upon family permission.[4] They noted that in light of the pressing need for organs, other countries had already changed their laws to an "opt-out" system where one would be required to file an explicit refusal to donate organs. Otherwise, doctors would be legaly entitled to remove organs for transplantation upon one's death. Due to small percentage of Israeli families willing to allow organ removal, they felt that such a legal change would be needed here as well.[5] It was explicitly the lack of familial cooperation that made legal change necessary. New legislation of the type argued for was not meant to *compliment* public attitudes, but rather to *override* them.

In 1981, under the auspices of the Meyshan Chair for the history and philosophy of medicine at Tel Aviv University, the first original Hebrew book devoted to modern medical ethics was published. It contained the protocols of several symposiums which the university had held on a variety of subjects in the late seventies.[6] A discussion on the determination of death presented one of the few conceptual *medical* critiques of brain-death sounded at this time. Dr. Korchin, the neurologist who had earlier warned against ignoring brain-death's ethical difficulties, here argued for examining these problems closely. The other participants all expressed full support for brain-death criteria.

Korchin began his presentation by noting how brain-death developed alongside of organ transplantation and was based upon something of a paradox regarding the end of organ viability. On the one hand, the notion of "clinical death," where the heart stops beating but can be later restarted, eliminated the use of cardiac criteria for determining death. However, the non-beating heart was essentially re-placed by the non-functioning brain. Brain-death relied on an assumption that this loss of function was irreversible, yet, Korchin asked, "Who is to guarantee ... as a result of medical progress that we will not reach a new idea: clinical death of the brain? Is it not possible ... that we may be able to restart the brain as we can do today with the heart? "

His point was that the medical definition of death depended upon medical prognosis, yet that it was treated as if it were some absolute which allowed doctors to "make use of the [dead man's] organs as we like." Korchin claimed that when doctors declared that a patient had suffered the death of his brain, they actually "mean that his body is alive." Organ donation, he argued, is what actually brings about the "death of the body whose brain has died."[7]

The other symposium speakers echoed a sentiment that had been the general attitude of the Health Ministry since 1968—that since the death of the brain was accepted world-wide as the death of the pa-tient—only proper *criteria* for establishing brain-death needed to be established.[8] One of the points made was that the need for many different criteria and tests revealed the problems of determining the brain's death. As all the criteria then in use were each in themselves reversible in many cases, it was only when several were taken to-gether that a "statistical probability" of death was reached but not an actual "scientific conclusion" that this was in fact the case.[9]

After hearing the position of the other speakers, Korchin continued in greater detail to outline the problems which ending the lives of the brain dead entailed. He argued that since kidney, heart and digestive function, all of which continue after the brain ceases to function do not do so in "isolation, but rather in an organized fashion each organ influencing the others" the equation of the loss of brain function with complete loss of bodily integration was false. [10] Without the brain,

# Really Dead?

Korchin explained, the body does not simply become a collection of cellular life.

Brain-death, then, for Korchin, was a "definition of convenience." In his mind, it was a worrisome slippery-slope where any signs of integrative life discovered among those so diagnosed would simply continue to be dismissed. He argued that while the spinal cord can in fact return to function as a major integrator of activity even if some trauma disrupts this for a time, it had simply been excised from the operative definition of life. Korchin added that this type of convenient exclusion was liable to "occur again and again; it is impossible to know to where it will lead."[11]

His proposal for solving all the complicated ethical problems presented by organ transplants lay in allowing for personal preference regarding brain-death. He wanted to let those who wished to become organ donors upon the end of brain function do so. This was the same position voiced by MK Kahana a decade earlier, yet still not accepted by either the medical or legal establishment. Korchin's arguments were unfortunately lost in the increasing general support for moving ahead with the transplantation project. The way in which the Israeli courts would address the questions of death determination make this abundantly clear.

Two similar court cases, one in a Tel-Aviv District court and the other in the Israel Supreme Court, became part of the debate on brain-death in the early 1980s.[12] In both of these cases the defendant was charged with murder. Each victim had been declared dead by neurological standards, but each had a still-beating heart which was donated to another patient.[13] In the former case, it was this victim's heart that had been transplanted by Morris Levy to Abdullah Azam. Both of the defendants were convicted of murder, but both had offered as part of their defense a claim that it was the removal of the victim's organs which had caused the actual death. Each victim, their attorneys

194

claimed, had been alive until then according to standard cardio-pulmonary criteria.

The former case was more straightforward in that while perform-ing a craniotomy to relieve pressure from swelling, the surgeons found that the victim's brains had "spilled out" rendering any further attempt at treatment moot. This being the case, the court held that in accord with Section 309 (1) of the Penal Code the defendant was guilty. This section holds an individual responsible for the death of a victim so long as the perpetrator had caused "bodily harm that re-quired medical treatment" even if such treatment itself "caused the death of the injured party," so long as the treatment was given accord-ing to normative standards of care.[14] Because the state of the patient was clearly untreatable after the actual loss of brain matter, the court saw no reason not to hold the shooter fully culpable. The defendant's argument was dismissed.

A much more detailed exploration of brain-death took place in the second case begun in 1982. The appeal was heard by a panel of three judges. Judge M. Beiski decided to make use of the opportunity offered by the appeal in order to offer a judicial appraisal of brain-death. Such a decision would carry precedential weight not only in other criminal cases, but would, due to the lack of legislation regard-ing determination of death, serve to effectively legislate the question at hand. Beiski wrote:

> It seems to us, that as this matter has reached us for de-liberation for the first time in a criminal context, and we must clarify the time of death and its causes, we are not free to merely note a final conclusion. The matter is not grounded in law in Israel, yet the problems exist here....[15]

# Really Dead?

As his decision consists primarily of citations of case law, legislation and articles which advance the argument for accepting brain-death, it is quite clear that the court did not set out to debate the various positions surrounding the establishment of death, but rather to advocate for the adoption of brain-death in Israel. The arguments for brain-death presented in Beiski's decision echoed the position that Frankel offered to the Knesset Committee: brain-death is accepted by the entire medical world, although there is some argument concerning the criteria used to confirm death of the brain.[16] This stance was strengthened over the verdict's 40 pages by citing the large medical and legal literature devoted to endorsing brain-death. The lion's share of the decision is devoted to an extensive rehearsal of the pro-brain-death literature.[17] Excepting the section of the decision devoted to the *halakhah*, there was no mention of any of the many objections raised to the use of brain-death criteria.

The trope of biological-death-as-process is stressed time and again in Beiski's decision. Stressing that death cannot be scientifically defined as a specific moment, the court built its case in support of brain-death conceptually. This was done by contrasting the way that heart and lung function could be artificially continued, while "no medical knowledge exists which can artificially support brain activity."[18] The loss of cardiopulmonary function, then, could no longer signal the end of life for it may be "restored" through a variety of "means that modern medicine has come to know" or it can be "artificially" continued.

> This is not possible in the case of irreversible brain-death; there is no regeneration of brain cells, and the brain cannot be resuscitated once its complete death has been established. The death of the brain is independent,[19] whether caused by trauma or stroke, and it will

bring within minutes the cessation of heart and respiratory function, if these are not artificially supported. In medical science today, it is accepted by all that irreversible death of the brain prevents life activities....[20]

The court did not choose to argue that the brain was more important in terms of it being the receptacle of personhood or the like. Rather, the court's description of brain-death was tautological. The difference between the brain and other organs, it argued, was due to the fact that resuscitation is not possible regarding the brain. But this is not true. A temporarily non-functioning brain (due to barbiturate poisoning, for example) can be 'resuscitated.' The court surely knew this. Therefore, it specified that only "irreversible brain-death" and "complete death" of the brain were under discussion. But, of course, the very term 'irreversible' means that no resuscitation is possible. *Heart function* could logically be substituted in the court's argument if it too were "complete" and "irreversible."

The inherent irreversibility that the court ascribed to brain-death describes medical futility. At whatever point damage to the brain was deemed untreatable, it was just at this point that the brain could be described as dead.[21] It could not—like a stopped heart—be resuscitated, nor did its cells regenerate. Once the brain has been declared dead, "life activities" falter. However, the court did not expand on what this last phrase actually meant.[22] Of course, without medical intervention, the loss of cardiac or respiratory function would also lead to loss of life functions. As the court did not privilege the brain over other organs because it was the seat of consciousness,[23] or the central organ devoted to integration of somatic function,[24] for example, the basis for their argument that brain-death is equivalent to the death of the patient rested upon the state of medical ability to care for the brain. This was just what Korchin had claimed was so ethically

# Really Dead?

problematic with the use of brain-death in determining the death of organ donors. Brain-death, Korchin argued, was medical futility which was being *presented* by transplantists as something more, something that allowed for the *dismissal* of somatic life *in order* to harvest transplantable organs.[25]

The brain-dead patient, according to the court, presented doctors with the (then) terminus of medical care. He cannot be healed; no more can be done for him – *ergo* he is dead. This standard argument of medical-futility-as-death, however, admitted of one difference. The difference here is that due to organ transplant interests – in *this* case the patient is not left alone as in other futile cases – rather the rest of his body is "artificially supported." This artificiality, I think, primarily describes the *uselessness* of such care. It is artificial, because it does not return the supported organ or body to health (see the way *restoration of function* is opposed to *artificial support* in the above quote. The heart can also be artificially restored to function). Anything done for the brain-dead patient cannot be considered treatment of the patient; he is beyond treatment.[26] So any care he is given cannot be said to be one of the many "means that modern medicine has come to know" which restore health or function: it is only an *artificial* prolongation of some *organ's* life in that it can never serve to heal the patient. Artificiality here is a function of the fact that treatment has no consequence for the patient himself.

By its own admittance, all that the court needed to decide in this particular murder appeal was

> whether death occurs when cessation of brain function
> is determined, which will in any case shortly cause ces-
> sation of heart and lung activity, or is the test [for death]
> that of the loss of pulse and breathing (according to the
> traditional criteria), which occurs with the disconnec-

tion of the apparatuses which are *artificially* [my empha-
sis] supporting them?[27]

If the former was true, the appeal would be rejected; if the latter, it would be accepted and the defendant found innocent of murder.[28] While this was the court's self-described task, its answer had already been supplied in the very way that it differentiated between real care and artificial support.

As I noted above, the only criticism of brain-death found in the judgment is found in the section of the decision devoted to the *halak-hah*.[29] As we have already seen, there were certainly halakhic positions which supported brain-death. From a formal perspective for the court, the most important may have been the opinion of the Chief Rabbi at the time when the appeal was being heard, R. Goren. After reviewing the basic Talmudic sources, the court quoted from him at length in order to show that cessation of respiration *per se* could not be used as the only indication of death.[30] While asserting both reluctance and incompetence in actually deciding any halakhic question, the court noted that all they wished to do was

> point out that the general inclination of *psaq* has been to adjust the signs of death, as they appear in *halakhah*, to the knowledge of physiological processes in the human body in each generation. ... Previous generations lacked the medical knowledge available today... and did not know of the dominance of brain function with regard to the function of other systems, such as respiration, central nervous [system] or heart.... The question which stands at the center of the debate today is whether it is possible to understand brain-death, as it is known today and in accordance with scientific-medical tests, as a ha-

# Really Dead?

lakhic criterion for the establishment of the time of
death.[31]

While it is understandable that the court was content with noting
some general impressions of a more complicated halakhic attitude, it
is noteworthy that in regard to the *halakhah* it narrowed its focus from
a general understanding of death to a particularly specific legal question regarding the "time of death" for which an affirmative answer
could be more easily found.

The court labeled unnamed brain-death dissidents as those who
"clung to the traditional tests for death... taking no cognizance of
progress in medical knowledge and technique, which allows for
reliable determination of the end of life and life activity with the
complete and irreversible death of the brain." In its final recommendations, the court advocated that *posqim* not ignore that "which is
universally recognized by the medical world."[32]

By the time the court had prepared its decision, the Rabbinate had
published its *psaq* regarding heart transplants which the court saw fit
to include in its verdict.[33] Judge Beiski concluded his judgment by
ordering the Court Bailiff to deliver a copy of it to the Health Ministry.
The court ignored nearly all of the readily accessible *debate* over brain-
death (Korchin's arguments which had appeared a year previous to
the beginning of this case, or Veatch's work, for example). For the
most part, the decision consisted of citations and enumerations of
positions, laws, or medical opinions which supported brain-death.
While at the time of the court's decision brain-death *was* well accepted
in Western medical practice, neither was this true "universally" (as
the court wrote several times) nor was this a practice without its
detractors. I think that by choosing to discuss any negative opinions
about the practice only in its section on Jewish law, the Court was able
to more easily present such opinions as (more readily rejectable)

reactionary opposition to "progress in medical knowledge and technique." The court viewed itself as a defender of modern medical techniques and the transplantation project against which only reactionary forces could conceivably raise any questions.[34]

The final piece of the Israeli discourse on brain-death at this time took place in the midst of the discussions among Hadassah Hospital doctors, Health Ministry personnel, and rabbis at an IMA sponsored symposium on organ transplants. Professor Joe Borman, who was busily working on getting his heart-transplant unit up to speed, was a featured speaker. Two other physicians involved in transplants, a rabbi, and a philosopher of ethics took part as well. This symposium was the last public discussion held by the medical experts before the actual start-up of Hadassah's new heart transplant program. While much of interest was said concerning transplants in general, I will focus only on the comments concerning the determination of death.

Asa Kasher, a moral philosopher, was the first to address this problem. Cutting to the chase early in his remarks, he described the brain-dead patient not as "a living individual with a dead brain, but rather as a cadaver whose heart is beating." Echoing the arguments offered by Frankel, he claimed that this was the case because such patients had lost their moral status as humans when they lost "nearly all" human capacities.[35]

R. Ravitz, speaking as a representative of the Jewish point of view, explained that establishing a "moment of death" had many practical implications in the halakhah – from inheritance to transplants. He argued that medical practitioners had decided to "make due with determining the death of the brain" alone before harvesting those organs, like the heart and liver, which needed to be removed while still functioning. He acknowledged that a final answer had not yet been formalized by those who were currently debating the issue of

# Really Dead?

death in *halakhah*, but foresaw that some similarity could be drawn between decapitation and brain-death in halakhah.[36]

It was in response to R. Ravitz's presentation that the discussion became animated. Dr. Tzahi Shapiro, a renal transplant surgeon, argued that it was not transplantation *per se* that created the problem of brain-death. Rather modern resuscitative technologies had turned death into a long process, thus creating seeming moral ambiguities. Borman added that if only Israel would join the rest of the "enlightened nations" in recognizing brain-stem death as equivalent to the death of the individual, these problems would be solved. S. Slovin, a Hadassah immunologist, claimed that the *halakhah* admitted of a paradoxical situation in insisting upon the end of cardiac function before determining death. He asked whether those with cardiac arrest had come back from the dead. The death of the brain, he argued, was irreversible and as such, a much better criterion of death from which there could be no return.[37]

The evening ended, as had the earlier symposium, still focused on the tensions between *halakhah* and modern medical practice over determining death. Kasher reminded his listeners that there was no unified halakhic position on this question (or fundamentally on any matter) as different rabbis held differing views. He asserted that multi-faceted *halakhah*, then, was not, and could not, just for this reason, regulate the behaviour of Israel's citizens. He also claimed that the issue of determining death was essentially a matter of public policy that the *secular state* needed to decide. These points seemed to be a warning of sorts (perhaps made in light of the halakhic position presented by R. Ravitz). Their implication was that Israel's secular majority would be able to find some halakhic basis for moving forward.[38] Ram Yishai, the president of the IMA, closed the evening by disagreeing with Kasher and stating that ultimately a *psaq halakhah* by the Israeli Rabbinate, the state's authority on these matters, could in fact offer an authoritative binding decision. Two months later they certainly tried to do so.

---

[1] A. Shekhner, Y. Ovil, and M. Levy, "*Shtilat Lev- Avar Ve'atid*," **Harefuah** 98:5 (March 2 1980): 225-227.

[2] Ibid., 225.

[3] A. Deveri and M. Levy, "*Shtilat Lev – Orot Vetslalim*," **Harefuah** 109:10 (November 15, 1985): 303-5, 304.

[4] Only five years previous the Anatomy and Pathology Law been updated to ensure that family members were consulted prior to the removal of a deceased's organs. See Hakohen, "*Mishpat Verefuah Bemedinat Yehudit Vedemokratit: Ben Antonomiah Shel Hok Lepatologiah Shel Yehasei Dat Vemedinah.*" **Sha'are Mishpat** 2, no. 2 (2000): 189-221. The IMA had led a bitter struggle against this change which impinged upon their liberty to do with cadavers as their members saw fit (206).

[5] Ibid. Another article called for a different change: making the request for donation incumbent upon all medical staff where appropriate potential donors were found (B. Segal, "*Mabat Hadash al Trumat Avarim Lehashtalah*," **ML** 47, no. 3 (1985): 7.

[6] Alon Ilai, ed., *Harefuah Tahat Izmel Hamusar* (Tel Aviv: Papyrus, 1981). The actual date of each symposium is not included, however.

[7] Ibid., 104.

[8] Ibid., 107. This was argued by a Dr. M. Shalit, from the Tel Aviv Medical School.

[9] Ibid., 108.

[10] Ibid., 120. This was an argument made by many in the history of opposition to brain-death. See D. A. Shewmon, "Brainstem Death, 'Brain Death' and Death: A Critical Re-Evaluation of the Purported Equivalence," *Issues in Law & Medicine* 14, no. 2 (1998) and the literature he cites.

[11] Ibid.

[12] Criminal Case 369/78 Tel Aviv and Criminal Appeal 341/82 Belker vs. the State of Israel, respectively. The first case was never published by the court and was cited in a 1981 article (see note 1).

[13] The first case involved the shooting of a robbery victim, while the second was a grizzly defenestration of the murderer's wife accompanied by an attempt to immolate her afterwards.

[14] *Hok Ha'onshin* (Penal Code), cited in Yosef Haled, "*Qviat Moed Hamavet L'inyan Ahrayut Haplilit*," **Meidah Lerofeh** 26 (June 1981): 30-33.

# Really Dead?

[15] *Criminal Appeal 341/82*, 14. See Menachem Mautner, *Yeridat Haformalism Ve'aliyat Ha'arakhim Bemishpat Hayisraeli* (Tel Aviv: Ma'agle Tsedek, 1993) for a classic study of the increased judicial activism that has marked the Israel Supreme Court beginning in the 1980s. The court, especially in its composition as the High Court of Justice, increasingly saw itself as defender of individual rights, the rule of law and the values of liberalism. Brain-death was viewed by the court as part and parcel of Western medical progress. The decision of the court also discussed the question of criminal causation and culpability, but this is beyond the purview of this study. The main focus and only instance of activist judicial legislation however, was on the acceptance of brain-death. The decision would end not merely with a rejection of the defendant's appeal, but with clear recommendations to the state to accept brain-death.

[16] *Criminal Appeal 341/82*, 2, 21, 38, etc. This is repeated many times in the decision, almost always emphasizing that the acceptance was "universal."

[17] The over-all effect is to swamp the reader with source after source in support of brain-death leading one to assume that there is no reason for the court not to accept it. Different sections of the decision are labeled as "acceptance of brain-death" in: US federal law; state law; other countries; etc. The court set out to defend a given position, not to investigate it.

[18] Ibid., 10.

[19] This is described elsewhere as meaning that even when a patient is on life-support, the death of his brain can be independently measured (Ibid., 10).

[20] Ibid., 13. "Life activities" is the translation of *pe'ilut hiyut*. As I will explain, *hiyut* is meant as something different from *hayim*, although both may be translated as *life*.

[21] This, in fact, was the description given of the actual medical case at hand by the attending doctor, Dr. Levinson: "At this point of death of the brain, we practically do not treat [the patient] any longer. Here the treatment ends. Even though there is heart function, because there is no brain function there is no reason to continue treatment" (Ibid., 8).

[22] It seems that this is an example of the problem which Korchin pointed out (discussed above). "Life functions" can be supported in a good ICU for some time, but the desire to end support brought about changing instrumental definitions of what exactly constitute important-enough 'life functions' so that death of the patient could be declared while his organs were still salvageable.

[23] This was Veatch's claim already in 1976 (*Death, Dying and the Biological Revolution: Our Last Quest for Responsibility*).

[24] As we discussed above, Korchin argued against this claim. See. note 9 above.

[25] The need, therefore, to add some other layer of explanation for equating the loss of brain function with the loss of life was well (and perhaps first) explicated by Veatch, and has been a constant trope in many of the discussions on the topic.

[26] We can easily imagine a case where the status of the brain and heart are reversed. I do not mean to be too morbid, but imagine a drugged person temporarily losing brain function who is then shot through the heart – destroying it completely. He is "clinically" brain-dead, but if he can receive proper treatment until his brain recovers he will certainly be considered to have been alive the entire time. Perhaps he will even be extremely lucky and a suitable donor heart can be found in time. He may completely recover. There is nothing here that suggests that while under cardiac support he is somehow less than in merely critical condition from which he can be saved. If, however, nothing can be done for him long-term — there is no heart available for transplant — but blood is temporarily pumped throughout his body, such "treatment" is really of no consequence. It is artificial because it does not lead him to recovery.

[27] Ibid., 1. This is actually the extent of what the court needed to find in order to accept or reject the appeal. The rest of its response was an activist position on the legitimacy of brain-death.

[28] Haled cites a similar American case where a California court acquitted the defendant of murder because the penal code stipulated cardiac criteria of death. (*"Qviat Moed Hamavet,"* 32.)

[29] The need to include a discussion of what is known as *mishpat ivri* (Hebrew law) in court decisions, while not mandatory, was encouraged by the passing of the Foundations of Law Act in 1980 which aimed both at weaning modern Israeli law from British Mandate precedent and offering the use of the "fundamental principles and ethical values of the Jewish heritage" as a complementary source for legal interpretation. See Menachem Elon, *Jewish Law: History, Source and Principles* (Philadelphia: JPS, 1994) volume four, for an overview of the use of *halakhah* in modern Israeli judiciary and legislative proceedings.

[30] Ibid., 34. The court cites from R. Goren, *"Hagdarat Hamavet Behalakhah."*

[31] Ibid., 34-35.

[32] Ibid., 36 and 38. The only person actually mentioned by name as a brain-death opponent was Dr. Y. Levi. The court referred to his article, *"Me'ematai Mutar Lehotsi*

*Evar Lehashtalah"* (discussed above), but only mentioned his doubts concerning the validity of certain *criteria* for establishing brain-death which it dismissed. No mention was made of his more serious critique of the misunderstandings of the CIOMS Geneva Conference conclusions or of his more radical questioning of the unity of *halakhah* and science in his earlier article, *"B'inyan Hashtalat Avarim Me-hamet."*

[33] The appeal had been filed in 1982, but the decision was not given until the end of 1986. The Rabbinate *psaq* was published a month earlier.

[34] See note 15 regarding Mautner on the court's understanding of its own role in Israeli society.

[35] Anonymous, *"Al Hashtalat Avarim," ML* 48, no.11 (Tishre-Heshvan 5747): 9-19, 13 and 16. R. Ravitz pointed out the slippery slope upon which Kasher tread. Kasher also clearly argued for the exclusion of such a patient's family from the morally important players in deciding whether his organs could be harvested for transplant. Only the patient's decision was relevant—and even this was not to be given "pride of place" in deliberations over harvest. He suggested that only those willing to donate organs should be allowed to receive organ transplants.

[36] Ibid., 15.

[37] Ibid., 15-16. Slovin's remarks are a good example of philosophical sloppiness—not differentiating loss of function from destruction of the brain. He also demonstrated halakhic ignorance in equating temporary "clinical death" automatically with halakhically defined death. We have seen that no *poseq* offered such a simplistic reading.

[38] Ibid., 18.

# Preliminary Conclusions

The first section of this study has been devoted to describing the conceptual history of brain-death in Israel over a nearly twenty-year period. I have attempted to give voice to the myriad opinions that players in the field of organ transplants expressed over this time by carefully reading the many documents that they produced. A consistent progress in the medical acceptance of brain-death can be noted. By the time of the 1978 Knesset committee discussion or the High Court of Justice deliberations a few years later, brain-death was considered a recognized medical "fact" that needed only some small adjustments to its implementation via proper criteria. Despite this, however, little conceptual agreement (or often, even coherence) could be found regarding what brain-death actually meant. Was it the actual death of the patient as had always been understood or was it a means of terminating futile treatment for the dying? Learned physicians confused prognosis with definition (see Durst's remarks above, in chapter eight); government ministers misread important documents (recall Barzeli's equation of neurological and personal death, recounted in chapter one); justices let their interest in promoting transplants lead them to avoid meaningful deliberation (as in Beiski's decision, see chapter nine).

In the realm of halakhic discourse too, little agreement could be found regarding the ways that resuscitation had changed halakhic categorizations of the dying (or even the actual treatment of resuscitated patients). R. Goren argued for a clear-cut rejection of earlier halakhic criteria of death and supported heart transplants. Others

# Really Dead?

(Rabbis Auerbach and Feinstein) offered varied interpretations of what the classic halakhic sign, cessation of respiration, meant.

Higher order questions, such as the ethical calculus regarding the care for the dying versus saving the sick, were also disputed. For some, this question was a matter of "rights" — with the dying losing any claims to care to those who could still be aided (Frankel and Asa Kasher). Others viewed this reassigning of claims as an affront to morality, and insisted that medical care should only serve the patient as an end in himself – and not as a means towards saving another (R. Weiss).

One noteworthy point is that throughout this fragmented history attention focused time and again on what the *halakhah* had to say. Halakhic scholars, while only a small fraction of the Israeli 'intellectual elite' that debated transplants and death determination, were responsible for a large proportion of what was actually written. While it is understandable that religious MKs might search for solutions to the ethical problems of organ transplantation by peering through the lens of religious thought, the concern evidenced even by secular physicians regarding the halakhic position on brain-death is intriguing. In two different interdisciplinary IMA symposia, the position of the *halakhah* became the focal point of discussion. Beiski's judicial decision dealt at length with the halakhic understanding of death. Those closest to actual medical practice well understood that advancing the Israeli transplant project would require reaching some type of halakhic consensus on the question of brain-death. Gutsman, the Hadassah cardiologist, felt certain that rabbinic permission would need to be obtained before heart transplants could safely (legally) be performed. Ram Yishai, the IMA's president in 1986, had expressed his hope that the Israeli Chief Rabbinate would in fact grant it. The next section of this study is devoted to exploring the Rabbinate's actual *psaq halakhah* upon which this hope was pinned.

# Section II
## The Israeli Chief Rabbinate Decision

# 10

# Approaching the Rabbinate

The *psaq* of the Rabbinate was written in response to separate queries from two different medical institutions: the Health Ministry and Hadassah Medical Center. The Rabbinate decided to answer both of these queries with one decision, but ultimately left each side frustrated. Professor Dan Michaeli, Director General of the Health Ministry, approached the Rabbinate first. Michaeli was a long-term player in the Israeli medical establishment, having held a number of important positions over a long career throughout the medical system.[1] He was granted a window of opportunity to effect a lasting change in the transplantation project when his close friend and associate, Mordechai Gur, became the Minister of Health in 1984. Gur, a celebrated army general and Labor-party politician, brought Michaeli in as the ministry's Director General.

The Ministry had been debating the question of "special transplants" through a committee devoted to examining their applicability and feasibility in Israel.[2] Special transplants were those of organs that needed to be harvested from heart-beating donors, ie heart and liver. In 1986, the Egoz Committee[3] submitted its findings endorsing the establishment of a liver-transplant program in the near future, and recommending that the program be established in Hadassah Medical Center. It was clear to Michaeli that one of the requisites for a successful transplant program was an adequate supply of organs from the public. As I have already discussed,[4] others in the medical establishment were also aware of the need for public cooperation. A 1985 newspaper interview with the visiting American transplant surgeon, Thomas Starzel, gave a short overview of organ transplantation progress, its author editorializing that:

> So long as we do not adopt the broader concept of death, so long as brain-death is not added to the Israeli law books—organ transplants, for the sake of saving the lives of the many critically ill—will never be able to become a part of the Israeli medical system.[5]

Additionally, it was clear that part of gaining this cooperation would entail receiving rabbinic endorsement for the removal of organs from heart-beating donors. It had been noted by many, that regarding death, even the usually secular Israeli grew more attentive to and interested in the position of the *halakhah,* which in general discouraged any use of cadavers and required quick and complete burial.[6] This, in part, accounted for the reluctance of deceased patients' family members (noted by Deveri and Levi)[7] to agree to organ donation.

MK Shulamit Aloni (*Tenuah Lezkhuyot Ha'ezrah* – Citizen's Rights Party), a noted civil liberties activist, who made her name as a defender of secularism and as a strong proponent of separation of religion and state in Israel,[8] had complained that the real difficulty with heart transplants originated in citizens' willingness to take outmoded religious thought seriously. During the Knesset Law Committee discussions which ensued following the 1978 transplant she claimed:

Approaching the Rabbinate

> There is a great deal of mythology surrounding the heart. ... These people treat scientists and rabbis like witch-doctors. That is, a certain measure of magic enters here. The fact is that these people still turn to rabbis with gynecological and other medical problems.[9]

The problem, in her eyes, was religious superstition of the kind that Ashkenazi had yearned to dismiss.[10]

Others, however, more expert in the field, expressed the view that it was not necessarily a sudden interest in the *halakhah* that made it difficult for families to agree to organ donation, but rather concern about the deceased's body. Baruch Modan, an epidemiologist and public health expert, who served as the Director General of the Health Ministry before Michaeli, insisted that the problem was not one of religion per se.

> A generally accepted opinion explains the lack of success in getting [enough] organs as opposition of a religious type and as religious-coalition legislation. However, this is not the root of the problem. Not a few rabbis have found the proper [halakhic] permission without desecration of the deceased. The anatomy-pathology law in Israel is also amongst the most liberal found in western countries, including the United States. ... The real resistance, from both religious and non-religious families, is emotional and stems from [their] hesitance to harm the body of loved ones at the moment of loss. This is also the source for the PR failure....[11]

The case can be made that this sentiment is connected to general Jewish-Israeli attitudes concerning the importance of the physical

213

# Really Dead?

Jewish body. On one level, there seems to be something about the traditional concern and respect for the physical Jewish cadaver which has found its way into the public consciousness, if it is possible to talk about such a thing. Traditionally, the deceased's body is carefully washed and wrapped before burial in a process called *taharah*–ritual purification. All body parts, including even blood stained clothing or bandages (in a case of injury), are also buried together with the body.[12] The body is never left alone up to the time of burial; it is at all times accompanied by a "guard" who usually chants psalms next to the corpse until the funeral procession begins.

Yair Loberbaum has argued that such concern with the physical Jewish body is part of the religious-philosophical tradition which sees the physical body as representative of what is called in the creation story of Genesis, the "image" of God. He collected traditional mishnaic and talmudic sources which describe the actual physical suffering that a corpse feels and sees them as grounded, in part "in the humanistic-somatic anthropology commonplace amongst the Sages that identified man and his spiritual powers—his personality, his consciousness, his feelings, etc.—with the body."[13]

The *mishnah* in chapter six of Tractate *Sanhedrin* describes the various death penalties meted out by the Rabbinic High Court. After certain criminals were stoned to death, the body was hung up, but immediately let down and buried. The *mishnah* explains:

> ... if he is left hanging, this is a transgression of a Biblical prohibition as it is written "Do not leave a corpse on the gallows, rather bury it hastily, for the curse of God is there-upon hung…" (Deuteronomy 21:23). That is to say, he has been hung for cursing God and [now] God's name is being disgraced.[14]

Most of the traditional commentary on this text cited by Loberbaum points to the way that the immanence of God was understood as residing in the actual corporal body. That a body is now hung in disgrace, then, reflects upon that immanence – the *image* of God that is part of the human even in his very physicality.[15]

This traditional concern with the sanctity of the body and its wholeness has been reflected in a variety of ways in Israeli-Jewish culture—from extreme devotion to procreation to extreme concern for the corpse. [16] One of the long-time participant-observers of the Israeli organ transplantation project, former Assistant Director of the Health Ministry, Dr. Yitshaq Berlovitz, described to me some of the tensions surrounding the use of cadaver organs (for research, transplant or therapy). He stressed that in his experience, the need to assure the interested parties that their loved ones were going to reach a *kever Yisrael*—a Jewish grave—was of prime importance.[17] Concern with the proper treatment and internment of the physical body is also evident in the great effort expended by the country in recovering bodily remains. The commander of a special IDF unit devoted to search-and-rescue operations (including the retrieval of those buried under rubble due to natural or man-made disasters) was incredulous that the victims of the London subway attack in the summer of 2005 were left un-retrieved for as long as they were.[18]

Overall, it may be that the special concern with the proper care for the Jewish body evinced in modern Israeli culture has its roots deep in the Jewish tradition. This concern seems to have become part of the general, and not just religious, Israeli culture.[19] Such concern makes itself felt in a number of ways—among them a general hesitancy among the Israeli Jewish population to part with body parts after death. In approaching the Israeli Rabbinate, the state representatives of traditional halakhic Judaism, those desirous of advancing the organ transplantation project were attempting to find ways of tempering this cultural aversion. Obtaining the cooperation of the Rabbinate, official state arbiters of Jewish tradition, may have been seen not just as a key to compromise with those who believed in "witch-doctors" (á la Aloni), but also as a way of grappling with a strong social and emotional connection of Israelis to the Jewish body. The desire for rabbinic authorization for heart transplants may have represented not merely a nod in the direction of religion, but was also aimed at touching a deeper traditional-cultural undercurrent of concern as well.[20]

More prosaically, however, a good part of Michaeli's motivation in approaching the Rabbinate was to avoid the types of confrontations with the religious community that he had witnessed in the Seventies over post-mortem examinations. As mentioned earlier, considerable tension over the proper care of cadavers and body parts had brought many religious Israelis to view the medical establishment with a good deal of suspicion, and frequently, even hostility. In an interview I conducted with Michaeli, he spent much time recounting (not without some measure of pride) how he had personally been involved in these "autopsy wars". He boasted of performing medically-indicated autopsies under police protection while groups of yeshiva students protested outside. As he put it (with a smile), he was a recognized "enemy of the *hevrah kadishah*."[21] By seeking official rabbinic approval of brain-death as halakhically legitimate, he felt that these former struggles could be avoided and the transplant project could move forward.

According to Michaeli, Israeli doctors by then had a clear view of brain-death and no further medical debate, concerning determination of death for organ donors, was needed. The question in his eyes was whether the rabbinic establishment would accept the medical establishment's conclusions. He and Gur both felt that attempting to change the actual law would be politically difficult and would waste valuable time. Legislative change meant going to the Knesset, opening formal debate and moving a bill through committee meetings. By changing public consensus, changes in the law would not be needed. Medical decisions concerning donor death would be accepted *de facto*. They envisioned that rabbinic acceptance would be part of this process.

In an article describing the process by which the heart-transplant project was established, Michaeli wrote:

> The question was, at this stage, essentially halakhic and the solution had to come from the side of the clergy. …we preferred to attempt to have the Rabbinate (which is the official state rabbinic institution) agree with the medical position that the death of the respiratory center [in the brain] is the moment of the individual's death. According to the *halakhah* and practically—there is equivalence between the "death of the respiratory center" and "death."[22]

For Michaeli, the question was whether or not the Rabbinate would agree with accepted medical fact. It was made clear to the rabbis with whom Michaeli and his colleague, the neurosurgeon Professor Abraham Sahar, met, that they were not asking "a medical question, but a religious question—if it is possible according to the *halakhah* to accept the death of the respiratory center as the death of the entire body".[23] He saw no need for any joint discussion or "committees" and claimed that the Rabbinate agreed that they would "deal with this question on their own." [24]

At the same time, Professor Joe Borman, a Hadassah cardiosurgeon, had begun to realize his dream of establishing a heart-transplant unit in the hospital. Hadassah's General Director at the time, Professor Shmuel Pinhas had given his approval and while

# Really Dead?

Borman worked on gathering and training his specialized team,[25] Pinhas also approached the Rabbinate. However, while Michaeli's strategy was to leave the rabbis alone to ponder his question, Pinhas approached the Rabbinate in a spirit of cooperation and tried to work together with them in reaching a mutually-acceptable method of performing these transplants. He himself met with the Chief Rabbis in their chambers a number of times and presented them with a proposed protocol for establishing death for potential organ donors. In an interesting analogy, Pinhas remarked that for him, turning to the Rabbinate regarding the determination of death was like turning to them regarding the kosher standards of the hospital cuisine. The Chief Rabbinate was an official state organ responsible for matters of religion, be they food or the determination of death. As the one responsible for the overseeing of a large, complicated medical center, for him, the involvement of rabbis was not just a matter of avoiding possible conflict and guaranteeing an organ supply, but also part of the regular functioning of an Israeli institution.[26] In response to a question, he even asserted that had he not been successful in getting halakhic clearance, he would not have gone ahead with the heart transplant program. As I will explain, in the end, however, this cooperation would only extend as far as a restrictive *psaq* issued by the Rabbinate.

---

[1] Michaeli (1933-2006), a medical doctor, served as the chief medical officer of the IDF and then as Medical Director of Icholov Hospital before joining the Health Ministry.

[2] Until then, Israelis who needed these organ transplants had to have these operations performed outside of the country at high cost.

[3] The Committee was commissioned by Michaeli to investigate the readiness of Israeli hospitals to carry out liver transplants. It was comprised of six doctors, each a specialist in a different field relevant to transplantation. They held a number of meetings over several months and visited a number of hospital sites before writing their report. The report was given to the Health Ministry on June, 8 1986. It was reported that certain staff members of Rambam Hospital in Haifa were angered at

the Committee's decision both to put off the immediate start of liver transplants and to plan on proceeding only later in conjunction with their rival hospital, Hadassah. See Areyeh Kizel, *"Rofe Rambam Zoamim al Miniat Hashtalot Kaved,"* **Yediot Aharonot** June 10, 1986, 2.

[4] See Segal, *"Mabat Hadash al Trumat Avarim"* and Deveri & Levi, *"Shtilat Lev – Orot Vetslalim,"* **Harefuah** 109, no.10 (November 15, 1985): 303-5.

[5] Shreiber, *"Idan Hashtalot Avarim Beyisrael,"* **Yediot Aharonot** March 16, 1985, 11.

[6] That is, all of the body's organs (and even clothing stained with blood in the case of accidents) need to be interred together with the body of the deceased. See *Shulhan Arukh* 349:2, 357, 364:4.

[7] A. Deveri and M. Levy, *"Shtilat Lev – Orot Vetslalim."*

[8] Others might less generously categorize her as a fierce opponent of organized religion in general and Orthodox Judaism in particular. Her often caustic barbs aimed at Israel's religious population contributed to her removal as Education Minister by Yitzchak Rabin in 1993 after serving less than one year in that position. She was even depicted as the "Wicked Witch of the West" chasing innocent religious "Dorothys" in a popular main-stream (secular) Israeli comedy show (*Zehu-Zeh*) during her tenure. This satire reflected both her image in the eyes of the religious camp and acknowledged this image among the secular.

[9] Protocols of the Knesset Law Committee (July 10, 1978).

[10] See section I, chapter three.

[11] Modan, *"Lev Basar Velev Even,"* **Yediot Aharonot** November 11, 1989. More recently, too, those intimately connected to the medical world in general, and to organ transplantation in particular, have dismissed the claim that *religious* attitudes are to blame for the dearth of willing organ donors in Israeli society, among them the previous director of the Israeli Transplant Center, Yonatan Halevi, in testimony before the Knesset Work, Welfare and Health Committee (Protocols [June 9, 2003]).

[12] I have witnessed first-hand the pains-taking process of collecting the bits and pieces of human tissue from accident sites. Hours are spent carefully searching for any sign of blood or other tissue that needs proper burial. Most of the nation has seen the work of the mostly Haredi ZAKA society that does this cleaning-up of sites after terrorist attacks.

[13] Loberbaum, *Tselem Elohim* (Jerusalem: Schocken Press, 2004), 282. Recall how R. Feinstein related to this physical suffering of the corpse as well.

[14] *Mishnah Sanhedrin* 6:6.

# Really Dead?

[15] This understanding can also shed light on the emphasis on physical sanctification through special types of eating, etc. that the Jewish tradition has stressed.

[16] See Susan Martha Kahn, *Reproducing Jews* (Durham: Duke University Press, 2000) for an intriguing description of the ways that traditional Jewish conceptions of motherhood, kinship, and the importance of child-bearing have influenced modern IVF technology in Israel—the country which offers the most liberal uses of that technology in the West. See Biale, *Eros and the Jews*, (Berkley: University of California Press, 1997) chapter eight "Zionism as an Erotic Revolution." He argues that Zionism's founding fathers were deeply concerned with the "body" of the Jew. See Orit Brawer Ben-David, "Ranking Deaths in Israeli Society: Premature deaths and organ donation," *Mortality* 11, no.1 (Feburary, 2006): 79-98. Ben-David discusses the changeable status of corpses in modern Israel.

[17] Interview with Dr. Yitzchak Berlovitz, June 21, 2005.

[18] Col. Gideon Bar-On quoted by Arieh O'Sullivan, "Israel's Insurance Policy," *The Jerusalem Post*, October 7, 2005.

[19] The ways that traditional cultural concepts work their way into the modern societies of which they are a part is confusingly complex. Attempts to understand them have been part and parcel of cultural sociology's work load at least since the time that one of its modern founders, Clifford Geertz, began to explore them. Geertz famously counted "the Plains Indians' bravura, the Hindus' obsessiveness, the Frenchmen's rationalism, the Berbers' anarchism and the Americans' optimism" as examples of what he saw as resultant national traits ("Thick Description: Toward an Interpretive Theory of Culture," in *The Interpretation of Culture*, 9). His seminal study of the influence of traditional religion on modern society, *Islam observed : religious development in Morocco and Indonesia* (Chicago : U. of Chicago Press, 1971), shows just how complex this influence may be. Many scholars have followed in Geertz' wake, pointing to similarly developed facets of modern Jewish-Israeli culture, yet not fully explicating the intricacies of the influence of tradition.

Kahn, for example, attaches importance to the traditional Jewish emphasis on procreativity as part of an explanation for modern Israel's uniquely liberal policy on IVF, even detailing some of the ways that traditional concerns become manifest in modern socio-medical policy. She argues that the "overwhelming desire to create Jewish babies deeply informs the Israeli embrace of reproductive technology" (Kahn, *Reproducing Jews*, 3). By noting traditional Jewish concerns with being fruitful and multiplying, it seems to be *assumed* that these ancient concerns have wended their way from the issues reflected in traditional texts to the modern IVF laboratories. She stresses how "consent for the new reproductive technologies is all but universal in Israel, a 'pronatalist state' where the despair of the barren woman has deep cultural roots. Indeed, one could argue that Ruti Nachmani's battle for motherhood [a celebrated Israeli legal case where a divorced woman fought to gain possession of frozen embryos fertilized with her ex-husband's sperm] echoes that of the biblical matriarch Rachel who lamented, 'Give me sons or else I am dead' (70)."

While I agree that this is indeed the case, a much deeper analysis is needed in order to explore *how* the traditional trope of fertility has made its way into the present. The search for the actual *mechanism* responsible for the transfer of these concerns and attitudes is ignored – it seems to be assumed.

Reticence to unravel this process is understandable. I would argue that such a search need be itself the aim of another complete study. Traditional tropes make their presence felt in modern societies in a variety of often contradictory ways (see Geertz' classic on Islam). To fully understand how any one such trope or conception percolates through a culture requires examining the multitudinous paths through which any such trope *could* be expressed –the arts, literature, legal traditions, political movements, educational methods – all those strands of human activity which taken together make up culture. This study is not devoted to such a search; indeed it is well beyond its purview of exploring the history surrounding brain-death.

One promising avenue of exploration for sociological studies of this type may very well lie in the work of Thevenot and Lamont who harness Swindler's theories of culture-as-tool-kit in order to contrast national strategies for dealing with social problems. If cultural responses to a given problem depend upon the "tools" available to participants in that society—we may want to understand that religious-culture traditions (in our case found in traditional Jewish texts, mores, and ways of thinking) offer a specific, readily available array of tools for dealing with questions facing Israeli society. The ways in which such tools are used, though, needs investigation. See Ann Swindler, "Culture in Action: Symbols and Strategies" in *American Sociological Review* 51 (1986): 273-86; Laurent Thevenot and Michele Lamont, *Rethinking Comparative Cultural Sociology: Politics and Repertoires of Evaluation in France and the United States* (Cambridge: Cambridge University Press, 2000); I.F. Silber, "Convergences and Cleavages in the Study of Cultural Repertoires: Theorizing the Inner-Structure of Tool-Kits, Symbolic Boundaries and Regimes of Justification," Paper presented at the Annual Meeting of the American Sociological Association, Anaheim, CA, August 18-22, 2001.

# Really Dead?

What is worth noting here, however, is the way in which concern for the dead Jewish body appears both in ancient Jewish texts as well as in modern Israeli practice. Some of these contemporary practices are near exact replications of older traditions reflected in normative modern Israeli burial rites; some certainly do *seem* to echo much older traditions – like the concern expressed by Berlovitz regarding proper internment. Is there a link between the ancient and modern? I would say yes. Is this the place to explore this link? Unfortunately not. Such a study must wait for another research project.

[20] The lack of willingness on the part of Israelis to sign "organ donation cards" and to donate organs after death has been bemoaned by many. While I have found no statistics from the earlier days of Israeli cadaveric organ transplantation, the lag of Israel's organ supply in relation to that found in other countries—directly related to (among other things) lack of donor willingness—has been mentioned frequently in more recent literature. Eytan Mor (Director of the Rabin Medical Center transplantation department), in a presentation on the phenomenon of Israelis traveling overseas to purchase organs, wrote that despite decades of success in actual transplant procedures, "Israel's organ donation rate ... remains one of the lowest in the Western world, averaging 9 donors per population of one million per year. The consent rate in Israel [referring to familial consent to donate organs from deceased relatives] is 40%...." He lists "*Cultural resistance to donation* [my emphasis] and objections of orthodox rabbinical leaders to the brain-death concept" as the two explanations for this state of affairs. (Eytan Mor, "Transplant Tourism in Israel: Effect on Transplant Practice and Organ Donation," http://www.elpat.eu/CDPraag/Presentation_Mor_text.pdf (accessed on May 17, 2005).

Another physician from the same hospital, P. Singer, wrote, that "The rate of potential and effective organ donors is low in Israel in comparison with other developed countries" ("Cadaveric organ donation in Israel: the facts and the perspectives," *Annals of Transplantation* 4 [1] 1999, 5-10). A survey of available information on organ donation per country in 2003 also found Israel ranking far below all other countries with similar health care standards (A. Kogan, et al., "Organ transplantation statistics in different countries: Internet review," *Transplantation Proceedings* 35 [2] 2003, 641-2).

A survey conducted in 1999 showed how Israelis were far less willing to sign organ donation cards when asked than the American public – 7% versus 28% (P.

Kedem-Friedrich and R. Rachmani, "Israelis willingness to donate organs: result of a survey," *Transplantation Proceedings* 31, 4 [1999]: 1910-11).

However, in a personal communication, the current coordinator of the Israel Transplant Center, Tamar Ashkenazi, expressed some doubt as to these two statistical studies. Primarily, she felt that they failed to take into account foreign countries' systems for donor inclusion (opt-in versus opt-out systems) or the ways in which they measured willingness to donate, reported on refusals to donate and the differences in criteria used in accepting or rejecting donor organs. Additionally, as the number of actual transplants in Israel is small (less than 200 per year), statistical variations appear more rapidly than in countries where a greater number of transplants are performed. In her opinion, it is therefore difficult to gauge where Israel stands in relation to other countries. However, in a study she conducted regarding Israeli attitudes towards organ donation (Tamar Ashkenazi, Nurit Guttman and Jacob Hornik, "Signing on the Dotted Line," *Marketing Health Services* [Summer, 2005]: 19-26), she noted that while the European refusal rate for donation is "approximately 30%" it is higher "than 50%" in Israel (19). She also noted that in a "preliminary test of 20 respondents it was found that when respondents were asked to participate in a survey on organ donation, most refused...." She subsequently had to change the survey's "topic" description to "saving a life" (21). Is this what Mor considered to be "cultural resistance?"

[21] Interview with Professor Michaeli, November 29, 2004. The *hevrah qadishah* (holy fellowship) is a group of Jews traditionally charged with the proper care and internment of Jewish cadavers. In Israel, there are many different private fellowships – usually belonging to, and taking care of, a specific ethnic sub-group. However, the majority of Israeli cadavers are cared for and interred by state-employed fellowships nearly always constituted of *haredi* Jews. As these fellowships are responsible for the care of the deceased in accordance with Jewish law, in the 1960s and 1970s, when post-mortems were the norm, they often conflicted with pathologists and others who dealt with the dead, but did not strictly adhere to Jewish law and custom.

[22] Michaeli, "*Qeviat Regah Hamavet,*" **ML** 49, no. 8 (Av-Elul, 5747): 8.

[23] Ibid.

[24] Ibid.

[25] In an interview, Borman stressed the exacting teamwork needed for a successful transplant program. Before performing their first human heart-transplant, his team had worked on dozens of dogs—up to four a week before he felt they were

# Really Dead?

ready to begin on humans. Concerning brain-death, he felt that it was a medically accepted concept no longer of any great interest (interview with Professor Joe Borman, November 15, 2004).

[26] Interview with Shmuel Pinhas, December 13, 2004.

# 11

# The Rabbinate Decision

Pinhas worked in two directions simultaneously, approaching both the Rabbinate and R. Tendler simultaneously. From R. Tendler, he requested affirmation of his (by-then-deceased) father-in-law's position supporting brain-death. This was supplied in a written reply dated July 5th, 1986. R. Tendler iterated three points in the body of his letter: one concerning organ donors, one regarding organ recipients, and one focusing on the entire transplant program. R. Tendler wrote that as long as "total cessation of all brain function including the brain stem" of the donor could be confirmed, no "ethical/halakhic" problems regarding removal of his still-beating heart existed. Second, he noted that R. Feinstein's dismissal of these procedures as too dangerous for the recipient had ended with more recent medical-technical improvements. As proof of this he offered anecdotal evidence that his father-in-law had in fact advised a "neighbor" to undergo a heart transplant in 1984. Third, he offered his own advice that Pinhas should "undertake a little *yahse tsibur* and *hasbarah* [public relations— written in Hebrew by hand]" to offset negative press from the "black" [meaning Haredi] press," basically by presenting the above two points to the public. He also added a post-script to his letter:

# Really Dead?

> I am not aware of any respected *"Poseq"* who now pro-
> hibits heart transplants. The therapeutic value is obvi-
> ous to all. Key concern is "killing" of donor. When
> made aware of "respirator brain" pathology (physio-
> logical decapitation), all should concur.[1]

R. Tendler split the controversy into two separate problems – the risk involved in undergoing dangerous surgery and the procuring of a donor heart. He claimed that the first matter had been solved with the advancement of medical technique and better survival rates for transplantees. However, not everyone accepted such a split. His prediction about expected concurrence was off. Several important *posqim* did react to the Rabbinate's *psaq* with strong condemnations. In fact, Rabbis Auerbach, Waldenburg and Weiss had already made their opposition to heart transplants quite clear—and certainly had not publicly expressed any change of heart.[2]

On Pinhas'other front, with the Rabbinate, a day of lectures for their transplant committee members was held at Hadassah in the fall of 1986. The Rabbinate committee was also presented with the hospital's suggested protocol for establishing brain-death.[3] Pinhas charac-terized the discussions with the Rabbinate as "difficult." He mentioned that he met with the Chief Rabbis a number of times in their chambers and described R. Avraham Shapira, the Ashkenazi Chief Rabbi, as "difficult, exacting, suspicious, sharp" continually asking questions concerning the medical procedures. It may be that the day at the hospital and suggested protocol was Pinhas' way of moving negotiations to a conclusion so that the transplants could begin.[4] It is not clear whether this meeting showed that he took R. Tendler's advice regarding PR, or that once he had a halakhic decision in hand (that of R. Feinstein), he felt more confident that his bargain-ing position had improved and so pressed forward.

# The Rabbinate Decision

The committee on transplants appointed by the Rabbinate was comprised of the two Chief Rabbis, two medical advisors and four other rabbis: R. Shaul Yisraeli and R. Yisrael Lau (municiple rabbi of Tel-Aviv), R. Chaim Shalush (municiple rabbi of Netanya) and R. Zalman Nechemia Goldberg of Jerusalem. The medical advisors were Professor Avraham Steinberg and Dr. Mordechai Halperin—both well acquainted with the problematics of *halakhah* and medicine. Rabbi Yisraeli, a long time member of the Rabbinate's High Council (since 1961), was a commanding figure among Israeli experts in *halakhah*, having authored many decisions, both theoretical and practical, on the questions that a modern state posed to *posqim*.[5] The other committee members left the actual writing of the *psaq* to him. R. Waldenburg, a *poseq* perhaps equal in stature to R. Yisraeli, had also been invited to join the transplant committee. He was less identified with the national-religious camp (those religious Israelis who see themselves as committed to both Torah observance and the ideals of modern Israeli Zionism) and so was more accepted by the *haredi* camp (those religious Israelis who do not identify with state Zionism and stress fealty to *halakhah* above all). Although R. Waldenburg had accepted the appointment, he declined to participate in the committee's meetings. He eventually published his own prohibitive injunction on the very day that the committee's recommendations were approved unanimously by the General Assembly of the Rabbinate. Two other important *posqim* were also approached by the Rabbinate—Rabbis Auerbach and Weiss. Neither of them agreed to participate.[6]

The committee met several times to discuss the issue at hand. In addition to its meeting with the Hadassah hospital staff, the members also met with medical experts from Shaare Zedek Medical Center in Jerusalem, a private, self-consciously religious tertiary-care institution.[7] After deliberations, this body approved a *psaq* that was divided into two distinct sections: one halakhic and one medical. The latter

# Really Dead?

section included additions to the protocol suggested by Hadassah. It was this section that brought both the Health Ministry and Hadassah into conflict with the Rabbinate. Each felt that the Rabbinate had no mandate to consider what they understood as purely medical issues.

After a short preamble describing the recent circumstances which brought about the establishment of the transplant committee (section 1), the *psaq* read as follows:

> 2) In the early days of transplants (17 years ago) it was decided to prohibit heart transplants [in keeping with the decisions of] the great R. Feinstein (of blessed memory) and R. Unterman (obm), as they were [considered] to be the double murder of both the donor and recipient. In the past 10 years a major change has taken place in the factual and medical data concerning heart transplants as follows:
>
> > a) The success rate of the procedure has reached nearly 80% of recipients attaining "permanent life" (life expectancy of at least one year post-transplant) and nearly 70% remain alive for five years.
> >
> > b) Today it is possible to determine in a certain and reliable fashion that cessation of respiration of the deceased is permanent and irreversible.
> >
> > c) Testimony has been brought to us that R. Feinstein (obm) permitted the performance of heart transplants in America, and we know of important rabbis who suggest that cardiac patients undergo heart transplants.

3) As this question is a true matter of life and death, it is incumbent upon us to reach a clear decision regarding this *halakhah* regardless of the consequences.

4) Relying upon the *gemara* in *Yoma* (85) and the ruling of the *Chatam Sofer* YD 338, death is established according to the *halakhah* with cessation of respiration. (See Responsa *Egrot Moshe* YD III 132) Therefore, it must be established that respiration has completely stopped in an irreversible manner. This is possible to ascertain by proving destruction[8] of the brain in its entirety including the brain stem which activates independent respiration.

5) Accepted practice in the medical world is that such a determination requires 5 conditions:

> a) Clear knowledge of the etiology of the trauma.
>
> b) Complete cessation of independent respiration.
>
> c) Specific clinical proofs of destruction of the brain stem.
>
> d) Objective proof of destruction of the brain stem through the use of laboratory tests such as BAER.
>
> e) Proof that the complete cessation of breathing and lack of brain stem function remain so for at least a period of 12 hours, while full standard treatment is given.

6) After examining a protocol for establishing death as proposed by the doctors of Hadassah Hospital in Jerusalem on July 15, 1985 and presented to the Chief Rabbinate on October 8, 1986, we find that it is acceptable

according to the *halakhah* with the addition of an objective scientific test (BAER) of the brain stem.

7) In accordance with the above, the Chief Rabbinate of Israel is prepared to allow heart transplants (from accident victims) in the Hadassah Medical Center of Jerusalem under the following conditions:

a) The fulfillment of all the conditions regarding the establishment of the donor's death as delineated above.

b) The addition of a representative of the Chief Rabbinate of Israel as a full member of the team that determines the donor death.

This representative will be appointed by the Health Ministry from a list submitted annually to the Ministry by the Rabbinate.

c) The obtainment of advance agreement in writing, from the donor or his family, to the donation.

d) The establishment of a review committee subordinate to the Health Ministry in concert with the Rabbinate to oversee all cases of heart transplant in Israel.

e) The Health Ministry must establish these procedures as nationwide regulations.

8) Until such time as these conditions outlined in section 7 are accepted, there is no permission to perform heart transplants in Israel.

9) In the event that permission is given in accordance with the conditions outlined in section 7, a review board will then be established by the Rabbinate whose task

will be to ensure that all the conditions are fulfilled completely.[9]

Two addenda were added as well: the first, the complete suggested brain-death protocol supplied by Hadassah with the additions required by the Rabbinate. The second was the protocol for the "brain stem auditory evoked potentials" (BAER) test which was written by Professor Chaim Sohmer.[10] I will return to these below.

Even at first glance, it is clear that the amount of space given to discussing extra-halakhic matters, such as medical protocols, review committees and the like, far exceeds that devoted to the actual halakhic question of defining death. The halakhic content is actually quite limited and expressed in section 4 using a mere three sentences. (Another few sentences dismantle a previously accepted prohibition of these procedures for reasons connected to their increased success.) This *psaq*, then, resembles more a set of administrative directives than a discussion of halakhic issues. This is testimony to the fact that as an *instituiton*, the Chief Rabbinate (then together with the now defunct Ministry of Religion) did and does indeed function as an administrative body devoted to proper administration of clearly delineated spheres of public life in Israel.[11] While Israeli law does recognize that the mandate of the Rabbinate includes the power to "give answers and opinions regarding halakhic issues to those who ask its advice," most of its personnel and resources are in fact devoted to the daily administration of the kosher standards of food and ritual items, marriage and divorce between Israeli Jews, supervision of local rabbis, and the like.[12]

The tension between the functioning of the Rabbinate as an administrative body and as "supreme religious authority" as it was originally constituted during the British Mandate has come to the fore in a number of cases, some of them reaching the Israeli High Court of

# Really Dead?

Justice. As Hakohen has outlined, perhaps the most famous of these was the Marbek case (*BG"Z* 195/64), wherein the Rabbinate conditioned its granting of a kosher certificate to a meat processing plant upon a number of stipulations regarding the distribution of non-kosher by-products from the same plant. The court (albeit in a divided decision) held that these stipulations were not part of the Rabbinate's legitimate legal and halakhic mandate concerning the granting of certification. Only the actual conditions for certifying that the meat was halakhically kosher could be stipulated, but not other factors which did not directly affect the state of the said meat.[13]

In certain ways, it would appear that the decision concerning heart transplants parallels the Marbek case: the Rabbinate was seemingly asked for its opinion regarding the halakhic validity of a given procedure and responded with a number of stipulations upon which it conditioned its approval. However, heart transplants reside completely outside of the normal *administrative* sphere of the Rabbinate. The query presented to the Rabbinate was not a request for normative "certification," such as a restaurant might require—despite the analogy given by Pinhas. Rather those doctors involved in organ transplantation knew that the success of the transplant project was dependent upon a supply of donors who would be influenced by the Rabbinate's decision. While the Health Ministry was not seeking kosher certification, it did want to establish that these transplants were indeed 'kosher.'

According to R. Mordechai Halperin M.D., an advisor to the Transplant Committee, the reason that the Rabbinate went to these extremes was because they mistrusted the medical establishment. He noted that previously the Rabbinate had given permission for certain halakhically complicated IVF procedures only to discover afterwards that doctors had ignored some of the conditions they had stipulated in order to ensure halakhic compliance.[14] This of course, came in the

wake of the long-standing tension over the proper handling of cadavers and body-parts.

Beyond this, however, while the Rabbinate was still debating its
answer, another dramatic transplant had taken place. Dr. Yigal Kam,
who had been training as a liver transplant surgeon for years, went
ahead with the first such operation in Israel on October 21, 1986 (the
Rabbinate decision was published on November 2, 1986). While the
Egoz committee report had proposed that Hadassah Hospital begin
preparations for liver transplants in the near future, the staff of the
Rambam hospital in Haifa lobbied the Health Ministry, received its
blessing and pushed ahead.[15] Kam performed two transplants in the
same week and each received front-page coverage in the daily press.[16]
The recipient's names and pictures were prominently featured in
dramatic stories and features. Kam was hailed as a hero.[17] The story
quickly turned from drama to tragedy as each of the liver recipients
died within three weeks of their operation. "THE PRICE OF BEING
FIRST" declared one headline in a sidebar of a long obituary of Mira
Shikhmanter – the first patient.[18]

All this took place while the Rabbinate Transplant Committee was
still in the process of writing its decision. The fact that the Health
Ministry had approached them with a query and had then gone ahead
with liver transplants in which the very same question needed answering, could not have escaped the Committee. It was certainly
noted by the religious press. Yated Ne'eman, a haredi daily, published a
two-part story detailing what the paper depicted as behind-the-scenes
small-minded competition between Hadassah and Rambam Hospital,
as each raced ahead with its own transplant program—ignoring
patients' well-being in the process. Their point was to expose the
danger inherent in blindly trusting the medical establishment, where,
they claimed, ethics were less important than fame.[19]

# Really Dead?

Referring to rumors that the complete medical records of the second liver-transplant patient had not been made available by Hadassah before his transfer to Rambam, another religious paper was even blunter:

> If it is conceivable that one medical center is capable of undermining another medical center when both of them are devoted to saving human lives, who can guarantee that halakhic stipulations, even the most minimal, can be kept when the ravenous appetite for success drives them beyond reason?[20]

Clearly, neither the longer history of tension between the rabbinic and medical establishments nor the immediate context of this *psaq* can be ignored. What remains unclear to me, however, is not why the Rabbinate *wanted* to exercise the regulatory "micro-management" that they requested, but why they believed that it would be possible? If the Health Ministry and hospitals were only hungrily seeking to advance the transplant program, why would they allow strict third-party supervision?

Additionally, the above question also touches upon the much broader subject of the legitimate boundaries of the *halakhah*. That is, what is the purview of the halakhic legal system in general and the Chief Rabbinate in particular? Are subjects with no clear-cut entry in the traditional codes of Jewish law—like matters of politics and economics on a state level—part of halakhic decisors' proper workload? Hakohen draws a parallel between this question concerning the Rabbinate and the same regarding the judicial branch of any parliamentary democracy.[21]

The problem of judicial boundaries is a fascinating question which cannot be addressed in this study. However, it is clear that R. Yisraeli was a proponent of a halakhic activism—arguing clearly since the early days of the State for the need to expand the *halakhah* from the private sphere, which responsa had traditionally dealt with, into the modern public sphere. He devoted most of his life's work to searching for halakhic answers to questions of politics, economics, and the like that are part of modern state life—moving beyond concern for the individual. Writing in 1950 he argued against the image of the *halakhah* as confined only to the private sphere.

> We hold that the hour demands of us our total commitment to the *halakhah* combined with worldly affairs, especially in those [unclear areas] that have arisen since the founding of the State. Anyone who is able to aid in the clarification of the *halakhah* and in its implementation in our daily lives is commanded to do so.[22]

And in the 1970's he expressed his opinion that:

> The principles of the *halakhah* can be applied in response to any question that arises in any time. Perhaps we may need to adapt some of the actual directives, but without losing the principles.[23]

The issue here, however, is not whether medical ethics is a legitimate concern of halakhic scholars or within the purview of the Rabbinate's mandate, but rather the way that the Rabbinate tried to take part in the actual process of determining the potential organ donor's death. After examining the halakhic and medical content of the Rabbinate's decision, I will offer an explanation for their desire for genuine involvement in the declaration of death.

# Really Dead?

The halakhic section of the *psaq* closely follows both the history and the logic developed in the responsa of R. Feinstein (as explained by R. Tendler). R. Feinstein and his work are mentioned three times. The determination of death is stated as primarily a question of discovering whether cessation of respiration is permanent, just as R. Feinstein outlined in his responsa.[24] In the historical section: "Today it is possible to determine in a certain and reliable fashion that cessation of respiration of the deceased is permanent and irreversible." In the actual halakhic definition of death:

> ...death is established according to the *halakhah* with cessation of respiration. (See Responsa *Egrot Moshe* YD III 132) Therefore, it must be established that respiration has completely stopped in an irreversible manner.

And finally in the actual brain-death clause: "This is possible to ascertain by proving destruction of the brain *in its entirety* including the brain stem which activates independent respiration" [emphasis added].

R. Feinstein claimed that the problem with the respirated patient was the inability to assess whether respiration had irreversibly ceased. He had agreed with his son-in-law's suggestion that evidence of destruction of the brain would serve as evidence for actual irreversibility. Once this was established, death (according to R. Tendler's interpretation) could be declared. However, destruction as evidence of irreversibility was read as the halakhic concept of decapitation. As we discussed above, for R. Feinstein, brain-death was "virtual decapitation." Halakhically, decapitation was understood as the most unequivocal determination of death. It allowed both for complete abandonment of the patient and for any bodily movement to be ignored as irrelevant "twitching." Interestingly however, while the

Rabbinate's decision followed R. Feinstein's language, insisting on complete destruction of the brain, it included no specific mention of the notion of decapitation—actual or virtual. The Rabbinate did insist, however, on both clinical and special "objective proof" of the destruction of the *brain stem* only and not the entire brain.

This would seem to be redundant if what was being sought was the "destruction of the brain in its entirety." One explanation may be that the stipulation to specifically include the brain stem was meant to exclude any possibility of confusing total brain-death with PVS (persistent vegetative state)–wherein all brain function excepting that of the brain stem is lost. (This was, in fact, the case with the famous patient Karen Ann Quinlan, who began to breathe on her own once respiratory support was removed.) In an article written by R. Yisraeli shortly after the Rabbinate's decision, he interpreted Rashi's gloss on the *sugya* in *Yoma* as presenting a similar call, for (over-)inclusive checking. Rashi notes that upon discovering a victim under the collapsed building: "If he [the victim] is like a dead individual, in that he is not moving any of his limbs, until where must he [the excavator] check to discover the truth?"

While many have understood this statement as setting up a precondition of general unconsciousness before respiration *need* be checked, R. Yisraeli reads Rashi's statement as an injunction to check beyond mere unconsciousness, which may have been mistaken for death. That is, he reads the gloss: "*Even* if the victim…," it is still incumbent upon us to check for breathing.[25] The only problem with this reading is that the word *even* is missing from the actual text. It seems to be a creative interpretation; reading in the *even* where the simpler understanding is that any movement at all obviates the need for checking respiration. The respiratory check is only necessary if no other signs of life are noted, but any movement is in itself taken as a sign of possible life and the excavation continues. This is not to say that the respiratory check is seen as unnecessary, *even* when no other signs of life are present—quite the contrary. The question is, though, whether Rashi is informing us that other signs of life—such as movement—may be taken as such, or whether the *gemara* is focusing solely on respiration to the exclusion of all else. For those advocating the removal of the still beating heart because independent respiration is the sole sign of life, the latter reading is certainly more valuable. Nevertheless, the stipulation that the entire brain, *including* the brain stem, be destroyed does follow this logic. Destruction of *just* the rest of the brain, while the brain stem is still alive, is not enough to determine the death of the patient.

Oddly, despite the original language in the Rabbinate's decision stating that its authors wanted to prove "destruction of the brain *in its entirety* including the brain stem," in fact, in the *definition of brain-death* supplied by Hadassah[26] – it was *only* the death of the *brain stem* that was being discussed and not the brain in its entirety. It was only the destruction of the brain stem itself that the Rabbinate desired to test. It seems clear that the Rabbinate found no need for the virtual decapitation, describing the complete destruction of the entire brain, created by R. Feinstein. Avraham Steinberg, one of the committee's two medical advisors, made this point explicitly in an explanatory article written the year after the publication of the Rabbinate decision. He described the question that faced the committee as whether the resuscitated patient "…with cardiac activity, when it can be determined that independent respiration will never return, is considered according to the *halakhah* as alive or dead?"[27]

In his review of the halakhic understanding of death, he asserted that respiration alone was the only true indicator of life or death.

> This definition was and will remain the sole halakhic definition, and no one has the power to change the es-

sential definition that our Sages determined in accordance with the Torah. Thus, as there are many situations in which it will be possible to revive respiratory function, we must strengthen the definition of our Sages through the proof that it has ceased forever.[28]

This proof could be attained either through showing that the heart or the brain stem have ceased to function. Steinberg argued that if either one of these organs has "died," respiration cannot be restored. In the case of the heart, this is because without circulation of oxygenated blood to the brain via the heart, the brain itself will die, thus ending respiration. In the case of brain death, the chain of causation is shortened: as the brain stem dies, its control of respiration ends and respiration ceases irreversibly. He argued that R. Feinstein's novel view regarding virtual decapition as death in accord with the *mishnah* in *Ohalot* was not needed.[29]

However, Steinberg's comment is not accurate in equating 'virtual decapitation' with *brain stem* destruction. R. Feinstein quite clearly described complete destruction of the entire brain and the complete severing of any brain-body connection. In *Egrot Moshe* he asked to test

> ...whether the connection which exists between the brain and the *entire* body has been severed. If it [the angiogram contrast dye] does not reach the brain, it is clear that the brain no longer has any connection to the body and [the brain] has *completely* rotted away so that it is as if the head has been virtually removed. ... If they see *any* connection between the brain and the body, even though he cannot breathe, he must be respirated even for a lengthy time period, and only when this test

> reveals no connection of the brain to the body can the
> loss of respiration render him dead [*emphasis added*].[30]

This inaccuracy aside, it is clear that for Steinberg and the Rabbinate, halakhic death was described by the end of respiration alone—which could be determined by the end of brain-stem function alone.[31] Death is described in an essentialist manner—as just that irreversible loss of respiration. As it is connected to brain-stem function, it may be correctly measured by brain-stem function loss alone. If this is so, however, conceptually at least, we can conceive of a patient with a very specific injury to that part of the brain stem responsible for respiratory control—where the rest of his brain remains unharmed. Such a patient, if properly respirated, may have a completely living brain absent the brain stem. If only the area of the brain stem controlling respiration is damaged, this patient fits the above halakhic description of death, despite the fact that most of his brain is intact and able to function. His capacity for independent breathing is irreversibly destroyed, never to return. He is then by definition dead.

If the reticular activating system (RAS) of the brain stem is damaged, then the rest of the upper brain may be unresponsive, but not destroyed or incapable of function. (The RAS is the portion of the brain stem responsible for "'switching on' the hemispheres" as Pallis, a staunch supporter of a brain-stem definition of brain-death, described its role).[32] Yet it will surely be alive. According to Sohmer, an EEG of such a patient would record tracings similar to those found in patients whose reticular activating systems have been suppressed through anesthetics or are merely sleeping.[33] A more recent critic of brain-death, the American neurologist Shewmon cited evidence of cases in which despite damage to the brain stem, full consciousness can be restored: "Patients comatose from pure brain-stem lesions have been restored to consciousness by electrical stimulation of the reticular formation above the lesion."[34]

So, if we subscribe to the formulation of death as only the death of the brain stem, we discover that we have the odd case of an at least potentially conscious patient who may be declared dead. Even if the *usual* presentation of the possibly brain-dead patient entails complete neurological unresponsiveness (perhaps suggesting death of the rest of the brain) this situation is only *contingently* related to the actual state of death. If we were to insist that this is not the case, because lack of consciousness is a *pre-condition* to actual death, it seems that this would deconstruct the essentialist equation of death with respiration.[35] It seems, then, that a halakhic analysis which based its understanding of death on complete or whole-brain death was at odds with what the medical staff of Hadassah presented quite clearly as their own interpretation of brain-death—brain-*stem* death alone. Yet, a medical or halakhic focus on brain-stem death was, as outlined above, conceptually quite difficult. It allowed for the (at least potentially) still conscious, but definitionally dead individual.

---

[1] Letter from R. Tendler to Shmuel Pinhas, July 5, 1986.

[2] As mentioned above, R. Tendler advocated a very strong naturalistic-legal position which made *conceptual* disagreement difficult to imagine.

[3] This protocol was written the previous summer as part of the general preparations for the heart-transplant program. The Rabbinate *psaq* notes that it dated from July, 1985 and that it was presented to them the day after the committee met with Hadassah staff in the hospital on October 7, 1986. I have not been able to locate in Hadassah's archives any interim protocols between this and the one adopted in 1974 – although there may have been one or more. The archives seem to be incomplete.

[4] Joe Borman felt that his team was well-nigh ready to start and that the main obstacle to doing so at this point was getting the formality of Rabbinic agreement to the "accepted medical practice" of brain-death. (Interview with Professor Joe Borman November 15, 2004).

# Really Dead?

5 Many saw him as *the poseq* of the national-religious camp. He took an unusually integrative view of halakhic theory, applying halakhic precepts to the problems—political, economic, and social—that the actual running of a modern state created. Not content to describe the halakhic requirements of the individual, R. Yisraeli often sought to explore and adjudicate halakhic questions on the national or public-policy level as well. See Efraim Auerbach, "*Samkhut Hahalakhah Beyamenu,*" in **Bein Samkhut Le'otonomiah**, eds. Ze'ev Safrai and Avi Sagi (Tel-Aviv: *Kibbutz Hameuchad*, 1997), 457-463.

6 In an article written after publication of the Rabbinate's decision, R. Eliyahu noted that two important Jerusalem *posqim* had declined to take part in the committee's deliberations. One felt that the medical establishment could not be trusted to adhere to any decision reached by such a committee; the other was pressured by his community to withdraw his initial commitment to cooperate with the committee. Several Jerusalem rabbis who have been involved in medical-halakhic issues have told me that the first was R. Auerbach and the second, R. Weiss – by then the *poseq* of the ultra-orthodox *Eda Haredit* ("*Hashtalat Averim Al Pi Hahalakhah,*" *Barkai* 4 (5747): 18-31).

7 Mordechai Halperin, "*Hashtalat Lev Beyisrael,*" **Assia** 42-43 (Nissan 5747): 70-80, notes 4 and 5, 70. Unfortunately, the actual protocols of these meetings are currently inaccessible as they were deposited in the Israel State Archives at the conclusion of the then Chief Rabbi's term in office. They are sealed for 30 years from that date.

8 The Hebrew original is *heres* whose literal meaning is physical destruction and not loss of function. This is the same word used throughout the document.

9 Ibid., 70-75.

10 This test was originally designed to test for various auditory nerve pathologies by tracing the electrical response of the nerve as it traveled from the ear-drum itself to the brain-stem. Sohmer had experimented extensively on mammals and had found that when blood pressure differentials between the cranium and body were altered so that blood flow to the brain was interrupted, the electrical response of nerve cells along the auditory nerve ceased as these cells stopped functioning and died. By testing at various points along the known path of the auditory nerve, the point at which the response ended could be discovered and death of the nerve cells at that point established. (Sohmer, "*Habasis Hamada'i-refu'i Leqviat Mot Hamo'ah,* **Assia** 42-43 [Nissan 5747]: 84-91 and interview with Chaim Sohmer, January 7, 2007).

[11] See Aviad Hakohen, *"Harabanut Harashit Leyisrael: Hebetim Mishpati'im"* in *Harabanut Harashit Leyisrael Shivim Shanah Leyesodah*, eds. I. Warhaftig and S. Katz (Jerusalem: *Heikhal Shlomo*), 159-219.

[12] Ibid., 188-194.

[13] Ibid., 204-207.

[14] Halperin, *"Hashtalat Lev Beyisrael,"* 74 note 33. The main halakhic problem regarding IVF treatments is keeping track of donor sperm identity. The chance of a women being accidentally impregnated with sperm that is not her husband's, or in the case of male infertility, of an unidentified donor, is greater without proper precautions and extra safeguards. See Susan Martha Kahn, *Reproducing Jews* for a discussion of how IVF clinics came to work together with rabbinical supervision.

[15] Devorah Namir, *"Hamilhamah al Hahashatalot,"* **Yediot Aharonot,** September 26, 1989, 8. In a personal communication, the head of the committee, Dr. Nachum Egoz, informed me that his committee had been given the mandate of determining which of the three competing centers, Rambam, Hadassah or Tel Aviv's Beilinson Hospital, would be granted the authority to begin liver transplantion. In choosing Hadassah, the committee chose the hospital with the best overall supportive abilities (immunology labs, blood banks, etc.) and general medical staff, despite their recognition of Kam's surgical skill. Egoz felt that Gur's decision to grant permission to Rambam and Kam was "reasonable," as Hadassah had "won by points, not by a knockout." However, this was not necessarily the perception of the public.

In a series of meetings of the Knesset Work and Welfare Committee the question of liver transplants in Israel had been discussed at length. One of the main arguments for beginning to perform these operations in Israel was the expected savings from the continued investment in subsidizing liver transplants overseas. However, the question of priorities regarding spending money for these advanced operations when many patients suffering from hernias and the like were kept waiting for treatment was also raised. The Committee's final recommendations reflected this conflict by noting both sides of the economic argument. (See the Protocols of the Knesset Work and Welfare Committee from December 30, 1985, February 24, 1986 and April 7, 1986.)

[16] Arieh Kizel, *"8 Shanim Hikinu Laregah,"* **Yediot Aharonot** October 23, 1986, 1.

[17] Devorah Namir, *"Hamilhamah Ha'ishit shel Dr. Kam,"* **Yediot Aharonot** October 23, 1986, 3. Kam's expertise was well acknowledged, but he became something of a medical diva in Israel, threatening to leave the country, actually leaving, and

# Really Dead?

holding out for extravagant compensation in order to return over the years. His comings and goings were always well-covered in the press.

[18] Anat Tal-Shir, *"Mirah Shihmanter,"* **Yediot Aharonot** November 11, 1986. Interestingly, in one of the few Hebrew books devoted to organ transplants, M. Kramer skips over this entire episode in his list of Israeli transplant history. While Morris Levy is noted as having performed the first heart-transplant and Borman the first *succesful* one, Kam is listed only in 1989 – when his liver transplant succeeded. Perhaps the difference is that Levi's failure in 1968 was on a par with medical ability and expectations of the time, while in 1986 livers were being successfully transplanted elsewhere—but not yet here. Is the omission a case of ethical embarrassment?

[19] *Yated Ne'eman* (Tishre 26 and 38, 5747).

[20] S. A. Eshel, *"Hashtalot,"* **HaModiah** (Hesvan 22, 5747): 3.

[21] Aviad Hakohen, *"Harabanut Harashit Leyisrael: Hebetim Mishpati'im,"* 207. The question of the Rabbinate's proper mandate has been the subject of much discussion. See for example, Uri Desberg, *"Haba'at De'ah Alyede Harabanim Harashi'im Leyisrael,"* in *T'humin* 11 (5750): 31-40. Here the discussion centers on the question of territorial compromise by the government during the era of the Oslo agreements. In a 1992 discussion of the state of the Israeli Rabbinate, R. Aaron Lichtenstein, a well known *Hesder Yeshiva* Dean (and Harvard Ph.D.), clearly supported a more limited, strictly "halakhic" role, when he asked rhetorically whether anyone could "imagine the Archbishop of Canterbury publicly determining who should be the Conservative candidate in Sheffield?" ("The Israeli Chief Rabbinate: A Current Halakhic Perspective," *Tradition* 26:4 [1992]: 26-38, 34). In general, R. Lichtenstein argued for some type of central authority as useful and necessary in the running of state-wide religious affairs, but held a quite low opinion of the Rabbinate at the time. He categorized it as "moribund" (34) and wrote how its authority, even among those most likely to support it as an institution, paled in contrast to that of recognized individual *posqim* like R. Auerbach (33).

More broadly, the question of the proper purview of the *halakhah* itself has been much debated. See Avi Sagi, *"Halakhah Veshikul Hada'at,"* and Yedidiya Stern, *"Nigishut Hilkhatit Lesugiot Mediniot"* both in **Bein Samkhut Le'otonomiah**, 195-217 and 218-243. (But see the critique of their thesis in Y. Y. Lifshitz, "Between Authority and Autonomy," *Azure* 7 [Spring 1999]. He argues that the authors' claims suffer from a reductionism that fails to take into account all facets of the *halakhah*.) For a discussion of the tensions in Israeli society surrounding the purview of the *halakhah* in public life see, Asher Cohen and Baruch Zisser, *"Bein Hescemiut Shevira Leshevirat Hahescemiut"* in ***Rav-Tarbutiut Bemedinah Demoqratit Veyehudit***, eds. Menachem Mautner, Avi Sagi, and Ronnen Shamir (Tel-Aviv: Ramot, 1998).

[22] R. Shaul Yisraeli, *"Hovat Hashaah,"* in ***Harabanut Vehamedinah*** (Jerusalem: Erez, 1991), 38-39. This essay was originally published as the introduction to the journal *Hatorah Vehamedinah* II (1950).

[23] Ibid., *"Kolah shel Harabanut Lo Nishma,"* 86.

[24] R. Yisraeli devoted most of an explanatory article published a few months after the Rabbinate's decision to explicating the stance of R. Feinstein. See R. Shaul Yisraeli, *"Beheter Hashtalat Halev Kayom"* in ***Barkai*** 4, (Spring 5747): 33-40.

[25] Yisraeli, *"Beheter Hashtalat Halev Kayom,"* 40.

[26] Halperin, *"Hashtalat Lev Beyisrael,"* 76. Section 3 of the Hadassah protocol's "definitions" section 3.1 reads: Brain Death—total lack of brain-stem function.

[27] Avraham Steinberg, *"Qeviat Regah Hamavet Vehashtalat Lev,"* ***Assia*** 44 (Nissan 5748): 56-77, 58.

[28] Ibid., 66.

[29] Ibid.

[30] EM YD III 132.

[31] Steinberg noted that actual physical destruction of the brain-stem was not needed, only the loss of function. This is parallel to the traditional cardiac criteria of death which required only the end of heart function and not destruction (63,72).

[32] Pallis, *ABC of Brain Stem Death*, 10. He did, however, admit that others reasoned that there may be actual consciousness without an active brain-stem – a locked-in condition of awareness without any expressive capacity. His only real defense against this idea is to disparage it as awful, a "hell" – seemingly vindicating the killing of a person in such a horrid state, 32.

[33] Personal communication, March 7, 2007.

[34] D. A. Shewmon, "Brainstem death, 'brain death' and death: a critical reevaluation of the purported equivalence," *Issues in Law &: Medicine* 14.2 (Fall 1998):125-48, 128. Unfortunately, we cannot ascribe the conceptual problematics of the brain-stem death definition of death only to then current understandings of the RAS. Despite Shewmon's proof (published only a decade later) Pallis was already all too aware of the potential problems with the RAS activity and, as noted above, chose to dismiss them.

[35] Traditionally, in terms of discussing brain-death, the lack of consciousness has been linked to the lack of independent respiration, as the respirated patient is also a

non-responsive patient. However, this has been true only contingently and not essentially. In terms of the halakhic description, the resuscitated patient has been the focus of brain-death discussion because of the stress on independent respiration. If this patient was also unconscious it was not *definitionally* important.

# 12

# The Hadassah Protocol

In order to understand how the medical team with which the Rabbinate was interacting conceptualized death, it is important to look more carefully at the actual medical protocol provided by Hadassah. A careful analysis of this document reveals how they connected consciousness with the brain stem. For them, the unconscious state of the patient was not a precondition of death, but led the medical staff back to its cause—the death of the *brain stem*.[1]

Their protocol started with complete unconsciousness before the exploration for brain-stem death began. The brain-death protocol devised by Hadassah was based upon a tri-leveled diagnostic description of the tested patient. These levels were labeled:

Stage 1: Existence of preliminary conditions.
Stage 2: Identification of circumstances liable to falsify establishment of death.
Stage 3: Essential tests for establishing brain-death.[2]

A given patient needed to satisfy the stipulations of each stage, in their proper order, before moving on to the next stage of testing in the protocol. The first preliminary condition (part of the content of Stage 1) was unconsciousness; the second, loss of independent respiration

# Really Dead?

(section 4.1.1); the third, evidence of actual (untreatable) physical damage to brain tissue (section 4.1.2). As the patient is comatose, neurological damage may be assumed (this is checked in Stage 2). Once neurological damage was introduced as the *assumed cause* of the observable state of the patient, it made sense to begin the process of establishing death by searching for its actual cause via the neurological pathway of the brain stem's death.

This new protocol was much clearer than the one from 1974, the clarifications answering the earlier criticisms that had been leveled against it. Most striking, though, was the change of focus in defining brain-death itself. While the 1974 document focused on destruction of the entire brain, brain-death was now redefined as just the loss of brain-stem function. This protocol represents a fundamental change in the logic of death. In the earlier protocol, Hadassah's Medical Board sought to find a "point of *death*." Its members had concentrated on showing how the patient had deteriorated into a "neurologically empty state" as collapse of biological system after system was observed. The end of this process required that the entire brain be inoperative. An EEG was administered twice to show "*complete* lack of *any* activity of the brain. An angiograph was to be administered to "demonstrate *complete* lack of blood flow in the vasculature system of the brain [emphasis added]." By 1985, however, *death* was never even mentioned, only time and again "brain-death." Here was something woven of a different cloth.

While the same early conditions of unconsciousness and lack of responsiveness were required (here listed specifically as "preliminary conditions") – brain-death, which did turn the patient into a "cadaver," was the very specific and localized loss of brain-stem function alone. No EEG was required; no invasive angiograph. These general tests were jettisoned for more specific ones as brain-death itself was localized. Its clear definition was given in section 3.1 simply as "Complete lack of brain-stem function."

While brain-death was narrowly defined in section 3, it is in section 4.3 that the specific tests for proving this are detailed. Control and observation were tightened, made more exact and more sophisticated every step of the way. The patient no longer needed to dissolve before us. Rather, it was enough to ascertain—beyond the shadow of any scientific doubt—that this patient has lost *something* essential to life, in order to determine his death. In a newspaper interview several years after these protocols were drawn up, one of their authors, the neurologist Professor Avinoam Reches described the choice of brain-**stem** death as a way of ensuring an early enough declaration of death to ensure viable organs for transplants.[3]

> The determination of brain-death rests on the understanding that brain-death does not occur at one point in time; rather it is an irreversible process that lasts a certain time. … Doctors who come to pronounce death must be certain that the patient has entered this "time tunnel" from which there is no return. The problem that stands before doctors is that the same patient who has passed through this time tunnel and exits from the other side is considered to be totally dead and his organs are of no use for transplant. Therefore, we must determine the beginning of the brain-death process as early as possible.[4]

If his description is representative of the thinking behind the move from defining brain-death as the end of the entire brain's function to the very localized end of brain-stem function alone, then this thinking is completely at odds with that of the Rabbinate.[5] Again, they viewed

# Really Dead?

brain-stem death as *inclusive* of the death of the entire brain (even though this was not a necessary, but only a contingent matter). Here, though, brain-stem death is explicitly described as being an earlier stage that specifically eliminates the need to wait for the end of brain function in its entirety! (As we noted, on a conceptual level, however, this may not be problematic for the Rabbinate.) According to Reches' reading, then, despite the meetings and discussions between the Rabbinate's representatives and Hadassah's doctors, clarity concerning intended meanings of brain-death was not achieved. In fact, there may have been more misunderstanding than not.

A close reading of the overall structure and content of the detailed protocol shows that it serves as a carefully designed attempt to scientifically banish doubt. Hadassah contructed less a general clinical process and more a controlled and structured experiment designed to prove the end of brain-stem function. The patient was first checked to ascertain whether he was a suitable potential participant for this experiment through the preliminary check. Contravening indications were then ruled out. Finally, the experiment itself, involving the testing of various brain-stem functions—most importantly independent respiration (apnea testing)—was conducted. The brain-death team entered the picture only at this point—as an oversight committee (or perhaps even as a professor ready to give a grade) devoted to checking that the experiment was, in fact, run correctly. Death was then declared—the successful end of the experiment.

The Rabbinate seems to have endorsed this very approach and sought to harness even better evidence that the brain-stem was in fact non-functioning. They proposed the addition of another test, of evoked auditory nerve-brain-stem responses, originally designed by Professor Chaim Sohmer for pinpointing auditory nerve damage.[6] This test stimulated the auditory nerve with a series of audible sounds and traced the nervous response along the known path of the nerve from the ear-drum into the brain-stem. If proper response was noted at the beginning of the pathway at the ear-drum and then ceased in the brain-stem, it could be assumed that general brain-stem function had failed. However, despite its objectivity (this was trumpeted by the Rabbinate) and visible available output (a graph of response peaks traced electronically) this test was dismissed as unnecessary by Hadassah.[7]

This represented an ironic reversal of positions. The Rabbinate stressed that the onset of *death* was cessation of respiration, yet looked for an objective test to measure its physical *cause* in the brain-stem. Hadassah, on the other hand, without mentioning actual death (not even the "point of death" used earlier) chose instead to define *brain-death* as the end of brain-stem function, yet stressed the measurement of its *effect*—apnea. So sure of brain-death were Hadassah's doctors after viewing apnea in the patient, they rejected the need for any other testing. The two sides moved in completely opposite directions. The rabbis started from clinically observed phenomenon and looked for a way to connect them to hidden biological causes. The doctors, on the other hand, started with a buried biological fact and looked for a way to move it outwards into an observed clinical expression.

Despite the absence of the actual term, it seems that for the doctors of Hadassah, *death* was a medical fact that existed deep within the hidden biological goings-on of the human body. As sociologists of medicine have pointed out, the creation of a "medical gaze" in modern bio-medical methodology has been presupposed upon the equation of the hidden bio-molecular processes with the observed medical symptoms of a given patient. For example, Bryon Good described the ways that imaging technologies have served to make biological processes more real for medical practitioners.

# Really Dead?

> Modern imaging techniques give a powerful sense of
> authority to biological reality. Look in the microscope,
> you can see it. Electron microscopy reveals histological
> concepts as literal. Look for yourself—there it is! [8]

The *actual* state of illness,[9] for some practitioners of bio-medicine,
is deep inside the human body. The realm of the *real* is that which
rests at the usually hidden cellular or even molecular level. Clinical
experience, clinical observation, are reflections of that reality; they
bring it up to the surface. However, the observable clinical symptom
is not what the underlying state of disease *is* in fact. The death of the
brain is a cellular event, but one that can be observed clinically. Scientific medicine "knows" that what is being observed is actually the
result of something taking place at a much deeper level. It is enough
to observe the symptom, to rule out other possible causes, and then
that cellular hidden event itself is known. It *must* be the case, for there
can be no such symptom without *that* very cause.

This is the path followed by the three-stage protocol of brain-death
developed by Hadassah. Observations are made, probable causes
checked and eliminated, and finally, the observed is subsumed into
the web of scientific knowledge and theory. This knowledge is the
product of the scientific medical project—the linking of what is seen
and felt by the patient (or doctor) with their underlying physical,
chemical, biological causes. Law-like chains of causation link the
visible with its *underlying* nature, so that it is enough to view the effect
and the cause itself is known, as it were, automatically.[10]

On another plane, though, despite the dramatic change in their
protocol, for Hadassah the resuscitated individual before them was
still essentially caught in a patient-donor dichotomy. There was no
real need to discuss death itself, for what mattered was whether the
individual should be treated as a patient and given "all normal medi-

cal treatment" or as an organ donor. The trajectory of his slide from one to the other is almost inevitable given the complex of pre-conditions. The main question was when this would occur. The patient moved slowly, but surely, from one stage to the other. Timing of observations was set "for a minimum fixed duration," as "advancement to further stages" was monitored. Brain-death was still the point where all obligations to the patient have been fulfilled. At that point he became part of the transplantation project where obligations to those waiting for his organs began. This echoed the original conception of the CIOMS statement discussed above in Section I.

---

[1] The full text is brought below in the Appendix.

[2] Halperin, "*Hashtalat Lev Beyisrael*," 76. All of the tests in stage three relate to brain-stem function. The Rabbinate wanted to add another test.

[3] Reches has been a vocal participant in many medical-ethical issues. He is currently the Chairman of the Israeli Neurological Association, and the Chair of the IMA's Ethics Committee. He has been involved in discussions involving end-of-life issues for many years.

[4] Aridor, "*Hashtalat Evarim–Hova Vezekhut*," **Haaretz** (December 28, 1989), 16.

[5] In a personal communication he told me that he was involved "from the very beginning" of Hadassah's formulation of the brain-death protocol discussed here. As I noted, no records beyond the protocol itself have been found in Hadassah's archives.

[6] For a detailed explanation of the test, its logic and history see Sohmer, "*Habasis Hamada'i*" which includes an English bibliography.

[7] While I have found no record of the reasons behind their rejection of this test in 1987 (perhaps it was overshadowed by the rejection of the Rabbinate's demand for representation on the brain-death team), a report submitted in 1993 by the acting brain-death committee encouraging the adoption of the BAER test was rejected by the Medical Board. The Medical Board claimed that the "cumbersomeness" of an additional test including the need for an additional staff member to administer it, worried them. They felt that the adoption of an additional test would slow down the process of determining brain-death and adversely affect the supply of donor organs (personal communication by Prof. Charles Sprung, ICU Director in Hadassah and

# Really Dead?

one of the 1993 committee members, and the unpublished report of Brain Death Committee, Hadassah Medical Organization, June 16, 1993).

8 Byron J. Good, *Medicine, Rationality and Experience* (Cambridge: Cambridge University Press, 1990), 72-74. See Stanley Joel Reiser, *Medicine And The Reign Of Technology* (Cambridge: Cambridge University Press, 1978), 169 for an earlier example of the same trend regarding the 'dethroning' of the stethoscope in favor of x-rays.

9 Obviously excluding *injury* where we can often directly observe trauma to a given organ or tissue.

10 This type of thinking about the universal laws of cause and effect in medicine are not exceptional, especially in the generation during which organ transplantation began and during which the doctors transplanting organs in Israel were trained. Consider, for example, this description of post-war medicine: "This increase in the power of medicine is conditioned by a philosophical basis. Disease and death were once thought to be Acts of God but they are now known to be brought about or determined by natural causes which *obey known natural laws*. This is *scientific determinism*. Increase in the detailed knowledge of Nature has widened the conception of the *Reign of Law*. Much of the work of men of science in general and of medical men in particular is done in a spirit which implies that these *predetermined laws* are universal and are wholly beyond ourselves [my emphasis]." (Charles Singer and E. Ashworth Underwood, *A Short History of Medicine* [New York: Oxford University Press, 1962], 747-8.) See also, Richard H. Shryock, "Changing Outlooks in American Medicine over Three Centuries" in *Essays in the History of Medicine Rx Honor of David J. Davis' M.D. Ph.D.* (Chicago: Davis Lecture Committee, 1965], 182-193.

In a rather caustic (yet characteristic) reply to a critique of neurological criteria for death, R. Tendler and Veith echoed some of this same medical philosophy. Arguing that loss of brain function must be linked to actual destruction of the brain they claimed against those who doubted this: "Their position opposes the great contributions of rational biomedical science that have been made during the last three decades. Discovering the interdependence of function and structure, as exemplified by the relationship of altered function to changes in cell membrane receptor sites, enzymes, or nucleic acid polymers, has been the great advance of our generation of biomedical researchers" (JAMA 243:18 [1980]:1808). Here is a clear echo of the bio-medical view described by Good.

However, later on, such a stance was not accepted or welcomed by all. In a careful study of American medicine Rothstein wrote how "Research in the basic medical sciences has emphasized a reductionism made possible by the electron microscope which permitted researchers to study genes' proteins and cellular and sub-cellular structures generally. Reductionism has adversely affected the medical aspects of the basic sciences" (William G. Rothstein, *American Medical Schools and the Practice of Medicine* [Oxford: Oxford University Press, 1987], 246). See also Alexander Rosenberg's discussion of the trend towards reductionism in biological sciences in chapter four of *The Structure of Biological Science* (Cambridge: Cambridge University Press, 1985).

Philosophers of science, biology, and medicine since then have hardly been satisfied with this picture either. The debate over essentialism in illness and medicine is tied to the debate over reductionism in science in general – a broad topic well beyond the purview of this study. I will return to the philosophic questions of essentialism regarding death itself below. For a short, focused discussion of the issues regarding medicine, see Daniel P. Sulmasy, "Diseases and Natural Kinds" in *Theoretical Medicine and Bioethics* 26 (2005): 487-513. For a broader picture in the biological sciences, see Dupre, *The Disorder of Things* (Cambridge: Harvard University Press, 1993).

# 13

# Death as a Status

As discussed above, both the Rabbinate and Hadassah adopted an essentialist definition of death in their respective brain-death protocols. However, this makes the Rabbinate's insistence on being part of the "brain-death committee" somewhat bewildering. True, because of the history surrounding their relationship, the Rabbinate did not fully trust the medical establishment. However, in order to make the best sense of their insistence (to the point of attempting to insert their own medical test—BAER), it is necessary to understand something more of the way in which the Rabbinate viewed its own role in assimilating scientific claims concerning death. On one level, it understood itself (at least in part) as functioning as a rabbinic court responding to the introduction of scientifically based claims of "fact" (just as secular courts do). That is, the acceptance of scientifically-produced evidence (the doctor's declaration of the patients death) was thoroughly filtered through its commitment to its own jurisprudential system. On another level, however, I will argue that there is a connection between the Rabbinate's desire to be an active participant in the actual declaration of death with both general sociological conceptions of death and more unique halakhic constructs of status.

In order to explain these relations, one must understand some of ways that scientifically-produced evidence and facts are subsumed

# Really Dead?

into the larger halakhic framework. For a rabbinic court they do not stand alone as objective representations of the real world. This chapter will argue that in contrast to the conception of biological death found in the Hadassah protocol, for the rabbis, the patient's status was not equivalent to biological fact. Rather, biology was used only to establish unequivocally the halakhic-legal *status* of the patient. Death remained a halakhic category whose presence or absence may have been *indicated* by scientific tests, but which ultimately belonged to the parameters shaped by halakhic reasoning and not the world of scientifically-measured potentials.

While the biological state of the patient was certainly important in determining his status, it alone did not supply what the rabbis would need to know in order to agree that this patient was halakhically dead. As Yaakov Levi had argued in his early article on brain-death, the *meaning* of death for the halakhah may not necessarily be reducible to biology. For Levi, it was a social-religious category which made use of biology in order to determine halakhic obligations towards the dying patient. It can be argued that the Rabbinate also held to a similar non-reducible understanding of death. For them, the meaning of death went beyond the physical state of the patient and was dependent upon how the halakhic system understood that state. What I will argue is that the *state* of death for the Rabbinate was not simply determined by medical-biological *facts*, but as these facts were understood through specific halakhic conceptualizations.[1]

As the halakhic system functions as a jurisprudential system, like any such system judicial fact is produced through the very specific rules of that system itself. (This is halakhic jurisprudence at work.) The Israeli halakhic religious-court system, as I will demonstrate, is remarkably robust in its adherence to its own particular conceptions when offered scientifically produced evidence. Historically, the *halakhah* has not balked at utilizing such evidence in order to reach halakhic conclusions. *Posqim* throughout the ages have utilized objective evidence and tests purported to establish facts in cases where halakhic decisions hinged upon obtaining objective knowledge in various ways. While the ideal halakhic evidence is eye-witness testimony of two competent Jewish adult males before a court, the instances of accepting a wide variety of other means of gaining what is known in the *halakhah* as "knowledge of facts despite the lack of witnesses" are so varied and many that eye-witness testimony is but one of many actually accepted types of evidence.[2] In varying degrees, the *halakhah* has accepted circumstantial evidence, presumptions and statistical inferences to arrive at halakhically valid evaluations of facts relevant to different cases.[3]

Already in the Second Temple period we find that the Sages used astronomical calculations to test the validity of testimony which they received from those who claimed to have witnessed the new moon's celestial appearance.[4] Another instance of "scientific" testing to obtain otherwise unavailable answers is a tale recorded in the Medieval *Sefer Hasidim* which described how one of the *Geonim* dipped the bone of a deceased father in the blood of two reputed offspring each of whom was claiming that he alone was his son and rightful heir.[5] When the blood of one, but not the other, was absorbed by the bone, that individual was proclaimed the real son.[6]

In line with this ancient tradition, at the start of the 21st century the Israeli Police Rabbinate turned to R. Wozner of Bnei Brak seeking advice as to the halakhic acceptability of DNA identification used both for the identification of otherwise unidentifiable corpses and for establishing the identity of crime suspects.[7] While a full examination of the ways in which scientific evidence has been used by halakhic adjudicators is beyond this study, I believe that the Rabbinate's concerns with Hadassah's protocol reflect the same general approach found in these instances.[8] Scientifically produced or objective proof has quite often been viewed not as evidence of ontological fact, but only as a means of confirming that the subjects of these proofs fit requisite halakhic categories.

The brief examination of a legal case which raised important conceptual issues regarding the use of Human Leukocyte Antigen (HLA) tests for the establishment of paternity will help to explain this approach. A case before the Ashdod Rabbinical Court in 1981 required that the court rule upon the paternity status of a recently divorced husband.[9] He had formerly both acted as father to, and claimed paternity of, a minor child, ostensibly the product of the now defunct marriage. HLA evidence was introduced which excluded the paternity of the father.[10] In his decision (which underwent revision regarding his understanding of the value of the exact results of this particular HLA test) R. Shlomo Dikhovsky clearly weighed the value of the scientifically produced evidence against other *presumptive* evidence in the case. He certainly did not treat the scientifically produced evidence as an absolute objective measure of reality.

The general halakhic arguments for assigning paternity are usually based on the presumptions that a- the majority of a married woman's sexual relations are with her husband; b- one who is accepted by the community as the parent of a child may be assumed to be the actual parent, despite any later denials on the presumptive parent's part. Both of these presumptions lead to the conclusion that a woman's children born during marriage have been fathered by her husband. R. Dikhovsky quoted from an earlier decision wherein blood tests to establish paternity were used.

> In the case where we find a child whose blood [type] is different than that of his [presumed] parents, against our will we must say that in this case the child is an exception to the usual majority where most children's

blood [type] is similar to that of his parents and according to this, the basis on which we understand that the child is of his [presumed] father is disturbed. … More exactly, we find here two presumptions of a majority of cases; if we say that the child is of his [presumed] father's lineage in order to uphold the presumption that the majority of sexual relations are with the husband, against our will, we must then say that the child has left the majority of cases wherein the blood type of children is identical to that of the blood type of one of the parents….[11]

In this decision, scientific evidence was treated basically as another legal presumption concerning the behavior of a given majority and not as a discovery that reveals to us something about reality on its own. With respect to the halakhic presumption, the subject of the presumption is the sexual behavior of the wife; in the scientific presumption, the subject is blood types transferred genetically between parents and offspring. Scientific evidence is not treated as descriptive of an ontological reality—but rather only as some statistical majority which must be weighed against other known statistical presumptions.

However, R. Dikhovsky differentiated between these two types of presumptions. One describes a "natural majority" and the other "a majority dependent upon custom and man's will."

If we come to weigh these two presumptions, the majority of tissue typing tests versus the majority of relations being with the husband, we see that the first presumption is certainly a natural presumption that does not depend upon man's customs, and it is an absolute

majority such that we need not be concerned with minority cases of exceptions.[12]

His conclusion is that sociological presumptions are made of flimsier
stuff than those found in nature. If we need to choose between the
two, exceptions to those presumptions which seek to describe human
behavior are more easily accepted than those dependent upon nature.
According to this, he was willing to dismiss the paternity presumption of the now divorced father and to absolve him of child support
payments.

On the other hand, however, logically such a dismissal would
mean that the child herself (who must have been fathered by someone) is the product of an adulterous union and could have the halakhic status of a *mamzer*.[13] Unless the woman could claim that she
had had relations with a Gentile, it would appear that the child had
the status of a *mamzer*. However, this did not occur in this case. In fact,
R. Dikhovsky's decision specifically excluded this possibility. He
noted that traditionally the application of *mamzer* status is avoided so
long as some reasonable doubt concerning the circumstances of
conception can be found. In this case, as the statistical certainty of the
HLA test denying paternity admitted of a .4% chance of error according to his sources, he was willing to conclude that this tiny margin is
enough to raise doubt as to whether the child is "absolutely not" the
offspring of the reputed father.[14]

This decision utilized the objective results of this test in a fascinat-
ingly complex way. They were not used to construct an ontological
picture of a certain, scientifically proven reality, but rather only as
part of usual halakhic jurisprudence. This meant that the results
became but one of various presumptions weighed against each other
when no direct testimony was available. The objectivity of the test was
acknowledged as trumping a more subjective presumption – but only

as part of the familiar halakhic process. The evidence created by the 99.6% certainty of the HLA test was not assumed to represent a complete biologically, ontologically valid portrayal of kinship relations. Rather, the test was used quite selectively in order to help construct a picture of kinship relations circumscribed first and foremost by halakhic ideas and ideals concerning paternity and *mamzerut*. It was another, albeit stronger, presumption concerning actual status.

By comparison, the Israeli Supreme Court, in its decision on braindeath, treated the medical establishment's embrace of these criteria as creating actual facts which defined death — not jurisprudential points for consideration.[15] Regarding paternity, the Israeli secular court system has utilized HLA tests as stand-alone tests even for positively establishing paternity (and not just eliminating suspect paternity lines). As Frimer pointed out, the Israeli civil courts were more inclined to assume that the objective scientific certainty (or near certainty) of the test was enough to disprove or prove familiar relation.[16] The Israeli secular court system was also aware of the problem of rendering a child a *mamzer* as a result of this testing, yet it dealt with this difficultly quite differently. As the weight given to HLA tests by the secular courts was so great, if the "good of the child" would be compromised by allowing their use when results could render the child a *mamzer*, they were either not to be used or their results were to be suppressed![17] That is, for the secular court system, these tests were a reliable reflection of a reality whose tracks had been covered by time and distance. Now, overriding concerns like the "good of the child" might lead the court to not use them at all; or perhaps the civil rights of presumptive parents may disallow their court ordered administration. However, once the results become known they carry the weight of *fact* — crushing anything else that may lead to different conclusions.

## Really Dead?

In his decision regarding the applicability of HLA testing in paternity cases, the High Court judge and Jewish law expert, Menachem Elon wrote:

> It is well known, with no need for proof, that the ways of proving facts in paternity cases, when they are based upon the testimony of the involved parties, are difficult and tiring. ... It appears to me that [due to] the difficulties ... the court should ... in every paternity case utilize, *as a first resort* [my emphasis], the test for tissue typing.[18]

However, due to the problems that may arise from proving paternity in cases where the results may prove problematic for the child himself, Elon, following precedent to value both the "good of the child" and the Jewish attitude which aims at not disturbing presumptions concerning the *kashrut* of families (not labeling already accepted families as *mamzerim*), he argued that the above objective test not be used in these cases. His argument is not based on the balancing of halakhic presumptions. Rather, for him, the scientific surety of the tissue typing may threaten the good of the child.

> In my opinion, when the question stands before us whether to privilege the obligation and right to arrive at the ***truth*** through the test or to prevent the possibility of undue harm to the standing of the child in exposing his legal disability, it is proper and correct to choose the good of the child... [emphasis added].[19]

The scientifically valid test cannot, in the secular court, be subsumed into the halakhic categories of "majority" and the like. It stands alone as a reflection of the true state of affairs. As such, the only alternative to prevent this truth from harming the child is to avoid the use of testing altogether in "dangerous" cases.[20]

The rabbinic court, however, viewed these tests quite differently. They represented not proven fact against which other claims about the status of those tested rang hollow, but rather they presented a certain picture of reality which needed to be inserted into the entire halakhic apparatus of majority presumptions. While "natural presumptions" (ie, those scientifically produced and proven) may be weightier than others, they remain presumptions.

Another example of this circumscribed use of scientific evidence in halakhic jurisprudence is found in the responsum of R. Wozner mentioned above.[21] The Israel Police Rabbinate had turned to R. Wozner with several questions concerning the acceptability of DNA-based evidence for a number of purposes. These ranged from identifying disparate body parts to ensure proper burial to establishing blood relations among the living. The experts consulted by R. Wozner's rabbinic court stressed that in terms of eliminating genetic matches between samples, the tests used were, "clear and certain, with no doubt" as to the result's validity. In other words, for the experts using DNA technology in Israel at the time, elimination of genetic matches could be considered full and final proof with no need for any other evidence.

However, just as R. Dikhovsky was hestitant to grant the HLA test automatic truth value, so too R. Wozner refused to view this scientific test as determinate of any actual physical reality. After asserting that any identification must be carried out in conjunction with a competent rabbinic court, he wrote:

> A DNA test—even though statistically it is considered a complete identification, in any case halakhically we

> cannot consider it as certain, rather it must be weighed
> as either a complete or simple majority, or as a fully
> clear, intermediately clear or weak sign.[22]

Apropos of this categorization, R. Wozner was conservative in the use of DNA evidence, only relying on it for the purposes of reassembling body parts for burial, but not for identifying *mamzerim*, corpses or for rendering a guilty verdict upon criminal suspects.[23]

Both here and in the earlier case, it is clear that scientific evidence is not something that circumvents the traditional halakhic evidentiary process by presenting to the rabbinic court or *posek* an unfiltered view of reality. Rather, this evidence is carefully assigned a role only as part of the web of traditional considerations which serve to determine the outcome of halakhic debate over unclear cases. In this fashion, the *halakhah* shares with other judicial systems a certain reservation over accepting scientifically produced evidence as certain fact.[24] Aside from the technical discrepancy between "fact" and "evidence" in terms of proper evidentiary rules, this difference reflects a different conceptual understanding of what a given fact *means*. A DNA mismatch may for the biological researcher produce certainty that an actually real state of affairs pertains, but for the *poseq*, it is only part of an essentially halakhic-judicial process and so must wait in line along with every other presumption.

All this, then, illuminates the way that the Rabbinate, adhering to its role as the highest rabbinic court in the land, viewed the process of declaring brain-death. While for the medical doctors of Hadassah, the measurements of brain-stem death were meant to establish the physical-biological *state* of the patient, for the Rabbinate measuring death could easily be understood as a matter of placing the patient into the proper halakhic, and not merely biological, category. Despite arguments that biological reality was equivalent to the halakhic definition of death made by R. Tendler and even by R. Yisraeli,[25] rabbinic expertise was needed not only to ensure that the doctors were exercising proper care, but to correctly identify the halakhic *status* of the patient.[26] Furthermore, because the question at hand was one of *status change*, from living to dead—and in an especially liminal case, the patient floating in an unclear comatose state—what was required was rabbinic *witness* to the change of status.

Witnessing is related to another conceptual point of halakhic jurisprudence. For the *halakhah*, as I mentioned above, the preferred method of providing evidence in any legal case is direct eye-witness testimony. When dealing with changes in personal status, archetypically marriage where the bride's status changes from single to betrothed to married through the wedding ritual, the act of witnessing the status-change itself is an essential part of the ritual. That is, without the very act of witnessing, no status change is or can be incurred, despite the proper performance of all parts of the ritual and the agreement of both parties. These witnesses are not part of a potential clarification process, watching to ensure that the wedding ritual was properly conducted in case of later disagreement, as are witnesses to the sale of property, for example.[27] Rather, their presence is part of the ritual itself. Without them, no change in status is possible.[28].

The reason for this insistence, especially regarding changes in status, is explained by the Rambam when discussing divorce—the converse of marriage—but its equivalent in terms of the change in status incurred.

> It is impossible that she will today [before divorce] be
> prohibited,[29] and one who has relations with her is li
> able for the death penalty and tomorrow she will be
> permitted with no witnesses. Accordingly, if she was

# Really Dead?

given a writ of divorce alone or even with one witness,
this is not considered a writ of divorce at all.[30]

In a comparative-law-based article on testimony in halakhic jurisprudence Shlomo Hafets labels this testimony "constitutive." "This
testimony is an integral part of the fact itself. The witnessing creates
this fact and without it, the fact has no independent legal existence."[31]
Hafets explains that the constitutive nature of this act of witnessing is
an expression of the true conceptual nature of testimony itself—a
combination of both observation and judging of facts.[32]

I believe that this peculiar need for constitutive testimony relates
to two different cultural planes. One is a sociologically-based desire to
have the ephemeral change of status—which is nowhere physically
noticeable yet carries very real cultural and legal consequences—
witnessed by the community at large. This is in line with the thoughts
concerning rites-of-passage rituals famously expounded by Victor
Turner.[33] From graduations to funerals, the need to open these rituals
to the public stems from the desire to grant social solidity to the new
status of those undergoing them. Here too the new status—a new
place in the webs of cultural meanings (to use Geertz's famous
phrase)—is granted by the gravitas of the presence of community
representatives in their act of serving as witnesses to this change.[34]
The new status is granted weight and depth—reality—by its public
perception.

This desire to concretize the ephemeral, to make it *real* by bringing
it into the public sphere, is not uniquely located only in the desire of
the Rabbinate to be part of the team that will declare the death of the
patient. Rather, it is part of the constitution and action of that very
team itself. As noted above, Hadassah's three-man team which would
finally sign the death certificate and declare death, functioned mostly
to affirm that all the conditions for brain-death had been fulfilled and

that all the tests had been completed. This team itself did not actually perform these tests. Rather, as an affirmatory body, one charged with concretizing the move from patient-to-donor by signing the proper forms, they acted symbolically as well. These "three wise men" (the traditional minimal number for a Jewish court) publicly affirm the patient's shift in status. To echo the words of Maimonides: It is impossible that today he is a patient, and any bodily harm to him is illegal and tomorrow he will be an organ donor, cut apart to help save the lives of others, without witnesses.

However, for the Rabbinate, this patient remains poised between the world of the living and the dead represented by the halakhic constructs of each. It is their expertise, their witnessing, which must be part of the death-declaring process—even more so than that of the doctors whose claim is based only the physical and the biological. Understanding this brings us to the more conceptually based second plane. Just as is true for other cultural systems, the case can be made for the halakhic system that it serves to construct the kinds or categories of things which make up its world and so, in turn, its own reality.[35] Such "construction of reality" has been the focus of much thought since Berger and Luckman's declaration that "social structure is an essential element of the reality of everyday life".[36] They described how "typificatory schemes" are used to classify others (and ourselves)—dictating our interactions on both local (personal) and global levels. Our actions, based upon these schemes, in turn reinforce those very classifications as our comprehension of our interactions in the world are understood as resultant of these classifications.[37] The very "lucidity" of our everyday world depends upon these classifications.[38]

Berger and Luckman exemplified this by describing the interactions of an *American* with a *European* or *Englishman*. On the personal level, each tailors his behavior towards the other in accordance with the expectations that such a typology suggests to him. The responses to these actions are similarly labeled as "typical" and so forth. On the more global, impersonal level, a picture of the *Englishman* is being created. Through habituation, these classifications become institutionalized—seeming ever more objective, more ontologically firm.[39]

As Peter Winch (writing about the same time) pointed out, it is the inseparability of our world from the language that we use to describe, discuss and detail it that makes it, our reality, very much a product of the classifications which we use as part of our language.

> Our idea of what belongs to the realm of reality is given for us in the language that we use. The concepts we have settle for us the form of the experience we have of the world.[40]

Following Wittgenstein, Winch argued that our "rule following behavior" is essentially a means of ascertaining what we mean by "the same."[41] That is, how we determine the classifications discussed above, how we group the distinct items we encounter in our experience, is what allow us to make sense of the world.

One of the most insightful contemporary commentators who has concentrated on the various ways that our own conceptions construct our world for us is Ian Hacking. In discussing a wide variety of social constructions, Hacking has focused just on this question of "sameness." For him, the often acrimonious disputes over the ontological weight of what we find in the world are reflections of our conceptions of the classifications and categorizations we use to understand the world around us. On the most basic level, he divides theorists into nominalists and, what he dubs, "inherent structuralists."[42] Strict nominalists view the "kinds" of things we find in the world as products of our own creation: All we can be sure of is that there are *things*, but any classification or grouping of them is our own doing. Those once called "realists," however, assert that the groups, classifications, *kinds* of things into which the world is divided, *discovered* by good scientific investigation—be they species, sexes, diseases or atoms—are ontological categories.[43] The world has "inherent structure" beyond (or beneath) what those who live in it may conclude. However, his most important point, exemplified through cases as disparate as child abuse, rocks and missile guidance systems, is that these classifications themselves (irregardless of their conceptual genesis), form the world for its inhabitants. Describing what a *child* is today, Hacking writes:

> Our idea of what a child *is* has been formed by a scientific theory of development. It forms our whole body of practices of child-rearing today, and, in turn, forms our concept of the child. Those ideas and practices form children themselves, and they also form parents. The child, its playmates, and its family are constituted within a world of knowledge about child development.[44]

What he means is that once a community ascribes to a *theory* (a "typificatory scheme") which supposes, proposes or proves that children develop through certain stages as they grow, the *meaning* of what it is to be a child is filtered through that scheme. The *child* is part and parcel of what is understand about development. Not only the *idea* of the child, but all the ways in which a culture or community interacts with *actual* children (schooling, play, food, clothing) are informed by their conception of "what a child is" (which help to reinforce these very conceptions, á la Berger and Luckman above).[45]

One final example will show how even in the "exact sciences" theoretical conceptions play a large role in constructing the real.

# Really Dead?

Philosophers who have discussed the problems of "natural kinds," have frequently used the identity of water as an example.[46] When one ascribes to a theory which groups things by molecular structure, and identifies things by their constitutive parts, one may come to identify water as $HRR_2O$. Water *is* $H_2O$; that is its essence. Now, such identification, as Soames has made clear, is actually a short-hand for a lot of complicated theory about atoms, electric charges and the like.[47] Clearly, our understanding of what water *is* depends upon all this theoretical information.[48]

However, as Canfield, Donnellan, Laporte and Khalidi have all pointed out, this theory-based identification suffers from theoretical indeterminacy.[49] For example, such a categorization ignores isotopes such as $H_3O$ (heavy water) from this definition of water and leaves one, when confronted by $H_3O$, wondering if there are two types of water or water and something else or perhaps that this identification of water is off in some other way. Here is a fine example (albeit simplified and streamlined) of the *construction of reality* via our theories about the world – even scientifically based theories. (I will return to this discussion below.)

Now, as the conceptual *forms* (to use Hacking's term) reality in this way, in accordance with theories about that reality, the claim that this holds for the system of *halakhah* as well is more readily understood.[50] The conceptualizations found throughout the *halakhah* form reality for the *posqim* who participate in halakhic discourse. As I discussed above, the importance of status and status changes in the *halakhah* is clear. The conceptual understanding of status is expressed in a rather unique fashion which ties it closely to the actual tangible physicality of the real objective world. This further anchors the halakhically constructed real to the physically experienced actual world in which the *halakhah* consciously operates. This occurs through the idea of *halut*, which describes the actual occurrence of status change that takes place upon the physical matter of this world as it moves from one halakhic realm to another. It is one of the cornerstones of halakhic theory in matters ranging from commerce to *kashrut* to marriage.

The conceptual construction of the object via its halakhic status is taken as seriously as that object's very physical construction. It can be claimed, in fact, that it is the halakhic status that exerts a stronger pull and carries more weight, in the eyes of the *halakhah,* than any mere physical property. Yohanan Silman has pointed out the realist tendency of halakhic conceptualizations of the physical world. Silman quoted Moshe Zilberg (an expert in what would come to be known as the field of "Jewish law"), one of Israel's first High Court judges, in his description of "halakhic realism."

> The changes that occur in the legal realm – for example: change in ownership (selling, gifting and inheritance) or changes in status (engagement, divorce, widowhood)… are seen not as something fictional, abstract – but rather as real actions in the real world, carrying with them, as it were, those [natural] laws which act in reality. Of course, no one thinks that through a legal act of declaring a lien, the molecular structure of the property changes…. However the legal conception of action and result – that is the relation between the writing of a document and the creation of a lien – is understood through categories of physical causation and the laws of nature which apply to energy, cause and effect, are applied to it.[51]

The Jerusalem Talmud (*Sanhedrin* 1:2) offers a classic example of this.[52]

# Really Dead?

> One who has sexual relations with a three-year-and-
> one-day-old girl is liable for the death penalty by ston-
> ing. If the rabbinic court decides to add a month to the
> year,[53] one who has sexual relations with her is not
> stoned. R. Abin said: "I will call to God on high, the
> God who completes me."[54] The three-year-and-one-day-
> old, [if] the court decides to add to the year, her virgin-
> ity returns. If not, her virginity does not return.

The control that the court has over the Jewish year is expressed as Zilberg asserted—using the language of "real actions in the real world." The girl is presented as having undergone a physical change – the *halakhah* does not speak of just the legal implications of the change of date. Rather it discusses the girl *as if* her actual physical state had changed. The rabbinic construction of legal-halakhic status is given the mien of actual physicality.

Halakhic constructions of actual persons and objects together with their legal-halakhic statuses are presented in this realistic mode using the language of *halut*. In an engaging exchange of articles in an Israeli journal devoted to Torah scholarship, R. Michael Avraham, a rabbinic scholar and former professor of physics, and R. Baruch Kahat, argued over how exactly to understand this status change of an object or person. For reasons that are not necessary to describe here, they disagreed whether *halut* was better understood as a "conceptual object" (Avraham) or an additional "layer of halakhic meaning" more akin to an additional name (Kahat). [55] However, both agreed that the transformation of status described by the *halut* of that status in objects and persons is primary. It is the halakhic status of an object or person which serves to create the variety of rights and obligations associated with those things in the *halakhah*. It is not that these collections of rights and obligations themselves define the object's status (although they may give us a clue as to what it is), but rather they are the product of that individual's or object's status.[56]

With this in mind, the reasons that the Rabbinate wanted to be involved in the actual pronouncement of death become clearer. It is not that the variety of changes in physical abilities, properties, and measurements bring the patient to a condition wherein his organs can now be harvested. These physical signs allow for the Rabbinate to recognize or perhaps name this patient as dead—a status which then enables a new set of actions—including the removal of organs.

R. Yisraeli himself made use of these same categorizations in discussing other cases at the nexus of halakhic status and science.[57] In an intricate and wide-ranging halakhic analysis of the talmudic-based discussion on whether a fetus is to be considered "his mother's limb" or not, R. Yisraeli grappled with a number of issues connected to the fetus' halakhic status—ranging from maternity in cases of embryo implantation to religious conversion of the fetus via the conversion of its pregnant mother.[58] Most of his article was devoted to exploring this latter problem. In doing so, R. Yisraeli made frequent use of the concept of *halut* in describing the change in status – from gentile to Jew – which takes place in conversion.

> …in his [Nachmanides'] opinion he [the fetus] requires for the *halut* of the conversion circumcision [as well as immersion]….
> So we have seen an argument of the *Rishonim* [medieval halakhic scholars] regarding the *halut* of conversion on the fetus ….[59]

There are other examples as well. However, the point is clear that also for R. Yisraeli, personal status change is something that occurs to or attaches to the subject in accordance with the various rules (of conversion in this case) just as described above. The subject (in this case a fetus) is seen as changed via the *halakhah* from a gentile to a Jew.

While both Hadassah's medical staff and the Israeli High Court viewed scientific tests as revelatory of actual physical states and relations, whether this was death or paternity, I have aimed at showing in this chapter instances of how halakhic jurisprudence does not necessarily subscribe to this view. Rather the *halut* of halakhic categories upon the physical objects in the world are often understood as having changed them in nearly physical ways. For those engaged in the halakhic process, the real world, ie that which is actually experienced, is constituted not just of the physical matter out of which it is made and which may be scientifically measured, but also of these physical objects to which halakhic concepts are attached. This attachment, this *halut* of the conceptual upon the physical, offers the halakhic thinker a radically different measure of the real. Halakhic categories and concepts are used to provide "raw" physical states with their actual meaning. This is evinced in the ways that Israeli religious courts were not quick to privilege scientific evidence over more traditional halakhic assumptions. This is also how R. Yisraeli understood the status of the converting fetus. For him the halakhic status was something which attached to the fetus giving it a new identity.

I would like to suggest, then, that this more realistic conceptualization of status can help to explain (beyond the historical circumstances) the differences between the Rabbinate rabbis and the Hadassah doctors. The medical and halakhic conceptualizations of the meaning of death in general differ in important ways. The focus on what is being discovered, pronounced or determined with the pronouncement of the donor's death is fundamentally different for each.

While the predominant view of death expressed throughout a wide array of sources ranging from medical journals to High Court decisions has spoken of death as some combination of biological state and cultural construct, I believe that the bio-medical view of death itself contained within the Hadassah protocol is understood more as biological state than as status. The ethical status of the patient-*cum*-donor is important, as competing medical obligations present an ethical dilemma to the medical staff which must be successfully handled. However, as the focus on death as a biological-medical state informs the ethical, it is primarily this state which concerned the Hadassah staff.

Conversely, the *halakhah* is concerned with status and not state. Death, regardless of its biological component, is primarily a legal status that involves different obligations and repercussions than does life. While status may devolve upon the physical and/or biological state of a given thing, it is not equivalent to that state. Status is understood as something both consciously conventional—dependent upon the witnessing of its *halut* for it to come into being—and yet as nearly physically real. The place that it holds in the conceptual grid described by that legal/halakhic system is one of utmost importance. The seemingly stubborn insistence of the Rabbinate to be part of the team that determines death can be better understood if this is taken into account. While physical states can be determined in different ways—through clinical observation or objective mechanical measurement—a change in status can accurately be recorded only by the expert in the complex web of relations of which it is a part.

The dismissal of the Rabbinate's request (and conditions) by Hadassah as unnecessary was, I believe, made by medical doctors who were intent upon measuring a physical state alone. They mistakenly thought that that was all there was to the measurement of death. As I have pointed out, however, even their own composition of the brain-death team seems to belie this. In pronouncing death, the liminal patient is ushered from one world to the next—from life to death and

# Really Dead?

from the status of patient to donor. The dissimilar view of death as medical fact was confusingly compounded by the Rabbinate's own inability to articulate their own uniquely halakhic realism. The halakhic joining of the physical world to religio-legal conceptualizations was ignored by the medical staff, and not fully explained by the rabbis. As a result, the two sides failed to reach full agreement.[60] The Rabbinate felt betrayed once again by untrustworthy doctors, while the Health Ministry and Hadassah were puzzled by the Rabbinate's intransigence.

---

[1] The question of what constitutes in itself a fact is not simple. Even without delving into the philosophic arguments over what something being true or real means, it is obvious that those measurements presented as medical facts are produced through the manipulation of a variety of technologies. That is, these facts are produced by individuals. It would be impossible to claim otherwise for the technically complicated measures used to ascertain the death of the brain by Hadassah's medical team; it seems obvious that regarding the social/halakhic fact of death that this is so.

[2] See Deuteronomy 19:15-21, Maimonides MT *Gerushin* 13:29.

[3] On evidence in general in the *halakhah*, see Menachem Elon, *The Principles of Jewish Law* (Jerusalem: Keter Publishing House, 1975). More specifically, see Cohen, "Scientific Evidence in Jewish Law," *The Journal of Halakhah and Contemporary Society* 39: 51-94 for a general introduction to these issues. Frimer, "Establishing Paternity by Means of Blood Type Testing in Jewish Law and Israeli Legislation," *Sefer Assia* 5 (1986): 153-195 provides a more Israeli centered view as well as a copious bibliography on different aspects scientific evidence in *halakhah*. Bleich, "New York City Water," *Tradition* 38:4 (Winter 2004): 70-111, offers extensive information on questions concerning an array of halakhic categorizations of scientifically proven facts. His conclusion that the "*Halakhah* is not based upon ontological reality but upon phenomenological perception" (83) is notable. It resonates with his outspoken criticism of brain-death; in America he has long been a counterpoint to the campaign for its acceptance by R. Tendler.

[4] See Maimonides MT *Qiddush Hahodesh* 1:6.

[5] The *Goanim* were post-Talmudic sages of the Babylonian Diaspora who, for the period from the mid-sixth century to the early 11th-century, were the effective arbitrators of *halakhah* for most of world Jewry.

[6] Frimer, "Establishing Paternity," 165.

[7] *Beit Horaah shel Rav Wozner, "Zihui Hilkhati al pi Bediqat DNA," **T'humin** 21: 121-122.

[8] See Elimelech Weistreich, "*Refuah Vemada'e Hateva Bepsiqat Bate Din Harabani'im*," *Mishpatim* 26, no. 3 (1996), for a review of a number of relevant and parallel historical cases in section two of the article.

[9] Case number 1245/81; Decision 378/82 of the Ashdod Rabbinical Court. The decision, written by R. Dikhovsky is found in his article, "*Shlilat Abahut Be'emtza'ut Bediqat HLA*," **Assia** 35 (February 1983): 16-31.

[10] For a more detailed discussion of the actual science of the HLA testing and presentation of the halakhic issues at stake in its use for establishing paternity, see Halperin, Brautber and Nelkin, "*Qeviat Abahut Be'emtza'ut Ma'arehet Ti'um Hariqamot Hamerkazit*," **T'humin** 4 (1983): 431-450.

[11] Dikhovsky, "*Shlilat Abahut*," 23.

[12] Ibid., 24.

[13] A *mamzer* is a child born of a halakhically married Jewish women from sexual union with a Jewish man who is not her legal husband. This child is a Jew, but may not marry other Jews, except for converts and other *mamzerim*. The question of determining the marital status of women is often compounded by the problem of consequentially pronouncing their children *mamzarim*. This status of *mamzer* has often been a point of contention in debates over whether secular marriage and divorce should be permitted in Israel. Those against the repeal of the near monopoly that the Rabbinate holds on marriage and divorce point to the real problem of creating situations wherein women could receive secular divorces and conceive children while still being married in the eyes of the *halakhah*. These children would become *mamzerim*. See Yitshaq Bar-Da, *Mishpat Vehalakhah* (Ramat Gan, 1978) for a detailed examination of the halakhic aspects involved in these cases.

[14] Dikhovsky, "*Shlilat Abahut*," 26. One of the other presiding judges, R. Y. Eliezrov, added a comment wherein he argued that the logic here was faulty. If it was determined that the child was not the offspring of the husband, then automatically she must be considered (at least) a questionable *mamzer* with nearly the same disastrous effects on her future ability to marry. He felt that R. Dikhovsky had argued for a logical contradiction.

Later on in the decision, R. Dikhovsky reversed his conclusion and rejected the validity of this particular HLA test as it was not clear. The child's results had shown, oddly, a complete match to her mother—with no indication of other genetic material. This was a result explained by a child's parents being themselves closely related and sharing much genetic material. However, here it raised a question as to the validity of this particular test result.

[15] Recall their language – "In medical science today, it is accepted by all that irreversible death of the brain prevents life activities...." And how they castigated brain-death opponents who fought "progress in medical knowledge and technique, which allows for reliable determination of the end of life and life activity with the complete and irreversible death of the brain."

[16] Frimer, "Establishing Paternity," 178. This was done in cases Civil Appeal 548/78, 705/79, and others. The court overturned a lower court decision on the basis of an HLA test alone in Civil Appeal 417/80.

[17] Ibid.

[18] Civil Appeal 548/78, 7.

[19] Ibid., 8.

[20] While the decision in general was accepted by the entire court, one of the three judges in the case disagreed with the inclusion of any discussion of a child's personal status. Justice Benito felt that as personal status was the purview of the religious court system, the secular court system could leave them to deal with these repercussions of tissue typing, (See pp. 16-17 of the decision).

It is also interesting to note that in the most comprehensive article on the subject of scientific evidence in the Israeli rabbinic court system (Weistreich, "Refuah vemada'e Hateva"), the author repeatedly claims that the continued use of presumptions in halakhic legal discourse is misguided. It reflects, in Weistreich's opinion, an outdated attitude towards science based on pre-modern assumptions that scientific evidence reflects expert opinion less than objective fact. "[Modern scientific facts] are essentially objective.... This is a new type of knowledge which was not known in traditional medicine..." (453). See also page 461. For Weistreich, a court which does not accept these facts is lacking. Unfortunately, so is his aquaintance with the large literature which explains how scientifically produced facts are, in fact, produced. See the works by Golan, Jasanoff, Lynch, Alder and Cole mentioned below. See Karin D. Knorr-Cetina, The Manufacture of Knowledge (New York: Pergamon Press, 1981) for a study of this issue.

[21] "Zihui Hilkhati al pi Bediqat DNA," 121-122.

<sup>22</sup> Ibid., 122. The terms "majority" and "fully clear, intermediately clear or weak sign" relate to the ways that traditional presumptions and identifying features respectively are classified in the halakhic analysis of evidence used for identification, whether it be of objects or persons.

<sup>23</sup> See also, R. Ovadiah Yosef, "*Heter Agunot Memigdal Hate'umim Benu York*" and R. Z. N. Goldberg, "*Heter Agunot Memigdal Hate'umim Benu York*," *T'humin* 23 (2003), 97-109 and 110-119 respectively for examples of how DNA evidence was used in actual cases of identification.

<sup>24</sup> The study of the use of scientific evidence by the judiciary has generated quite a large literature. One of the better collection of case studies that I have read is Tal Golan's multi-site work on the judicial uses of blood typing, pictures and x-rays in courts, *Laws of Men and Laws of Nature* (Cambridge: Harvard University Press, 2004). See also the works of Sheila Jasanoff and Michael Lynch who have both written extensively on the issues of science and law. See Ken Alder, *The Lie Detectors* (NY: The Free Press, 2007) and Simon Cole, *Suspect Identities: A History of Fingerprinting and Criminal Identification* (Cambridge: Harvard UP, 2001) for studies of these technologies and law.

Additionally, we might note that halakhic jurisprudence in general often interestingly delimits what it will consider as evidence for the establishment of a halakhic-legal fact. Most famously, it disallows the admission of guilt by a defendant himself in any capital case (see *b. Sanhedrin* 9).

<sup>25</sup> R. Yisraeli, "*Beheter Hashtalat Lev Kayom*," **Barkai** 4 (Spring, 1987): 32-41, 41.

<sup>26</sup> Lynch has made the interesting point that legal defense against "certain" scientific evidence of guilt, such as O.J. Simpson's crime-scene DNA, has often focused on the ways that such evidence is not a given, but the product of a process. The focus on the process and protocol—the handling of samples, chances for contamination and the like—all serve to put the onus of proof for the accuracy, and more importantly, the validity of results, on the prosecution. But more than this, defense lawyers act as sociologists of knowledge in proving how seemingly unassailable scientific facts are indeed humanly constructed artifacts. (Michael Lynch, "The Discursive Production of Uncertainty," *Social Studies of Science* 28:5-6 [October-December 1998]: 829-68.) This defense strategy may also shed light on the close attention that the Rabbinate paid to Hadassah's protocol. It represents a powerful way of asserting an equivalence between legal (or halakhic) constructs and medical facts: both are human-made artifacts. (See Ian Hacking's discussion of what he dubs the 'unmasking' of scientific fact in *The Social Construction of What?* [Cambridge:

# Really Dead?

Harvard University Press, 2000]: 92-95 and *passim*.) If this is stating the case too strongly, it does serve, at least, to create a more level playing field between adversarial positions when one side comes armed with "scientific proof." However, I am not sure, despite the history of suspicion between the two sides to the Rabbinate decision, that the relationship was as adversarial as that of the prosecution and defense in a murder trial. To a large degree, both rabbis and doctors were attempting to advance the organ transplant project in order to save lives. I am not satisfied with reducing this conflict to a power struggle over authority—I think that the differentiation between state and status serves to better describe the conceptual differences between the two sides.

[27] *Cf.* R. Aryeh Leib Heller, *Qtsot Hahoshen* 241:1. This classic commentary relegates all witnessing to the level of potential clarification only. But he is alone in this conception.

[28] As the Talmud succinctly states in Tractate *Qiddushin* in the name of R. Nahman quoting Shmuel: One who betroths a woman with one witness, we have no doubt that there was no betrothal, even if both of them [bride and groom] agree [that a proper betrothal had taken place] (65a). The Rambam's gloss on this statement, "and all the more so with no witnesses," explains that the change in status must be witnessed by two proper witnesses – in accordance with the ideal expressed in the Torah—"by two [witnesses] will the thing be established" (Deuteronomy 19:15-21).

[29] His actual term here is *rvh*- a halakhic term describing in this case her status vis-à-vis men not her husband. Note that he does not write that relations with her are forbidden, but rather that the about-to-be-divorced wife has a certain status which renders relations with her forbidden.

[30] Maimonides MT *Hilkhot Gerushin* 1:13.

[31] Shlomo Hafets, *"Meqomo shel Edut Bemishpat Ha'ivri," **Dine Yisrael*** 9 (1978-1980): 51-83, 75.

[32] Ibid., 76. He goes on to discuss the evolution of the British jury system as another example of the combined functions of testimony and judgment. *Cf.* Yehoshua Ben Meir, *"Re'ayot Nesibatiot Bemishpat Ha'ivri," **Dine Yisrael*** 18 (1995-1996): 90-142. This technically dense article serves in part to deconstruct the notion of constitutive testimony by searching for instances where the various halakhic authorities have been willing to forgo such acts of witnessing for more circumstantial evidence.

[33] Victor Turner, *The Ritual Process: Structure and Anti-Structure* (Chicago: Aldine, 1969).

[34] See Daniel Wolf, *Minhah Le'Aharon* (Alon Shvut: Yeshivat Har Etzion, 2005), 14. He describes that the granting of gravitus to the witnessed ceremony is one of the central traditional explanations given for the need for constitutive testimony.

[35] So much has been written on questions of social construction that an attempt to explicate all of the arguments surrounding it is well beyond the purview of this work. What follows is but a brief tracing of one line of thought. The first three chapters of Ian Hacking's *The Social Construction of What?* provide a good overview of these questions.

[36] Peter and Thomas Luckman Berger, *The Social Construction of Knowledge* (New York: Doubleday, 1967), 33.

[37] Ibid.

[38] Ibid., 44.

[39] Ibid., 64-5.

[40] Peter Winch, *The Idea of a Social Science and Its Relation to Philosophy* (London: Routledge, 1999), 15.

[41] Ibid., 27. This relates to, of course, in Quine's phrase, "the perennial philosophical problem of induction" (W.V. Quine, *Ontological Relativity and Other Essays* [New York: Columbia University Press, 1969], 117).

[42] Ian Hacking, *The Social Construction of What?* (Cambridge, Mass.: Harvard University Press, 1999), 83.

[43] Ibid.

[44] Ian Hacking, *Historical Ontology* (Cambridge: Harvard University Press, 2002), 21.

[45] Ibid., 22.

[46] Saul Kripke and Hillary Putnam are two of the most prominent.

[47] Scott Soames, *Beyond Rigidity* (Oxford: Oxford University Press, 2002), 273, 79. See also Jarrett Lepin, "Is Essentialism Unscientific?" *Philosophy of Science* 55 (1988) and my conclusions for more on this.

[48] Kripke himself noted (discussing gold and not water) how theory-laden and dependent such identifications are: "Certainly we could find out that we were mistaken. The whole theory of protons, of atomic numbers, the whole theory of molecular structure and of atomic structure, on which such views are based, could *all* turn out to be false" (Saul Kripke, *Naming and Necessity* [Cambridge: Harvard UP, 1980], 124-5).

[49] John V.Canfield, "Discovering Essence," in *Knowledge and Mind*, eds. Carl Ginet and Sydney Shoemaker (Oxford: Oxford University Press, 1983), 107. Keith S.

Donnellan, "Kripke and Putnam on Natural Kind Terms," in *Knowledge and Mind*, 99-103. Joseph LaPorte, "Essential Membership," *Philosophy of Science* 64, no. 1 (1997): 97. Muhammad Ali Khalidi, "Carving Nature at the Joints," *Philosophy of Science* 60 (1993).

[50] It constitutes one of the "subuniverses" which make up society as a whole in Berger and Luckman's phraseology (*Social Construction*, 87-88).

[51] Yochanan Silman, "*Hiqavuyot Hilhatiot ben Nominalizm Verealizm*," **Dine Yisrael** 12 (1984-1985): 246-266, 250.

[52] Unfortunately this most classic of examples may seem perhaps difficult and coldly over-analytical in a case where, if it were an actual one, we would expect the registering of some moral condemnation beyond the actual technical discussion of the legal point herein. Sexual vaginal penetration of a girl less than three-years-old is not considered to be categorically a 'sexual' act. In the words of the *gemara* – 'it is as if one poked a finger in an eye' (Talmud *Bavli Nidah* 13a). An injury such as this, then, to the under-three girl does not change her status to a non-virgin. The same act, however, done to a three-year-old, is considered sexual in nature and the girl is no longer considered a virgin and the perpetrator is liable for full punishment as a rapist of a virgin—the death penalty.

[53] In order to conserve the lunar months of the Jewish year (which lacks approximately 11 days as compared with the solar year) with the actual time needed for the earth's orbiting of the sun, a 13th month is sometimes added to the Jewish calendar. Ideally, this is done on an ad-hoc basis by the sitting high rabbinic court— the Sanhedrin. This may be done at various times, but the month that is added is always another Adar, the last month of the Jewish calendar, such that there is an Adar I and an Adar II. Accordingly, time-related halakhic events measured by year (like maturity) which have already taken place in Adar when it was the 'only' last month, may suddenly be "revoked" by the insertion of Adar I and the renaming of the now real last month, Adar II.

[54] Psalms 57:3. It seems that R. Abin puts this cry into the mouth of the girl whose maturation is not dependent upon nature, but rather upon the religious construct of time.

[55] Michael Avraham, "*Mahi Halut?*," **Tsohar** 2 (Winter 1990): 71-86. A status itself (whether an object is owned or ownerless, a woman married or single) is, in Avraham's understanding, akin to a Platonic idea: a conceptual 'object' and not merely a form or description. Avraham wants to describe metaphysical status in this way so as to understand a number of seemingly difficult cases wherein a woman may be

considered, for example, in the process of being betrothed, upon the fulfillment of some condition by her, to be both married and not at the same time. If "being married" and "being single" are considered as "conceptual objects" and not descriptions, we can understand that in this same woman reside two separate statuses — which do not create a logical contradiction which would arise if "married" and "single" were descriptions. As descriptions, these terms are contradictory; as conceptual metaphysical objects we can acknowledge that one person can contain both of them. Avraham likens this to a soup which cannot be both sweet and salty (descriptions) but must be either one, but can contain both sugar and salt at once (79-81).

R. Baruch Qahat wrote a rebuttal to Avraham's argument in which he dismissed the Platonic notion of 'halut' as wrong and unnecessary ("Od B'inyan Halut," **Tsohar** 6 [Spring 1991]: 175-180). Instead, he claimed that halut represented an additional level of halakhic meaning which is added onto a person or object giving it additional meaning in the halakhic world. For example, a certain structure may gain the new halakhic status of sukah, (a ritually significant booth) resultant of the actions of an individual, despite the lack of any physical change. A new halakhic layer of meaning (a new name) is added to the same physical object, which has legal-halakhic results. Contradictions of status, like married and single, are explained as being unclear as to whether the pronouncement of the name "married" in relation to a woman has been removed or not. Unclear cases are just that — unclear.

56 In contrast, the idea of ownership in secular legal discourse has often been defined as that set of usually exclusive rights to use of an object. Ownership stems from these rights. See, for example, Joshuah Weisman, "Organs as Assets," *Israel Law Review* 27:4 (Autumn 1993): 611-623 and the rebuttal by Tedeschi in the same issue. The halakhah, however, would tend to describe ownership as a certain status of an object. It may be an owned object or an ownerless object. But it is from the status of this object that rights of use (and obligations for damages it may cause) stem and not the reverse.

57 R. Shaul Yisraeli, "Ha'ubar Umamado Hahuqi-Mishpati Vekeger." This work is part of the CD database T'humin + (version 2.0) and was accessed digitally. Therefore references are to the digital version. It also appears in print as "Ha'ubar Umamado Hahuqi-Mishpati Vekeger," **Havat Binyamin,** ed. Neriah Gutel (Qfar Drom: Makhon Hatorah Vehaaretz, 1992).

58 If the fetus itself is merely one of the limbs of his mother, in an animal for example, an injury rendering the mother ritually unfit affects the fetus as well. In

# Really Dead?

humans, if a pregnant gentile mother converts, so too does the fetus. However, if the fetus has some measure of independence from the mother as a separate being, this may not be the case.

[59] R. Yisraeli, "*Ha'ubar*," sections three and four respectively. The first quote opposes the opinion that for a male, fetal conversion is complete without circumcision, as it is impossible at the time of conversion. His circumcision at the age of eight days is like that of any other Jewish male infant and not for the sake of conversion.

[60] As we will see, from the point of view of the Rabbinate, no agreement was reached.

# 14

# Reactions to the Rabbinate

This chapter explores the reactions engendered by the publication of the Rabbinate's decision. In general, these served to highlight the split between state and status, bio-medicine and religion discussed above. This was evident both in the tactical maneuvering undertaken by the Health Ministry (and the Rabbinate itself in response) as well as in further halakhic commentaries and explanations produced by rabbis who felt the need to respond directly to the Rabbinate's position. (R. Yisraeli himself wrote a dense theoretical defense of his *psaq* which aimed at collapsing this split, but, as I will demonstrate, actually reveals the difficulty in taking such an approach). I will also explain how the Rabbinate's *psaq* put them in a difficult position. They painted themselves into an odd corner—getting themselves stuck between those who endorsed the Health Ministry's scientific under-standing of death and other more Haredi-oriented *posqim* who argued that such a position was halakhically untenable.

On November 3rd, 1986 Michaeli personally went to the Rabbin-ate's chamber to receive their decision. More than one newspaper remarked on the fact that he did so with a *kippah* upon his head. For the secular press, this religious sign of respect was perhaps less a symbol of humility before God and more a sign of humiliation. Re-ports that the Director General of a government ministry was forced

# Really Dead?

to make a "pilgrimage" to the rabbis were used to reinforce the feeling that secular society was once again being taken advantage of by the rabbinic establishment.[1] As the staunchly secular daily, *Haaretz,* editorialized:

> The rabbis can mark this day as a victory which they never would have dreamed of ten or twenty or even five years ago—but the majority of the state's citizens and Jews world over are shocked by this new expression of the 'rabbi-ization' of Israel—a secular country.[2]

This attitude reflected only upon the granting of the decision by the Rabbinate and not on its actual content. The very fact that the a religious council was asked for its opinion on a subject which rightly belonged to the realm of secular "scientific" medicine was viewed as an affront to the secular citizenry of the country.

It was merely a matter of days, though, before both the Health Ministry and the IMA expressed deep dissatisfaction with the content of the Rabbinate's decision. They bristled at the Rabbinate's request to add their own observer to the medical team charged with declaring donor death. Michaeli claimed that the Ministry was under no legal obligation to adhere to any of the Rabbinate's conditions and that in their negotiations they had never agreed to abide by any and all stipulations that the Rabbinate might have. The IMA's head, Dr. Ram Yishai, was even blunter, arguing that his doctors had no need for "watch dogs" as they had taken upon themselves the most stringent of conditions in defining death.[3]

So despite *Haaretz*'s rhetoric, Michaeli and Hadassah's staff did not see themselves as having lost any sort of battle between themselves and the rabbis. Pinhas, as well as others involved in the transplantation project, felt that they had asked for rabbinic cooperation and had in fact received it. At Rambam Hospital's liver transplant center, the feeling was that the Rabbinate had indeed decided to give a greenlight for any and all transplants.[4] At Hadassah, plans went ahead for their first heart transplant as they waited for a suitable donor to appear. This would happen in the summer of 1987, not only without any "rabbinic supervision," but with the clear message from the Rabbinate that they had rescinded any perceived permission for these procedures.

In a strongly worded letter from the Rabbinate Secretariat to Pinhas a little over a month after the publication of the *psaq*, the Rabbinate reiterated their stance that without the full involvement of their own representative on the brain-death team, "no permission to perform a heart transplant according to *halakhah* exists." [5] If Hadassah refused to accept their conditions, they threatened to make the absence of permission public.

Neither Michaeli nor Pinhas seemed to have been disturbed by this threat. Pinhas explained that as a hospital director it was ethically impossible for him to accept the Rabbinate's condition. Inserting a rabbi into the process would undermine his own doctors' authority. Alternatively, inserting a religious doctor, as one suggested compromise recommended, was unacceptable. Pinhas felt that this would amount to privileging one doctor over another for non-medical reasons. This, he claimed was akin to "racism" — allowing a doctor's race or religion to influence the medical role that he could play.[6]

Michaeli saw the implementation of the Rabbinate's condition as impossible on a practical level. He stressed that both morally and legally, it was impossible to obligate either secular Jews or non-Jewish Israelis to agree to this non-medical condition.[7] In his opinion, the Rabbinate had agreed that heart transplants were fundamentally permitted by the *halakhah* and more importantly:

# Really Dead?

> The implication of this decision is that a *"psaq halakhah"* [was granted] explicitly determining that the determination of death lies in the "respiratory center," in accordance with accepted medical criteria and [that this] is acceptable for the *halakhah* as the determination of death.[8]

In other words, Michaeli saw the Rabbinate's decision as an agreement to accept the modern medical definition of death as proper in terms of the *halakhah*.

In an official letter to the Rabbinate he attempted to differentiate between the purely medical and the public-ethical aspects of the determination of death.

> As noted in the correspondence between us, the issue of determining death, through relying on the diagnosis of damage to the brain made by doctors, is concluded. On the other hand, procedures such as this, as they are in many ways sensitive matters, require the utmost attention and understanding on the variegated ethical and public planes.
>
> ...
>
> I understand the need for an option to consult with authorized representatives of the Rabbinate with expertise in organ transplantation. The role of these representatives, who will have received our authorization, will be to be available, after the fact [of death determination], to those Jews who are so inclined to turn to one of those representatives in order to advise the family and to affirm that the decision concerning transplantation was indeed in accordance with the *halakhah*.

These representatives need not necessarily be doctors as
they are not determining death nor are they partners to
any medical decisions, rather they are [there] to assure
the interested public that all the decisions and actions
are in accordance with the *halakhah*....

This definition of the representatives' standing is intended to prevent the need for the Health Ministry to
automatically give similar standing to the representatives of other denominations, including other rabbinic
court representatives,[9] or those of gentile communities....[10]

For Michaeli, then, the role of the Rabbinate was to serve both as a
rubber stamp for the transplantation project and to calm the nerves of
any concerned citizens. The medical decision of determining death
was not something that rabbis need fret over—it was in the capable
hands of the doctors. Michaeli echoed here the same conceptualization
of death that I described above—a biological state to be measured by
those expert in scientific evaluation. How could the rabbis have
mistakenly thought otherwise? Their "representatives need not necessarily be doctors as they are not determining death nor are they
partners to any *medical* decisions." It is not hard to understand why
the Rabbinate would be insulted and angered by the patronizing tone
of Michaeli's letter. In essence, while the Rabbinate had expected to
play an active role in determining death, once they had pronounced
that in theory brain-dead patients could be used as organ donors, in
Michaeli's eyes their role was over.

Just over a month later, Michaeli issued a general directive to the
entire medical community stipulating official guidelines for "special

transplants." Included were the Rabbinate's decision, a summary of the World Medical Association's position on organ transplantation and his own response to the Rabbinate (quoted above). The actual directive included five points.

1. Determination of death will be performed separately and independently by three doctors...

2. Each of these doctors will prepare a document written and signed by him addressed to the hospital director, regarding the findings upon which death was diagnosed, which affirms that the determination of death was performed correctly.

3. The hospital director will ensure that informed consent of the donor's family is received, signed by two doctors or a doctor and a nurse of the department in which the donor is hospitalized.

4. In the event that the family wishes to consult with a representative of the Chief Rabbinate, one should refer them to the hospital administration or chief of hospital services [in the ministry] or the Rabbinate, to allow the family, without delay, to consult with one of the advisors from the agreed upon list that will be supplied by the Rabbinate to the hospital services and office of the General Director of the Health Ministry.

5. The hospital director will appoint a doctor to be responsible for recording all relevant cases and collation of all relevant documentation. Upon the receipt of permission, as noted above, the surgical staff will be authorized to perform the actions necessary for transplant. Authorization will be given in writing by the hospital

director and recorded in the medical chart of the donor.[11]

These directions are essentially administrative and seem to have
been written with an eye towards potential legal problems by insisting on establishing a clearly written paper trail of decisions and
authorizations. Any actual commentary on brain-death and transplantation was supplied by the attached Rabbinate's decision and a summary of the World Medical Association's position paper from their
annual meeting held the previous year in Buenos Aires. This paper
was concerned primarily with ensuring the doctor's ethical obligation
to his patient, whether donor or recipient, by stressing that donor
death must be determined by those uninvolved with the actual transplant procedure. Regarding the actual determination, it was noted
only that: "Death shall be determined by the judgment of each physician."[12]

From the Health Ministry's perspective, brain-death was now an
established fact; it was also socially acceptable. The search for a likely
heart donor could now begin. This was hardly the 'rabbi-ization' of
Israel so feared by the *Haaretz* editorial writers.

While those advancing the transplant project attempted to present
the question of brain-death as so medically sound and ethically sure
that there was no room for any debate, a number of influential rabbis
did not agree. On the very day that the Rabbinate presented their
decision to Michaeli, R. Waldenburg published his own strong dis-
sent.[13] After expressing his shock and dismay at the recent liver
transplant and the intent to begin heart transplants, he opened with a
comprehensive review of his previous *pisqe halakhah*. The major addition here was his argument concerning supposed support for heart
transplants by other *posqim*. He claimed that the reported reversal of

opinions by *posqim* who had previously forbidden heart transplants were all related to cases outside of Israel.[14] These *posqim*

> ...felt that there was room to allow these operations as they [the gentiles] had permitted them and one cannot forbid [for them] that which they have permitted. [These *poskim*] have reasoned that such procedures are permitted even when the recipient is Jewish. But to come here in our holy land and do such a terrible deed by the hands of Jews, through a Jewish donor and recipient, it is completely shocking and it could not have possibly occurred to any of our luminaries to permit such a thing.... [15]

This argument represents an interesting reversal of the ethical claims put forth earlier by R. Weiss and R. Feinstein against heart transplants in their early responsa. These authors had noted that that even the gentiles had forbidden heart transplants. This fact was presented as proof of the *universal* immorality of the sacrifice of one patient for the sake of another. R. Waldenburg's claim, however, dismissed the gentile world's ethical import. If *they* are willing to behave immorally, so be it—even if in the end a Jew may reap the benefit of such behavior.[16] His argument also revealed the particularism of which the *halakhah* often admits. Waldenburg's statement pointed to an ethic which may very well differentiate between Jews and gentiles.[17] As such, it once again revealed the difference between the halakhic construction of death and its interpretation as medical fact.

As Michaeli and Pinhas argued, death was a biological state. It was based upon scientifically discovered, universally applicable laws. How could one differentiate between death by religion, culture, or race? As discussed above, the IMA's Scientific Advisory Committee's 1969 report on criteria for organ transplants understandingly noted that cross-cultural differences accounted for actual differences in death criteria. Citing the case of the Catholic Church's influence on French transplant proceedings, its members questioned whether Israel should follow international precedent without paying attention to its own special cultural attitudes.

However, this was not the approach that Hadassah or the Health Ministry adopted. The Ministry itself consistently pointed specifically to internationally accepted ethical standards as proof of the correctness of its own approach to organ transplants. The Hadassah protocol was not designed to 'match' any particularistic Jewish viewpoint, but rather to facilitate transplants based upon universal modes of biomedical testing. The use of brain-stem death criteria was deemed scientifically valid, not culturally so. This approach to determining death gained *ethical* legitimacy exactly from its presentation as universally applicable.[18] Even if these criteria did not measure "death," they at least indicated a *medically* normative point where patient-care could be replaced with donor-care. For the Rabbinate, however, only the fact that brain-death did indeed correspond to the quite particularistic halakhic definition of death allowed for its adoption.

Michaeli's protests to the Rabbinate over the use of a culturally particularistic determination of death pointed to two different problems—one conceptual and the other ethical. His shunting of the rabbis to an ex-post-facto advisory position ensured that the actual determination was medical, scientific and universal.[19] Allowing halakhic representatives to participate in the determination of death would make the death of the donor (at least in appearances) a "Jewish" death—something quite impossible from his point of view.

The desire to find a moment of death that contains some measure of choice, but is ultimately *biologically* based (reminiscent of what

# Really Dead?

Gervais advocated), has appeared as one of the 'leitmotifs' in the Health Ministry's discussions of brain-death. The conceptual solidity of this choice of death is anchored in its biological standing, its scientific universality. Michaeli had asked only if the scientifically determined brain-death could satisfy the rabbis' own definition of death. That it had (to his thinking), meant only that the rabbis had finally accepted scientific fact. To begin to enter into negotiations about that death itself made no sense—it was a medical fact, not a cultural opinion. To admit of a Jewish death would unravel this position, conceptually and ethically. This is because a part of the ethical claim for the transplant project is that the organ donors are absolutely— scientifically proven—dead. To admit that this death may be something of a cultural construct would open up the project to more difficult debates than are engendered when brain-death is presented as universal, scientific fact.

The week following the publication of the Rabbinate's position, another *psaq* was issued that directed attention at the halakhic understanding of science and its proper role in halakhic decision-making. R. Shmuel Wozner argued against the Rabbinate's decision in a responsum which included an interpretation of the *gemara* from *Yoma* alongside a strong condemnation of the improper use of science. The former was a familiar explanation of the singular validity of the respiratory test only in the case of complete absence of other signs of life – including those from the heart. The *gemara's* reliance upon a test for respiration alone could be interpreted either as a declaration that the statistical anomaly of continued cardiac activity could be ignored, or as actually being inclusive of cardiac activity. Here, R. Wozner mentioned both of these interpretive strategies.

In his argument against the adoption of scientific standards, R. Wozner pointed to the limitations of scientific claims concerning non-scientific categories. For R. Wozner, scientifically produced evidence

was only valuable as a means of deciding between competing halakhic statements. Such evidence, however, could not be used to
"disprove" halakhically valid statements.

> In this case, has any one of the *Rishonim* determined dif-
> ferently than the *Hakham Tsvi* and the *Hatam Sofer*…
> here, however, we, as students of our rabbis, declare to
> these doctors, that the reality which you wish to deter-
> mine is not real at all and [as such] it does not refute our
> received tradition that so long as the heart lives, the pa-
> tient is still alive. The death of the brain establishes only
> the death of the brain and not the death of the person.[20]

The *real* was a halakhic construct and not something for doctors to
discover.

R. Wozner picked at the same place that other brain-death critics
had: the movement from assessment of organ function to determining
the broader meaning of such an assessment. The "death of the person"
was not primarily a scientific determination – but rather a socio-legal
fact that the *halakhah* had already determined. The equation of the
biological state of the brain with the status of the individual was a
mistaken reliance on science to tell us something that was beyond its
capabilities.

The immediate halakhic responses to the Rabbinate's decision
called both the ethics of transplantation into question and pointedly
accentuated the differences between biology and the *halakhah*. In his
differentiation between death in Israel and elsewhere, R. Waldenburg
stressed the culturally dependent aspect of defining death. R. Wozner
clearly asserted that death was not merely a question of scientific
measurements. These two reactions to the Rabbinate's *psaq* again

opened up those very questions which the Health Ministry sought to suppress in order to proceed with heart transplants.

The rabbis responsible for the *psaq* did not remain silent, however, in the face of this halakhic criticism. In 1987, articles written by R. Yisraeli and both Chief Rabbis were published explaining the rationale and some of the history behind their decision.[21] R. Yisraeli's and R. Eliyahu's articles provided novel halakhic analysis and deserve attention.[22] Each in his own distinct way attempted to properly position both *halakhah* and science in his respective defense of the *psaq*. R. Yisraeli aimed at collapsing the distance between the two. R. Eliyahu focused upon the *halakhah's* dependency on scientific input.

R. Yisraeli addressed the main part of his rebuttal to proving that a clear moment of death, dependent solely upon absence of respiration, with no regard for continued cardiac activity, had been precisely what death had meant for the Talmudic sages, for R. Sofer and R. Feinstein. His approach combined textual analysis with certain historical assumptions. I will focus first on the former and then return to the latter.

In interpreting the responsa of R. Feinstein, R. Yisraeli strove to show that the *gemara* in *Yoma* pointed in the direction of using a singular respiratory definition of death. First, he stressed what he understood as a general agreement in the *gemara* regarding testing only for respiration "at the nose" of the buried victim if his *head* is uncovered first. "...when starting to check from the upper extremities all agree that once his nose is checked that is sufficient. As it is written: 'all that the breath of life is in his nose' (Genesis 7:22)."

He then presented a very clever interpretation of R. Feinstein's reading of the *gemara* designed to prove that only respiration has meaning for determining death. He asserted that there are two options for understanding the disagreement concerning the need to check for respiration when the *lower* extremities are uncovered first. One opinion holds that despite discovering no sign of life at the *heart* we must continue to check "at the nose," while the other is satisfied with this first test. Relying on a traditional commentary on Maimonides' *Mishna Torah* cited by R. Feinstein,[23] R. Yisraeli suggested that for those who held the position requiring that even when no cardiac activity could be detected respiration must still be checked, cardiac activity itself could be understood in one of two ways. Either, one: it was not an important sign of life/death or, two: even though it was an important sign, so long as a more thorough test could be completed (checking the nose) it was necessary to do so—even on Shabbat. In the first case, this would mean that those who argued against them, then, claiming that *only* the heart needed to be tested, viewed lack of cardiac activity itself as a sign of death. In the second case, however, the argument centered not on the importance of cardiac activity as a sign of life/death, but rather on whether or not it was necessary to perform even extra meticulous checking. For those who claimed that even with no cardiac activity, respiration must be checked this was true even on Shabbat. But for those who were satisfied with checking cardiac activity, it was, he argued, only the need to safeguard the sanctity of Shabbat which prevented further checking. Those who argued against further checking on the Sabbath (beyond the heart when a victim was uncovered feet-first) would not argue against further checking—until the nose—on a weekday. To summarize: the argument over the need to check the heart for signs of life focused either on the importance of cardiac activity itself or on the scope of checking required by the halakhah. In the first case, cardiac activity was either a sign of life or not. In the second case, those who were satisfied with only checking for cardiac activity held this position only on the Sabbath—when further checking involved further Sabbath desecration.

The accepted halakhic conclusion drawn from this *gemara* requires that in the case of discovering lower extremities first one must also check until the nose. R. Feinstein himself wrote that the second interpretation of the argument seemed to him to be the better one. That is, the reason for not checking beyond cardiac activity was based on concern for the sanctity of the Sabbath. It did not reflect upon the worth of cardiac activity as a criterion for death. From this, R. Yisraeli drew his conclusion regarding respiration for R. Feinstein. As the argument in the *gemara* centers on the need to check beyond any doubt and not over the value of the cardiac criterion itself, one should assume that if a cardiac based criterion of death was truly important, then when a buried individual was uncovered from the top one would also need to continue to remove rubble until everything that can be checked is uncovered. However, when moving in this direction—from the top down—there is no disagreement. Both sides of this talmudic dispute agree that checking at the nose is sufficient. This proves, then, that this respiratory check is enough to eliminate doubt *despite* any cardiac activity—even for those who want to exercise extra-caution whenever possible, ie those who insist upon moving beyond the heart when discovering a body feet-first. The head-first case, R. Yisraeli argued, proves that checking anything other than respiration "at the nose" is not needed, for lack of respiration "leaves not the slightest of doubts and in this case, the [victim] is certainly dead."[24]

One interpretive problem in R. Feinstein's dismissal of cardiac activity according to R. Yisraeli remained, however. That is the section of his responsum where R. Feinstein admits that discovered cardiac activity cannot be ignored.

> Therefore regarding an individual in whom life activity is seen through the use of an electric radiogram [sic]... he is alive even though he is not breathing. This is like the man who was entombed because he stopped breathing, yet lived afterwards for 25 years. Since there is af-

ter all a real case here, even if it is a unique case – it is still real. Therefore, it would be forbidden to declare such an individual [dead]. On the contrary, we must endeavor to heal him.[25]

Here R. Yisraeli claimed that this is only true when no etiology for the cessation of respiration exists. The doctors may suspect that the patient may again start breathing. The archetypical case presented in *Yoma*, however, is a case wherein the etiology is known – we find a buried victim with a "crushed skull and brain damage." In this case, even proven heart activity will have no bearing upon determining that the victim is dead.[26]

This is an intriguing reading which concurs with the fact that in this section of R. Feinstein's responsum he is discussing resuscitated patients whose status, as well as the nature of their breathing, is indeed unclear. However, R. Yisraeli's conclusion that etiology related to brain injury is enough to override any cardiac activity merely returns one to the argument over the need for actual and complete brain destruction as a necessary condition for characterizing these patients as decapitated and dead. R. Feinstein was unequivocal in demanding the complete severance of any connection between brain and body in order to categorize a patient's continued heartbeat as meaningless. This was discussed at length above.

R. Yisraeli concluded his halakhic arguments by offering an interpretation of R. Sofer's opinion that brought it in sync with the use of brain-death as well. He read the triad of symptoms/tests that R. Sofer suggested not as a list of concurrent tests, but rather as stipulating the inclusion of a respiratory test despite other evidence of death. R. Sofer, in R. Yisraeli's reading, was actually stressing the need to check for the loss of respiration *even* in the absence of pulse and movement.

# Really Dead?

> The meaning of his words is not that we specifically re-
> quire three signs; rather the words teach that if the first
> two signs occur, they [alone] are not sufficient. We
> should not think that if the loss of respiration is enough,
> all the more so the loss of circulation....[27]

R. Sofer's opinion, then, represents the *halakhah* learned from the Talmud's discussion in *Yoma* as explained by R. Yisraeli above. Even if a victim lacked signs of cardiac and neurological activity, as in the case where he is uncovered from his lower extremities, respiration must be tested.

The interpretive agility demonstrated by R. Yisraeli in this discussion is quite impressive. However, his readings, while reasonable in terms of their internal coherence, entail some reverse engineering designed to shift various 'proof-texts' so that they correspond with brain-death conceptions. The question of the validity of such an exegetical strategy is fascinating, but cannot be discussed here. What I would like to point out, however, is that his readings depend upon a number of historical speculations as well, designed, it seems, to bolster his presentation of these sources as in line with contemporary science. In his presentation of the *gemara* from *Yoma* he wrote, for example:

> There is no doubt, that it was also known to our Sages
> that even when respiration had ceased, it was possible
> that the heart would still be beating. ...it was possible
> for this to be proven in the time of the Talmud by [ex-
> amining] those put to death or who had been decapi-
> tated. ...since respiration has completely ceased, even if
> the heart is beating, [the victim] *ayn alav torat chai* [is not
> legally considered to be living]....[28]

As Edward Reichman has written, the Talmudic Sages, who lived in the temporal and cultural milieu of Greco-Roman Galenic medicine, almost certainly did not understand respiration and cardiac function as two separate systems.[29] In Galen's view, the heart generated heat which had to be cooled by the introduction of air through the nose. It seems more likely that the checking of the heart and/or the nose was a test for different aspects of some heating-cooling-of-humors function alone.

The parallel text found in the Jerusalem Talmud replaces "heart" with "navel" which also seems to indicate that what was being investigated were signs of breathing, and not circulation. These Sages may have assumed that respiration itself as reflected in the continued function of *any* respiratory organ in the body served as a sign of actual continued life. They may have assumed, even if they discovered beating hearts in decapitated bodies, not that cardiac activity in the absence of respiration was meaningless, but that in such cases it was obvious that no *respiration* could possibly be taking place. The *gemara* in *Yoma* may very well have been seeking to determine which sign of respiration must be checked. Dismissal of cardiac activity as understood today as unimportant in light of the end of respiration seems dependent upon a completely different conceptualization of the function of the heart.

It is then difficult to argue that historically the beating of the heart was ignored because it represented something other than the singular sign of life/death found in respiration. Reichman himself suggests that the argument in the Talmud is perhaps more theological than physiological as in the end it devolves upon a Biblical verse describing the source of life as respiration.[30] It is not at all clear what a beating heart with no other respiratory signs would mean under Galenic concepts.

# Really Dead?

R. Yisraeli, however, unlike others who promoted singular respiratory criteria,[31] chose to build his argument upon a reconstructed past wherein notice was taken of the beating heart, yet dismissed. He did this regarding R. Feinstein, as well, who wrote in 1970 that even if a heart was available for transplant which had been removed from a "certainly dead individual" the recipient was still forbidden to undergo surgery as the patient's chances for survival with his own heart were still better. For example, "There is no doubt that the author of the *Egrot Moshe* knew that the heart which was taken for transplant was still beating, since only this heart was suitable for transplant...."[32]

Here R. Yisraeli uses the hypothetical notion that the Sages of the Talmud knew that hearts *could* still beat in spite of the individual's actual death to presumptively reconstruct some speculative knowledge about what R. Feinstein "no doubt" knew. This, too, regardless of the logic behind his presumption, may not have been the case. As we have seen, some early commentators on the halakhic implications of heart transplants assumed that a heart could be revived after a few minutes of systolic silence and then used for transplantation.[33] It is certainly open to debate, then, what exactly R. Feinstein 'knew' about the state of the heart to be used for transplantation.

It seems that R. Yisraeli used these historical reconstructions to buttress his view that the *halakhah* corresponded to his own understanding of what modern medical discourse had presented as the essential key to life—the brain-stem's respiratory function.

> It is amazing that our Sages, despite the lack of medical instruments used by doctors in our day, relying on their "spiritual powers," found, through the study of writings, those very mysteries of the Creator which reside in the bodies of animals and men.[34]

For R. Yisraeli, then, the decision of the Rabbinate was not merely halakhically valid because it correctly read the relevant halakhic sources. Rather, it was also true – because these readings corresponded to the actual physical world uncovered by scientific medicine. This same world, these same "mysteries of the Creator," had in fact already been discovered by the Talmudic Sages of old. As the traditional texts described a reality which corresponded just to that described by modern medicine there was really no room left for dissident opinions.

However, the interpretive gymnastics that R. Yisraeli required in order to reach the conclusions of his Talmudic and halakhic readings seem to admit of a certain lack of robustness. The argument that he presents necessitates abandoning a simpler reading of the actual Talmudic texts in order to read them as presenting a logical puzzle to be deciphered by weighing logical alternatives one against the other. Only if the sources are passed through a very particular logical prism—assuming that those who held that lack of cardiac signs of life were sufficient did so only on the Sabbath—do they read as R. Yisraeli argued. As he was surely aware, these very same texts could be, and had been, interpreted quite differently. Therefore, he may have added his historical reconstructions, aimed at strengthening his textual analysis, in order to show how his own readings did in fact correspond with modern *medical facts*. This double-sided defense of the Rabbinate's *psaq*, however, did not note that the medically described reality with which it identified was dependent upon a certain type of modern medical theory, which seeking an ethical path for harvesting organs, had only then found in the brain's respiratory control center one essential indication of life.[35]

R. Mordechai Eliyahu, one of the two Chief Rabbis in 1986 and a transplant committee member, wrote a quite different halakhic analysis backing its decision. Although he touched on a large number of

# Really Dead?

topics related to determination of death,[36] the main argument that he developed in his article was concerned with the interesting question of whether the employment of resuscitative technologies on patients who may or may not be saved by their use is permissible. This question was discussed years earlier by R. Weiss in his responsum prohibiting heart transplants. R. Eliyahu pointed out the tension between the obligation to save even a dying patient, even for a short period of time (*hayei sha'ah*) and the prohibition of needlessly extending the life (and suffering) of a patient for whom there is no hope of recovery.

R. Eliyahu maintained that the allowance made in the *halakhah* for the removal of an impediment to death (salt on the tongue and the like) should not be taken as a directive against extending the life of a patient. The *gemara* in *Yoma* certainly advocated transgressing the Sabbath in order to save even those whose long-term survival is not possible. The rescue of these victims, even if they may only live for a few moments is incumbent upon the rescuers. R. Eliyahu wrote: "In the case where the *hayei sha'ah* of the patient is certain, even though shortly afterwards he will die, in any case it is permitted to work to save this patient, even in the face of doubt whether he may only live for another hour."[37]

Recalling the prohibitions against artificially sustaining patients noted by R. Feinstein and R. Weiss, R. Eliyahu maintained that these *posqim* had only prohibited this in the case where there was absolutely no hope at all for the patient. However, if any life at all (even only temporary *hayei sha'ah*) could possibly be saved through the use of resuscitation, R. Eliyahu argued that the *halakhah* required its use.[38]

He then worked his way from this position to the question of determining death in two steps. First, he discussed the different physical statuses of the wounded and dying in *halakhah*. He pointed out that the establishment of a status of *traifa* for humans depended upon the medical decisions made by the anatomical experts in each generation. He cited Maimonides' statement to this effect.[39]

> One who kills a *traifa*, even though he [the victim] eats and drinks and walks in the market—the murderer is exempt from punishment at the hands of man. However, every person is considered to be healthy and one who kills him is executed, unless it is known with certainty that he is a *traifa* and doctors have stated that the injury from which he suffered had no known cure in humans and would have killed him, if something else had not.[40]

The point that R. Eliyahu wanted to make here, as others had done before him, was that the concept of the *traifa* in *halakhah* was a flexible one, linked to current medical knowledge and abilities.[41] While the consequences of establishing such a status lay in the realm of halakhic jurisprudence, the establishment of the status was essentially a medical decision entrusted to medical experts.

The second step in R. Eliyahu's argument was to link this example of deference to medical opinion to the case at hand: establishing the death of resuscitated potential organ donors. The successful resuscitation of a patient who had ceased breathing should not, R. Eliyahu felt, be understood as a "rebirth," but rather as proof that the individual, despite cessation of respiration, had not yet actually expired. Successful resuscitation, then, established that the "test for the loss of respiration that we had performed earlier had not been definitive."

> ...if they [the doctors who may be able to successfully resuscitate a given patient] state that the loss of respiration is not yet an indication of death because it is possi-

ble to revive the patient, then, if the doctors state that a particular loss of respiration is complete and cannot be repaired, because the brain stem has been damaged, and this has been checked and re-checked, they have spoken and they have spoken. They have said that sometimes the respiratory apparatus may restore life, so if they say that in a certain case resuscitation is impossible, then [the patient] is dead.[42]

The logic of R. Eliyahu's argument is only apparent when placed against the backdrop of his previous discussion concerning the very permissibility of resuscitation. If the purposeless extension of life is halakhically prohibited, yet doctors are permitted to resuscitate patients in the hope of extending their lives even by a matter of minutes (hayei sha'ah), it follows that the halakhah has allowed for these doctors to decide whether a given patient's life is to be extended or not. The doctor is not only permitted, but obligated, to use resuscitative technology based on his own medical discretion. If medical opinion is that which allows for the extension of life, then the converse should also hold. A decision against extending a life also rests on medical advice.

The original decision concerning the use of resuscitative techniques and technologies is not made, according to R. Eliyahu, in an arbitrary or automatic fashion. Rather it is the result of weighing two competing obligations: that of extending even fleeting life against not needlessly keeping a patient from dying when there is no chance for any recovery. The halakhah has entrusted medical experts with this initial vital decision. The application of resuscitative procedures is decided upon by a doctor, not just in practice, but in accordance with halakhic theory as well. The question of whether resuscitation is needlessly prolonging a life or has a chance of reviving the patient and restoring some measure of life (even if only temporary) is a medical decision. In this way it is similar to the establishment of *traifa* status. The *halakhah*, then, according to R. Eliyahu, acknowledges that medical experts are required to determine when resuscitation is no longer keeping a patient alive, but is merely forestalling his death.

R. Eliyahu presented the resuscitated patient with no chance of survival as a case which calls out for decisive medical action.

> We must deliberate if it is permitted to play with the individual who is already a *gosses* and has no chance of living. One for whom all medical tests indicate that there is no connection between his brain stem and heart and breathing and has no chance that his respiration will ever return. Yet in spite of this, we continue with the respiratory machinery, which is merely a pump and causes this "patient" pain. He has no life expectancy and no hope of recovery.[43]

This 'patient' (note the scare quotes), by every medical indication, is hardly a patient anymore. He is not able to derive any benefit from the medical care that he is receiving. This being the case, medically, as well as halakhically, his status is no longer that of patient. Rather, medical technology is just preventing him from actually dying. Medical *care* for him is a misnomer; medical *interference* is a more apt description of keeping such a patient artificially resuscitated. Once medical opinion is certain that there is no longer any hope for recovery, the patient's *status* changes from that of one who must be rescued to that of one who must be left to die. This change in the patient's status means that the very same medical technology once dedicated to saving his life is now only an encumbrance to his passing and should be removed.

# Really Dead?

R. Eliyahu agreed with the earlier *posqim* that it is unconscionable to keep such a patient resuscitated merely for the sake of study or organ harvesting. However, keeping the patient respirated for some time in order to make sure that the dismal prognosis is indeed certain is permissible as this is done for the patient's own sake. After some reasonable time period, though, continued respiration is not only unbeneficial, but halakhically contraindicated. That, coupled with his agreement that an individual whose spinal cord has been severed renders him halakhically decapitated, allowed R. Eliyahu to conclude that the removal of life support from such a patient and the harvesting of his heart was halakhically permitted.[44]

The Rabbinate's decision, then, according to R. Eliyahu, correctly reflected the tension in the *halakhah* which mandated both patient care for those capable of sustaining even the most minimal amount of life, while also insisting upon letting those with no hope of any life die. The way that R. Eliyahu constructed his halakhic understanding of the brain-dead heart donor interestingly echoed the very same tensions described 18 years earlier in two of the first *pisqe halakhah* on heart transplants written by Rabbis Feinstein and Weiss, yet reached the opposite conclusion. R. Eliyahu endorsed heart transplantation from those declared brain-dead by medical experts only because the resuscitation that was keeping these donor's organs functional was also improperly keeping the patients themselves from the grave— prolonging their suffering and thus necessitating its cessation. A very brief window of opportunity opened just when the patient had surely died, but his organs were still viable. This window would close when resuscitation would be used only for the sake of organ and not life preservation.

Paradoxically, his endorsement of the doctor's critical role in declaring the *patient* a patient no longer, seems to at least theoretically undermine his insistence upon reserving a role for rabbis as well in that declaration. However, this insistence is better understood given that the window of opportunity for viable transplant organs is provided by the patient's time on resuscitation. The *halakhah* only allows for continued resuscitation when needed to confirm the irreversibility of lack of respiration due to brain damage. Medical confirmation of 'death'—a prognosis of no possible recovery—for R. Eliyahu, is a doubled-edged decision. Once such a prognosis is medically confirmed, the *halakhah* obligates the removal of any impediments to final expiration. Thus the keeping of organs viable through artificially resuscitating a now dead body being denied its final rest can no longer be sanctioned.

The declaration of death, then, both allows for the removal of organs for transplant yet disallows continued artificial resuscitation for organ transplantation's sake. Secular medical ethics have often envisioned the brain-dead patient as "beyond harm."[45] This allowed the ethical harvesting of their organs in order to save the lives of those seriously ill and still very much in harm's way. If the brain-dead donor is conceptualized as such, it is quite reasonable to allow for the continuance of resuscitation until a proper recipient for his organs can be made available. As I have pointed out above, the movement from patient to donor has often been the ethical movement from care of the patient to care of his organs for the sake of another. This "abuse" of medical care, directed not towards the patient himself, but towards another, was that which was so vehemently opposed in earlier halakhic decisions. R. Eliyahu, following Rabbis Weiss and Feinstein, also rejected this secular moral calculus. He repeated R. Feinstein's admonishment that despite the denials of medical experts, the suffering of the already dead-yet-kept-resuscitated, is very real and must be avoided.[46]

That it was halakhically valid for a *medical* declaration of death to be made, then, was not at issue for R. Eliyahu. Interestingly, he saw

# Really Dead?

death as a medical *prognosis*—a way of describing brain-death which had found some supporters in the secular world of medical ethics as well. The fact that such a declaration was so fraught with *immediate* halakhic and moral consequence for the once cared for patient-now-donor, however, was what necessitated rabbinic involvement in this decision.[47] As one of the two Chief Rabbis, R. Eliyahu was directly responsible for endorsing the Rabbinate's decision and its implementation, on his watch, so to speak. The tension inherent in such a declaration, one that paradoxically changed the *status* of the life-support measures taken up until that moment from permitted to forbidden while allowing the slimmest of opportunities for the saving of another life required expert halakhic input. For R. Eliyahu it was not the *status* of the *patient* himself that required rabbinic supervision (this was a medical task), but rather the *status* of the *treatment* given to that patient resultant of the doctor's declaration. Resuscitation was permitted only so long as the patient could benefit from it—even if only doubtfully. The declaration of death removed even that doubt. Artificial life support then became support not of doubtful life, but of a donor's organs. While secular ethicists may have seen no harm in continuing resuscitation for some time so as to allow for the successful preparation of a transplant recipient, this was halakhically prohibited. The patient ceased to be an end and became merely a means. This, in R. Eliyahu's moral construction of the heart transplantation project, could not be halakhically condoned.

The heart-transplant program at Hadassah continued despite the lack of cooperation between the Rabbinate and the medical staff of the hospital. Professor Joe Borman got his chance to transplant a human heart less than a year after the Rabbinate had effectively withdrawn their permission for such operations. On August 25, 1987, Ovadiah Mitzri, a factory worker from Be'er Sheva, became the first successful heart recipient in Israel. While the secular dailies played up this historical event with front-page headline coverage, the religious paper belonging to the Mizrahi religious-zionist party, *Hatzofe*, devoted much less space to this operation, preferring to lead that day's news with coverage of religious-secular tensions over the public screening of movies on the Sabbath. In a small anonymous article, they did quote a statement made by Pinhas at a press conference thanking the entire hospital staff including Hadassah's chaplain who ensured that, "all halakhic obligations" were indeed fulfilled in this operation.[48]

Despite the protests of both the Rabbinate and *haredi* groups, some of whom did not shy away from calling Borman a murderer, no huge public outcry like that which had erupted over the seemingly more benign autopsy practices occurred. The difference may have been that no matter what one thought of brain-death, ultimately, in the case of organ transplantation, lives were being saved. A new medical era in Israeli medicine had begun.[49]

---

[1] Devorah Namir and Gad Lior, "*Or Yaroq Lehashtalat Lev*," **Yediot Ahronot** (November 4, 1986), 3.

[2] Anonymous, "*Rabinizatziah shel Harefuah*," **Haaretz** (November 5, 1986), 7.

[3] Devorah Namir and Michal Politi, "*Harofim Dohim Teviat Harabanut*," **Yediot Ahronot** (November 6, 1986), 3. Michaeli framed this claim as a legal technicality. He cited his Ministry's inability to force doctors to consult with non-medical staff. This is an interesting claim, as the ministry was committed to and had established a Helsinki Committee for the review of human experimentation. This committee, like others world over, was constituted both of medical doctors and other ethical experts including rabbis, lawyers, and academics. Regarding the IMA's claim, we know that the level of "stringency" did not include the additional BAER test desired by the Rabbinate. The criterion itself—brain-stem death *alone*—was also specifically chosen not as a stringency, but rather as a measured expediency in order to move the transplant process along.

[4] Devorah Namir and Gad Lior, "*Or Yaroq*."

[5] Letter from Rabbinate Secretariat to Shmuel Pinhas (Kislev 13, 5747). Note the claim was not just about the rescinding of permission – but that this in itself rendered the unauthorized procedure as non-halakhic.

# Really Dead?

[6] Interview with Shmuel Pinhas, December 13, 2004.

[7] Pinhas, "*Qeviat Regah Hamavet Vehashtalat Avarim Meyuhadot*," **ML** 49:8 (Av-Elul 5747): 8-9, 8.

[8] Ibid., 9.

[9] This is probably a reference to *haredi* groups disinclined to accept the authority of the state rabbinate.

[10] Letter from Dan Michaeli to the Rabbinate Secretary General, R. Yehiel Halevy (December 11, 1986).

[11] Health Ministry General Directive 11/86 (December 11, 1986).

[12] Ibid. Just over a year later, Professor Yoram Less, who replaced Michaeli as Director General of the Health Ministry, issued, for the first time, specific government instructions for the actual determination of death. This directive followed the lead of the U.S. Presidential Commission's Report from 1981 and proposed that both brain-death and cardio-respiratory death were each acceptable ways of determining the "death of the person" (*Misrad Habriut, Hozer Mankal Haklali* 15/87 [November 29, 1987]). This document is deserving of attention, but is beyond the time frame of this study.

[13] Advertisements containing this opinion were placed in a variety of print media paid for by an organization called the Public Committee for the Protection of Human Dignity. It is not clear who in fact was behind this group which was based in *haredi* circles and enjoyed the support of many prominent rabbis. It was through this group that R. Waldenburg's response was so quickly disseminated, but he included it in his formal halakhic work later on.

[14] This refers to R. Tendler's assertion concerning R. Feinstein.

[15] R. Waldenburg, *Tsits Eliezer* 17:66.

[16] There is a large amount of halakhic literature which attempts to delineate the sometimes fuzzy line between ethical and unethical enrichment. See Nachum Rakover, *Unjust Enrichment in Jewish Law* (Jerusalem: The Library of Jewish Law, 2000) for an overview and Aaron Kirschenbaum, *Equity in Jewish Law* (NY: Yeshiva University Press, 1991) for other aspects of this problem. See an interesting exchange concerning societal benefit from Nazi experimentation by the late British Chief Rabbi, R. Jakobovits, in Jeffery Cohen, *Dear Chief Rabbi* (Hoboken, NJ: Ktav Publishing House, 1995), 147-152. It is open to discussion whether accepting an organ taken from one pronounced dead by standards that one would not accept himself is an example of this same type of problem or not.

[17] See Avi Sagi and Daniel Statman, *Ben Dat Lemusar* (Ramat Gan: Bar Ilan University Press, 1993), for a phenomenological treatment of the tension between particularistic and universal ethics in the *halakhah*. See David Novak, "Bioethics and the Contemporary Jewish Community," *Hastings Center Report* 20:4 (1990): 14-17, for a discussion of the pertinence of a particularistic halakhic worldview to general medical ethics.

[18] It is worth noting that this is not always the case in Israeli medical care – even at Hadassah. The current head of the Hadassah ICU, Prof. Charles Sprung, has written a number of articles for professional journals on what he described to me as a Jewishly influenced approach to ICU practice that emphasizes the withholding of care over the withdrawal of care—as the latter is halakhically and, in Israel, culturally, more difficult. See Phillip D. Levin and Charles Sprung, "Cultural Differences at the End of Life," *Critical Care Medicine* 31, no. 5 (Supplement) (2003).

[19] In his article, *"Qeviat Regah Hamavet,"* Pinhas consistently discussed a "medical" (read scientific) definition of death, but also acknowledged the "critical public aspect" of convincing the public to accept this "medical definition" as one of the conditions for the transplant project's success (8).

[20] R. Wozner, *Al Hashtalat Lev*, **Assia**, 42-43 (Nissan 5747): 92-4. He also noted that continued heart function was indicative of actual brain activity which has gone unnoticed.

[21] R. Yisraeli, *"Beheter Hashtalat Lev Kayom,"* **Barkai** 4, (Spring 5747): 33-40 and R. Mordechai Eliyahu, *"Hashtalat Avarim al pi Hahalakhah,"* **Barkai** 4 (Spring 5747): 18-31.

[22] A third brief explanatory article written by one of the Rabbinate's transplantation committee members appeared in the form of a letter addressed to the world's rabbis in the quarterly *Or Hamizrah* in the fall of 1987. Written by the Ashkenazi Chief Rabbi, R. Avraham Shapira, this brief article did not offer much in the way of original analysis, however (*"Harabanut Harashit Leyisrael B'inyan Qeviat Regah Hamavet Vehashatalat Halev,"* **Or Hamizrah** 31:1 [1987]: 66-70). It seems that as Chief Rabbi, R. Shapira merely wanted to reiterate the Rabbinate's stance to the rabbinic public-at-large. Aside from criticizing R. Waldenburg's willingness to publicize his own opinion without consulting with the Rabbinate's committee members or Hadassah's medical staff, the main argument that he offered in support of the Rabbinate's decision was to point out the qualitative difference between natural and artificial respiration. Following the *psaq* of R. Feinstein, R. Shapira argued that only "independent God-given respiration" was a sign of life. However, because of the

masking effect of artificial respiration, only when the "destruction of the brain-stem" was proven, could one be certain that a respirated patient was indeed dead. So long as brain-stem death was not proven, any respirated patient was considered alive and should be treated as such (68-9). Brain-stem death, then, established that the original loss of independent respiration could be understood as the death of the patient. (This was the approach taken by R. Auerbach). R. Shapira concluded his article by noting that the severity of the life and death questions involved in the heart transplant project required rabbinic supervision (70).

[23] This is the *Qesef Mishnah* written by the great halakhic codifier, R. Yosef Karo, author of the *Shulchan Arukh*.

[24] R. Yisraeli, *"Beheter Hashtalat Lev Kayom."*

[25] EM YD II 146.

[26] R. Yisraeli, *"Beheter Hashtalat Lev Kayom,"* 36.

[27] Ibid., 40.

[28] R. Yisraeli, *"Beheter Hashtalat Lev Kayom,"* 33-34.

[29] Edward Reichman, "The Halakhic Definition of Death in Light of Medical History," in *Torah U' Madda Journal*, ed. J. Schachter (NY: Yeshiva University Press, 1993), 148-174, 149.

[30] Ibid., 154.

[31] Avraham Steinberg and Mordechai Halperin both focused on the need to test only for respiration as proof that its cessation alone was indicative of death. However, it is possible to read this source as advocating reliance upon a respiratory test alone only after no other bodily functions – including heart beat – are noticeable.

[32] R. Yisraeli, *"Beheter Hashtalat Lev Kayom,"* 35.

[33] See the comments of R. Rabinowitz during the first IMA symposium, or, even later, those of Prof. Durst: "It is not right to say that we need to transplant a beating heart. The heart needs to beat, but even if we are discussing the death of the brain ... there is a certain moment of cessation of function in the heart. ... After a few minutes we can revive the heart" (*Knesset Law Committee Protocols* [July 5, 1978]: 4-7).

[34] R. Yisraeli, *"Beheter Hashtalat Lev Kayom,"* 41.

[35] Let us recall Reches' statement concerning the flexibility of brain-death criteria.

[36] These included the dismissal of continued heart beat after the cessation of respiration as mere twitching and not a sign of life, as well as arguing that modern certainty of the end of respiration displaces any need for waiting to establish death. Both of these points had been made previously by other authors.

[37] R. Mordechai Eliyahu, *"Hashtalat Avarim al pi Hahalakhah,"* 21.

[38] Ibid., 22.

[39] The main import of such a status in persons is that one who kills a *traifa* is not punished in the same way as one who kills a healthy person. The logic behind this halakhic rule is that the *traifa* is not fully living, as he is suffering from an injury or disease that will be responsible for taking his life in the near future. There is much debate as to whether this status, however, renders the life of the *traifa* less valuable than healthy people in terms of priority in triage and other medical decisions. See Yehudah Dik, *"Trumat Avarim Migosses Lehatsalat Haye Adam,"* **Assia** 53-54 (Elul 5754): 48-53 and Halperin, *"Hashtalat Lev Beyisrael"* who both suggested that brain-dead potential organ donors be considered *traifot*. This would mean that any removal of essential organs from their bodies could not be constituted as actual murder.

[40] Maimonides MT *Rotse'ah* 2:8.

[41] See R. Feinstein, *Egrot Moshe*, HM II: 83 and the index of the Frankel edition of the *Mishneh Torah ad loc* for a comprehensive listing of traditional commentaries on this *halakhah* of Maimonides.

[42] R. Mordechai Eliyahu, *"Hashtalat Avarim al pi Hahalakhah,"* 30.

[43] Ibid.

[44] Ibid., 31. It is not clear to me whether R. Eliyahu required that a donor's heart must have stopped beating at some time previous to the start of artificial respiration before it is permissible to harvest it for transplant, even if it is actually beating at the time of harvest. He noted that the beating of the heart in the brain-dead patient is only vestigial twitching (page 24). However, he referred to this cardiac activity as such seemingly as the result of being renewed from a once silenced heart beat now dependent upon artificial respiration. On page 31 in his conclusion he summarized the two most important medical conditions that permit organ harvesting as being the certainty that respiration has irreversibly ceased and that cardiac activity "will not continue in a *natural fashion"*[emphasis added]. From this statement it does seem that he required some initial loss of cardiac activity so that its continuation could be understood as artificial. If this is the case, this seriously undermines the historical reconstructions proposed by R. Yisraeli, who claimed that the naturally beating heart was observed and disregarded by Talmudic Sages and halakhic authorities.

[45] See D. A. Shewmon and Elisabeth Seitz Shewmon, "The Semiotics of Death and its Medical Implications," in *Brain Death and Disorders Of Consciousness*, eds.

# Really Dead?

Calixto Machado and D. Alan Shewmon, 89-114 (NY: Kluwer Academic Publishers, 2004). The authors list several such tropes in bioethics.

[46] R. Mordechai Eliyahu, "*Hashtalat Avarim al pi Hahalakhah*," 21.

[47] Technically, R. Eliyahu cited the Rabbinate's insistence on participation in the declaring of death as stemming from the *psaq* of the *Shvut Yaaqov* (III:75) mentioned in the earlier discussion of R. Weiss's responsum. The *Shvut Yaaqov* concluded his own responsum by insisting upon cooperation between the local rabbinic authority and medical experts in determining whether medical assistance to a given dying patient was actually permitted or not depending upon whether it would hasten his death or prolong his life. However, as I have described in my analysis of R. Eliyahu's article, it was this very tension which, in his view, lay at the root of the permissibility of heart transplants. His linking of the Rabbinate's decision to the *Shvut Yaakov* is not merely technical, but conceptual as well.

[48] *Hatsofe* (August 27, 1987), 1.

[49] According to Pinhas, despite the anger and frustration of the Rabbinate, when it came to individual cases of organ donation, rabbis could be found to endorse the declaration of brain-death and the removal of organs (interview with Shmuel Pinhas, December 13, 2004). In a personal communication on August 9, 2007, Rabbi Mordechai Halperin related that after the rejection of the conditions outlined in the Rabbinate's *psaq halakhah* by Prof. Michaeli, both he and Prof. Steinberg did, on several different occasions, check on presumptively brain-dead potential organ donors after being asked to do so by one of the Chief Rabbis – either R. Eliyahu or R. Shapira. As he explained to me, on different occasions concerned family members of the presumably brain-dead patient had made contact with a member of the Rabbinate (who I am assuming notified one of the Chief Rabbis). At the request of one of the Chief Rabbis (R. Eliyahu was more often involved than R. Shapira), R. Halperin, M.D. would examine the brain-dead patient in order to determine whether or not this patient did in fact meet the medical conditions outlined by the Rabbinate in order to be considered brain-dead in accordance with its *psaq halakhah*. R. Halperin would then report his findings to the rabbi on whose initiative he was sent. R. Halperin related to me that there were times when he agreed with the medical diagnosis of brain-death, but also times when he did not. In response to a question, he related that he knew of no cases wherein he felt that the diagnosis of brain-death was not correct, but the patient's organs were donated. He noted that there were also cases where he agreed with the diagnosis, but for various reasons no organs were harvested.

# 15

# Really Dead

The tensions surrounding brain-death have not disappeared in the forty-years since they were first discussed in Israel or in the twenty-years since heart-transplants have become part of standard medical procedure. The Israeli organ transplantation project has continued apace, with additional transplant centers operating across the country, performing more complicated procedures on a wider array of difficult patients, still relying on brain-dead organ donors for the awaited "gift of life." The ever-expanding need for donor organs has led to constant efforts to increase the yield of available organs. These have ranged from public relations campaigns run by the Health Ministry and the private organ transplant advocacy group, ADI,[1] to the establishment of a centralized transplant center with specially trained nurse representatives in every hospital,[2] to suggestions by Knesset members that the laws governing the harvesting of cadaver organs be changed to an opt-out system making presumed consent the norm.[3] Additionally, there have been nearly continuous negotiations between rabbinical representatives and the Health Ministry. Sometimes gaining more ground, sometimes losing traction, these talks have aimed at arriving at an agreement concerning the determination of death. However, despite the establishment of an official public committee devoted to this issue by the government in the 1990s,[4] the experimental decapita-

# Really Dead?

tion of pregnant animals aimed at scientifically demonstrating the truth of halachic categorizations[5] and more recently the establishment of a government funded religious-secular think-tank, *Yachad* ("together"), which devoted hundreds of hours to studying the issue of brain-death,[6] the percentage of Israelis willing to 'sign-on' as cadaver organ donors has remained quite low compared to most other Western countries. It has consistently hovered between 3-4%.[7] Those involved in the transplant project decry this as an unfortunate waste of valuable resources.[8]

Yitshaq Berlovitz, the long-time assistant Director of the Health Ministry, has been involved in these discussions for decades and has grown pessimistic that any real accommodation with the leading halachic figures will be reached.[9] The increasingly fragmented rabbinic world, lacking any universally recognized *poseq* willing to accept that, in Berlovitz's words, "the death of the brain is actual death," and the weakened status of the Chief Rabbinate, headed for years now by rabbis with low standing in the eyes of many religious Jews, have made it unlikely that this will occur.[10] Instead, new growth areas for organ donors have been found amongst the non-Jewish population of Israel. It was this group which was largely responsible for the increase in donations after a large and lengthy public relations effort by the Health Ministry in 2004, dubbed by the ministry "The Year of the Transplant."

Suprisingly, just as I was finishing this manuscript the Knesset passed a bill into law establishing a standard review board for training doctors who would be authorized to establish brain-death in potential organ donors. This review board would include both medical and rabbinic personel.[11] It was soundly criticized both by the IMA and the *haredi* camp. Whether this law will actually help increase the number of organ transplants in Israel remains to be seen.

# Really Dead

The difficult questions surrounding the multiple meanings of brain-death have not been answered. Death is still a polysemic cloud: for some, prognosis, for others, biological fact, for yet others, social construct. Recent renewed attention to the subject in the medical and academic worlds coupled with the growing awareness of the burgeoning third world black market for organs may lead to reassessments of transplantation ethics and practices in much of the world, Israel included. Yet different assessments of what the medically-situated dying human body *means*—ethically and practically – do not seem to be converging on any one standardized concept. As Lock wrote, "death is not a self-evident phenomenon."[12]

This study has detailed the history of the multi-leveled discourse which surrounded the beginning of the age of heart transplantation in Israel. By analyzing the wide variety of documentation that this discourse produced, I have attempted to offer a fuller picture of the difficult debate over brain-death in Israeli society than has been available until now. In conclusion, I want to describe how the historical record can be understood as paradigmatic of both a classic "boundary dispute" as well as representative of the philosophical difficulty in naming that which is death. As I will explain, these two readings of the struggle over brain-death are closely related.

In discussions concerning the ways in which various communities develop or produce knowledge, attention has been focused on how certain questions, often those with consequences of public concern, have produced what have been labeled as boundary disputes between different parts of these communities.[13] That is, different groups have claimed that the problem at hand properly belongs to them as it is constituted of just that with which their own level or type of expertise is meant to deal. It is often the case that the very definition of the problem itself is part of the struggle over its ownership—for if the building of a road is defined as a engineering problem and not one of proper resource allocation—the expertise of the engineer is that which is required and not that of lawyers or philosophers trained to discuss the latter and not the former field.[14] Boundary disputes between medical doctors and non-medical theorists and practitioners have been one of the more prevalent types. The questions regarding classification of homosexuality, child abuse, or attention deficit disorder as medical problems or not, have already become classic examples of this same issue.[15]

Regarding concerns over brain-death, Thomas Brante and Margareta Hallberg, two Swedish scholars, have depicted the 1986 debate relating to legislation on this issue in their country as an example of the same type of boundary dispute over knowledge.[16] They argued that many contemporary societal controversies of this type in the West can be understood as following a three stage path of competition, crystallization and termination.

> The *origin* of controversies is often characterized by competition between various disciplines, or parts of a discipline, about the *jurisdiction* of a specific field or problem. ... it concerns who has "the right to speak," who is the real expert on the issue... (392).

> The second phase within controversies typically emerges with the *crystallization* of differences. ... During this phase, the social and argumentative structure of the controversy is crystallized. Most often, we are faced with two opposed parties, each possessing a number of excellent arguments for their position (392-3).

The third is the phase of *termination*, which also can be effected in several ways. ...resolution, abandonment and closure (393).

Resolution occurs when one side to the argument concedes to the other, abandonment when one side simply quits the struggle and closure is reached when outside intervention (like the passage of a law by the government concerning the conflicted issue) decides the argument in favor of one or another side (394-6).

Regarding the history the Israeli brain-death debate presented here, it seems clear that even today (and I would also argue that this is the case in the West), [17] despite the general acceptance of brain-death in medical practice and in organ transplantation in particular, there was never any conceptual agreement between the various parties who participated in the debate.[18] Essentially, despite much concerted effort to find a mutually acceptable way of measuring donor death, the jurisdiction over death remained contested. In Brante and Hallberg's scheme, this study described the first stage of public controversy. The Health Ministry's Michaeli (as well as the Hadassah medical staff) clearly argued that death was a scientific medical issue—one for which only medical expertise was relevant. Logically then, only the medical profession should have jurisdiction over death.

Such a claim for jurisdiction is part of the medical "professionalism" described by Eliot Freidson in his classic sociological analysis of modern medical practice. Freidson argued that claims for autonomy are the benchmark of what it means to act in a professional manner. Three claims are made for complete autonomy of action by any professional group.

# Really Dead?

> First, the claim is that there is such an unusual degree of
> skill and knowledge involved in professional work that
> nonprofessionals are not equipped to evaluate or regu-
> late it. Second, it is claimed that professionals are re-
> sponsible – that they may be trusted to work
> conscientiously without supervision. Third, the claim is
> that the profession itself may be trusted to undertake
> the proper regulatory action on those rare occasions
> when an individual does not perform his work compe-
> tently or ethically.[19]

Following Freidson, the brain-death debate can be understood as
an attempt at a professionalization or as the medicalization[20] of death.
Doctors alone should diagnose death: they alone were competent to
do so; the three-man brain-death committee would be composed only
of doctors—requiring no other supervision; they would be held
responsible only to other medical doctors.[21]

One difference, however, between the 'classic' presentation of jurisdiction and boundary disputes presented above and the actual case
here is the real interest that many of those who argued most strongly
for the medical-professionalization of death had in attaining the
approval of those who were, according to the above scheme, their
natural enemies in the dispute. As I have demonstrated, some commentators, like MK Shulamit Aloni and H. M. Ashkenazi, felt that
properly medicalizing death meant dismissing the view of outdated
"witch-doctors" and outmoded laws. However, others, including
Michaeli and the High Court, felt that attaining the halakhic authorization for heart-transplants was important. They did not aim at
dismissing the *halakha*, but wanted to show that medically defined
death was in fact halachically permissible and compatible. (I have
discussed the reasons for this above.)

Unless one adopts an extremely cynical attitude as to their motivations,[22] it seems that while those involved in the medicalization of death were interested in accord on a theoretical level—finding a definition of death that fit *both* medical and halachic understanding— it was on the practical level that the boundary dispute (re-) erupted. As I have noted, though, this practical dispute is connected to the essential conceptual differences between those involved. Brante and Hallberg describe these differences that they encountered in studying the Swedish case by referring to the incommensurability of opposing views. They found a dichotomy between those who advocated an analytic view of death – asserting that death could be defined scientifically and those who argued that death was not only a medical-scientific category. The former claimed that "death"

> … identifies a distinct, absolute difference between life and death, achieved by instruments that go beyond the immediate, "surface" appearances, observable by sense impression. …[it] separates appearance … and essence….[23]

This, they asserted, is basically a "scientific" stance—concerned with attaining the essential elements of any of the phenomena which it studies. Regarding brain-death—death, studied scientifically, was reduced to its essential component—the loss of brain function, understood as standing behind (reductively) that which had been observed previously as death.

The Swedish opponents of brain-death saw death not as a moment, but "as a process in which no absolute point can be discerned."[24] The loss of brain-function may be a part of this process, but it could not be death—for death was not a single essential point. As I have shown, this same split between those who viewed death as a specific moment versus those who viewed it as a process was characteristic of the Anglo-American discourse over brain-death as well. For Brante and Halle, this split was incommensurable in that the two views were conceptually exclusive: there was no way of bridging the conceptual gap between the two. "It is difficult," they wrote, "to imagine an argument from one party that would be viewed as a falsification of the arguments of the opposed party."[25]

The Israeli history described in this study reveals that despite the numerous attempts at fruitful exchange of ideas between doctors, lawyers, legistator's and rabbis – these concerned commentators talked past each other rather than with each other. Conceptual differences in understanding what death was—a measurable moment, a matter of rights, a legal-halachic status—kept the discourse incommensurable despite the best efforts at accommodation.[26] As I have argued, this incommensurability is what caused the seemingly most promising of these efforts—the halachic decision of the Israel Rabbinate—to fail to bring about full cooperation in the heart transplant project.

I feel, however, that the reasons behind this conceptual incommensurability have not been adequately analyzed. I would like to conclude this study by offering one philosophically-based explanation for the "missing of the minds" that I have described throughout this history. The Israeli debate over brain-death (like its counterpart in other Western countries), in addition to being about proper jurisdiction, was dependent upon the conceptual stance that the parties to it took regarding death itself. That is, their understanding of what it meant to define death resulted not only in different definitions of death, but in conceptually incommensurate definitions. In this way the debate over brain-death is paradigmatic of philosophical arguments over what it means to define (or re-define) *natural-kind* concepts (which is in some ways at the root of broader debates over modern science and its role in Western culture).

The advent of resuscitative technology and vital organ transplants brought about the need for reassessing what was meant by death in order to harvest the organs of dead donors with still-living vital organs. My claim is that discussions followed the contours of claims over the uses of language to define what was meant by other natural kinds like water or gold or sex (to name some of the more famous examples of these debates).[27]

Contention over natural kinds has revolved (and still does) upon the now well-known work done by the philosophers Saul Kripke and Hillary Putnam on the ways that man-made language reflects onto-logical reality. The next few pages will briefly outline their argument for a causal theory of reference as it relates to natural kinds and then return to the Israeli debate over brain-death. I want to show how some of the very same philosophical tensions regarding other seem-ingly ontological facts and the vocabulary used to talk about them can be found in the debate over brain-death detailed in this book. (As the work done by Kripke was more self-contained, I will use the case he made in his classic *Naming and Necessity* (*N&N*) to explicate what has been called the Kripke-Putnam thesis).[28]

Kripke built upon the notion that the meaning of language is refer-ential. That is, our words *mean* something because they refer to some-thing else.[29] His main philosophical intent was to explain how linguistic reference can be understood as creating *a posteriori*, yet *necessarily* true, statements about our world. He argued that the reference function of language is not monolithic, but that words can be used to designate either contingently or rigidly. One may refer to an individual as the one who ate that whole pie yesterday, for exam-ple. This is a contingent reference, because one can envision different circumstances wherein *this* individual can be correctly referred to as the one who ate a different pie or no pie, yet one would still consider him to be the same individual. When one refers contingently or non-rigidly, one is *describing* the object of his reference—often by pointing out some notable property possessed by that object—big eater—or some historical fact concerning it (like pie consumption). In using this type of reference one says something about an object, yet does not say what that object *is*.[30] Something *about* this object of reference could change, yet it would still *be* the same object.

Language, however, is also used to rigidly refer to people or things.[31] Proper names are usually (but not always)[32] used in this fashion. When a community or individual *names* something or someone, they are attempting to label it in a way that will constantly and consistently pick out *that* object correctly through the use of that label.[33] This is true whether astronomers are naming a new found star Alpha Centauri, or parents their new born son Dudley van Humperdink.[34] However, aside from such first dubbings, things are usually more complicated than this. Kripke writes:

> In general our reference depends not just on what we think ourselves, but on other people in the community, the history of how the name reached one, and things like that. It is by following such a history that one gets to the reference.[35]

As words are meant to designate something[36]—sometimes descriptively, sometimes rigidly—they seem to leave some type of trail to follow—back from them to that which they designate. In developing his theory of reference, Kripke strove to demonstrate the workings of this trail.

Kripke chose "gold" as an example of how one may follow this trail from word to object. The word "gold" does not refer to merely a particular example of a substance but rather to a certain *kind* of substance of which an individual piece of gold is but an exemplar of this kind of thing.[37] I will quote at length from one of the key passages from *N&N* that builds upon the difference in types of designation. Here Kripke traces the way that meaning functions regarding *kinds*.

> ...we use 'gold' as a term for a certain kind of thing. Others have discovered this kind of thing and we have heard of it. We thus as part of a community of speakers have a certain connection between ourselves and a certain kind of thing. The kind of thing is *thought* to have certain identifying marks. Some of these marks may not really be true of gold. We might discover that we are wrong about them. Further, there might be a substance which has all the identifying marks we commonly attributed to gold and used to identify it in the first place, but which is not the same kind of thing, which is not the same substance. ... Such a thing is, for example, as we well know, iron pyrites or fool's gold. This is not another kind of gold. It's a completely different thing which to the uninitiated person looks just like the substance which we discovered and called gold. We can say this not because we have changed the meaning of the term gold, and thrown in some other criteria which distinguished gold from pyrites. It seems to me that that's not true. On the contrary, we *discovered* that certain properties were true of gold in addition to the initial identifying marks by which we identified it. These properties, then, being characteristic of gold and not true of iron pyrites, show that the fool's gold is not in fact gold.[38]

# Really Dead?

Here is a basic outline of reference theory. First comes the discovery of a "*kind* of thing". That is, rather than the name of a particular individual, one finds a certain name of a type or kind. In naming this *kind* (or in a community's relation to this naming some time down the road), there is a rigid, rather than contingent reference, similar to the usual usage of proper names. In fact, Kripke stresses that he considers that "terms for natural kinds are much closer to proper names than is ordinarily supposed."[39] Using Mill's conception of proper names, he insists that names for *kinds* are also "*not* short for the conjunction of properties a dictionary would take to define them."[40] That is, the term "gold" does not *mean* a yellow, metallic rock often found in etc., etc. This is a description of "gold", but not its reference. Its reference is, rather, necessarily to a certain and specific "*kind* of thing."

Kripke is arguing that the terminology of particular kinds is not built up step by step as one learns more and more about, in this case, rocks and metals. Whether one is discussing gold, tigers or water (to name three of his favorite examples) these terms are conceptualizations of kinds, even before much is really understand about them. Tiger or water or gold might have gotten their start in language by referring to some *certain* sample of these kinds and so speakers may have gotten used to associating the term with fuzzy, striped, four legged jungle predators, but what they *mean* by "tiger" is a certain "kind of thing" picked out rigidly.[41] The rigid connection between a word and its referent is the *essence* of that very thing. It is not a contingent property of that thing — but what that thing *is* — what it cannot lack and still be that same thing.

Regarding gold, scientific study has learned that it is an element with a very specific atomic weight, molecular structure, etc. Kripke wrote:

> Gold apparently has the atomic number 79. Is it a necessary or contingent property of gold that it has the atomic number 79? Certainly we could find out that we were mistaken. The whole theory of protons, of atomic numbers, the whole theory of molecular structure and of atomic structure, on which such views are based, could *all* turn out to be false. Certainly we didn't know it from time immemorial. So in that sense, gold could turn out not to have atomic number 79. ... Given that gold *is* this element, any other substance, even though it looks like gold and is found in the very places where we in fact find gold [that is iron pyrite or fool's gold], would not be gold. [42]

For Kripke this holds not only for what appear to be simple natural kind terms and their constituent substance, such as water=$H_2O$, but also for theoretical identifications, such as "lightning is an electrical discharge" or "light is a stream of photons." These identifications also show how necessary truths about natural kinds can be discovered.[43] These kinds, "lightning" or "light" are also picked out by a Millian naming function. These terms refer rigidly to some *kind*, like a name does to some individual or object, picking it out for us and holding it while we may discover more details about it. Some of these details may include its substantive or theoretical make-up.

Jarret Leplin correctly asserted that the rigid link between word and object in this type of referential language structure described by Kripke aims at finding the essence of the object that it names. However, while in some cases essence is understood as the constitutive substance of that thing, it is difficult to assert that this is true regarding more theoretically complex constructions like lightning or light.

# Really Dead?

Rather, it is best to understand that rigid reference is meant in a *causal* fashion.

> All that need be known about [the original referent] $r_0$ at the time [that the referring term] $t$'s reference to it is fixed are the experientially accessible features that pick it out or that pick out what it is introduced as the cause of. So [causal reference theory] CTR connects the idea of essence with the causal explanation of those reference-fixing features. The essential features of $r_0$ then, are those that scientific investigation reveals to be causally responsible for the features involved in the ostensive element of $t$'s introduction. If $r_0$ itself were not experientially accessible but rather causes some [other experientially accessible artifact] $o$ which provides the ostensive element in $t$'s introduction, then either [an essential feature] $f$ is a composite of all of $r_0$'s features, or there is a second level of causation at which we ask what features of $r_0$ caused those of its features that were manifested in $o$. In either case, there is the strong suggestion in CTR that the properties for lack of which nothing can be $r$ are those properties that produce the experientially accessible element in reference to $r$.[44]

More simply, what is meant by the rigidity of essential reference is that which is discovered by scientific investigation to lie behind (in a causal fashion) those observable characteristics of a given object. Since scientific study has told us that what makes gold have the characteristics which we first observed is its molecular structure and atomic weight – that is what we consider to be its essence. In Kripke's view that is what was meant by *gold* all those eons ago when someone picked out the *kind* gold by pointing to one example of this kind.

One of the semantic strengths of aligning identifications this way is that it enables the *meaning* of the kind term to remain constant. The meaning of the simple kind term is always referential to that which is ultimately the cause of what we can experience about this kind and not those changing experiences themselves. This is open to better discovery as more is learned about this kind, but what is discovered is the cause of what was meant when this *kind* of thing was originally identified.[45]

Now returning to the case of death—it is clear that in the debate over brain-death many of those involved treated death as a type of natural kind rigidly referred to by the word *death*. That is, the kind *death* was something with which people were intimately familiar and were used to describing it in various ways. When brain-death began being debated some claimed that this was a clear example of discovering a more essential way of understanding that which had always been meant (that is referred to) by the word *death*. This claim was made by R. Tendler in describing brain-death. In his coauthored article in JAMA, he claimed:

> ...the Harvard criteria or other neurological criteria for determining death can be viewed as the <u>scientific expression</u> [emphasis added] of those observations that, until recently, were the actual way a patient was known to be dead.[46]

That is, brain-death did not represent a change in what it meant to be dead—it was a more essential expression of that which had always been meant by death. The end of neurological function was a better way of expressing what had always been meant by the term death.

# Really Dead?

Brain-death was a step towards finding something more *essential* about the natural-kind *death*. This instead of reliance upon a conglomerate of experientially available phenomena to differentiate between the dead and living. In this view, just as *describing* gold as yellow, shiny, etc. was originally adequate to pick out the kind *gold* until the discovery of fool's gold, so too was a reliance upon cardiac and somatic signs of death adequate until doctors were confronted with beating-heart resuscitated bodies.This brought scientists to search for something more essentially—more rigidly—meant by the term *death*. As the British brain-death advocate David Lamb wrote,

> …the term brain death can be used as a better formulation of the concept of death. When fully articulated it is not so much a new concept as the formulation of a definition of death where previously none existed. [47]

One of the fascinating things that occurred over the course of the Israeli brain-death debate is how many of the voices (far and away the majority) which proclaimed death not as the type of natural kind of which brain-death was its better expression, but as something more ontologically obtuse and ethically complex, were in the end hushed by the move forward with vital organ transplants. These included the medical doctors: Neufeld, Depres, Levy, Ouaknin, Durst, and Korchin, as well as the expressed opinion of the IMA itself. The High Court also viewed death as something fluid that could change with medical capabilities. The majority of medical opinions expressed in this discourse over brain-death understood that there was both a biological-scientific *and* conventional-cultural aspect to determining death (much like Gervais argued). This stance meant that there was room for negotiation about where it seemed best to draw this conventional line. That is, both biological and philosophical arguments for the best life-death distinction were to be considered. Of those who expressed opinions on the matter, only Ashkenazi argued (somewhat problematically) for an essentialist understanding of death.

However, when Michaeli and Pinhas began to proceed with their plans for heart-transplants—the many-tiered discussions of ethics—especially those which viewed death as prognosis (and thus flexible)—were simply ignored. Instead, Michaeli claimed that "the medical position [is] that the death of the respiratory center [in the brain] is the moment of the individual's death." By asserting an essentialist stance which equated a very particular moment with death—and claiming, as I discussed above, that this is a scientific *fact*—there could be little (or even no) room for discussions about defining death. I believe that such a stance was one that those interested in moving forward with the heart-transplant project felt was necessary to take, in order to accomplish their goal. If death was malleable, part of a prognosis, then how could doctors remove the vital organs from a donor whose death was not a scientific-medical *fact*—something scientifically proven beyond reproach? Although there was much else to be said about death and brain-death, conceptual essentialism may have seemed the safest way to 'prove' to a hesitant public (whose cooperation was needed for donor organ supply) that donors were already, actually, truly, factually, scientifically, medically DEAD.

Ironically, the Rabbinate itself also chose to follow an essentialist path. It formulated its decision in accord with the only *psaq halakha* which itself offered an absolute definition of death. Anoxia measured by brain necrosis (R. Feinstein's approach as interpreted by his son-in-law, R. Tendler) was the most rigid of halackic statements defining death. (See R. Tendler's statement on the rigidity of death above.) By asserting such a definitive essentialist understanding of death, the Rabbinate (perhaps unwittingly) played into the hands of those who sought to professionalize or medicalize death. For if death was a

# Really Dead?

matter of a certain measurable fact—all that was needed was for a trained technician to measure it. No rabbis, philosophers or others need apply. The Rabbinate, like the medical personnel involved, actually wanted to advance the transplant project and offered their cooperation in order to do so. However, by stint of the reductionist element of their *psaq*—they almost guaranteed their own dispensability in the eyes of the medical practitioners. This ended any chance of actual cooperation, anticipated increase in the number of organ donors, and more saved lives through rabbinically-endorsed heart-transplants.

Over the years researching modern death and the transplant project, I have become convinced that the continuing gap between transplant need and the availability of donors is a result, in part, of the way in which neurological death has been presented as scientific fact by many of those involved in the procuring of organs. Such a presentation is still the subject of some controversy among doctors and other scientists involved in neurology and transplant.[48] It is also, from the point of view of those most interested in advancing organ transplantation, counterproductive. Such a stance helps to stifle ethical debate surrounding death, care of the dying, proper use of scarce biological resources, and public policy vis-à-vis individual rights. Medical practitioners who need the cooperation of the public in order to ensure a supply of cadaver organs should not be surprised that this is difficult to come by when that same public is told that it has no place in the discussion of death itself. This has led some to lobby for what I view as disturbingly coercive measures aimed at increasing organ supply, like enabling automatic organ retrieval from any and all cadavers. Essentialist reductionism regarding brain-death, by cutting out productive debate, may be also cutting out the very donors so sought after by those who endorse such a view.

---

[1] This is an organization established by the parents of a young man who died for lack of a suitable organ donor. ADI has been responsible for promulgating the use of organ donor cards in Israel. Its representatives have worked hand in hand with the Health Ministry and the Knesset in a variety of activities aimed at raising the number of organs available for transplant. Its web site is hosted by the Health Ministry, and is an interesting example of the private-public face of transplants (http://www.health.gov.il/transplant/index.htm).

[2] The National Center for Organ Contributions and Transplants known as "Israel Transplant" was officially founded by the Health Ministry in 1993 (Mark and Rivka Amado Cohen, "Organ Procurement and Transplantation in Israel," [Jerusalem: JDC-Brookdale Institiue, 1994], 43). It is devoted to coordinating all organ transplant efforts in the country. For a description of the problems with its actual functioning see the Annual Report of the Israeli Ombudsman 51b (2001) in the section devoted to the Health Ministry, http://80.70.129.40/51b.htm (accessed September 4, 2005).

[3] For example, a private bill introduced by MKs Ilan Leibowitz, Eliezer Zandberg and Ariella Golan in 2005 sought to do just this. The logic behind such legal changes is that the inherent indifference of the general population makes it more likely that many more will not take the trouble to register their disagreement to organ donation upon death than are willing to register their express consent in the present opt-in system. The ethical concerns surrounding such a change need to be seriously examined. *Cf.* Knesset Protocols (July 23, 1997) wherein the suggestion to give preference in receiving transplant organs to those willing to sign a post-mortem organ donation card was dismissed.

It is also worth noting the changes that have occurred regarding the internationalization of the organ supply. In 1989, the Health Minister, Y. Tsor, bemoaned the fact that Israel was lagging well behind Western Europe in the percentage of organ donors and was becoming increasingly seen as a country which requested organs from, but did not provide them to, other countries. He felt that this would certainly lead to dire consequences of acute organ shortages as Israelis would be barred from receiving organs in the future (Knesset Protocols [November 28, 1989]). By the 21st-century, however, the acquisition of donor organs from other (usually developing) countries, seemed to be a settled, standard procedure. Worries were ethical and financial and less about losing actual organ sources. Arrangements to receive organs overseas were made and paid for by government sponsored and private health insurers. See Knesset Protocols (July 30, 2003) section 521 and Knesset Protocols

(December 9, 2003) which includes a fascinating presentation of the first reading of a government-sponsored bill governing organ transplants. *Cf.* Knesset Work, Welfare and Health Committee Protocols from November 2, 2005 for a long discussion of many of the difficult issues involved.

[4] Such a public committee was established to encourage discussion of transplant issues between doctors and rabbis after the tenure of the Chief Rabbis involved with the original *psaq* ended. Unfortunately, its records are not available having been deposited and closed in the government archives.

[5] For a description of this experiment, see A. Steinberg and M. Hersch, "Decapitation of a Pregnant Sheep: A Contribution to the Brain Death Controversy," *Transplant Proceedings* 27, no. 2 (1995).

[6] See their unpublished report presented to the President of Israel, Mr. Moshe Katsav, on November 23, 2003 and the accompanying background position papers.

[7] One of the closest observers and participants in the entire question of transplants over the last 30 years, Professor Avraham Steinberg, has claimed that in spite of everything done in this time no real change can be seen in this low percentage of Israelis willing to donate organs. (Knesset Work, Welfare and Health Committee Protocols [June, 9, 2003]: 16). This statistic is quoted in the same protocol by the then Health Minister, Danny Naveh (6).

[8] Ibid.

[9] He retired after over 20 years in this position in 2007.

[10] Interview with Dr. Yitzchak Berlovitz (June 21, 2005).

[11]*Hok Mavet-mohi Neshimati* (The Brain-death Respiratory Law)-2008 (http://www.knesset.gov.il/privatelaw/plaw_display.asp?LawTp=2). Interestingly, the media coverage of this law was divided as to whether this law represented a victory for religious elements or their capitulation. The IMA expressed its dissatisfaction with the law. It was viewed as encroaching upon medical prerogatives.

[12] Lock, *Twice Dead*, 11.

[13] There is a huge literature related to the production of knowledge in the sciences, as well as in other arenas. One of the classic works on the philosophical-sociological understanding of this subject, Peter Berger and Thomas Luckman, *The Social Construction of Knowledge* still provides a solid grounding in many of the issues related to the sociology of knowledge. The works of Steven Shapin and Ian Hacking (see bibliography) also address and develop a wide variety of related issues.

[14] Eliot Freidson, *Profession of Medicine* (New York: Harper & Row, 1970), 336.

[15] See Simon LeVay, *Queer Science : The Use and Abuse of Research into Homosexuality* (Cambridge, Mass: MIT Press, 1996); Ian Hacking, *The Social Construction of What?* (Cambridge, Mass.: Harvard University Press, 1999), chapter five, 'Kind Making: The Case of Child-Abuse,' 125-62; Thomas Armstrong, "Add: Does It Really Exist?," *Phi Betta Kappan* Feburary (1996).

[16] Thomas Brante and Margareta Hallberg, "Brain or Heart? The Controversy over the Concept of Death," *Social Studies of Science* 21, no. 3 (1991).

[17] A recent *Newsweek* magazine cover story was devoted to new resuscitation techniques and featured a caption reading, "This man was dead. He isn't anymore," http://www.msnbc.msn.com/id/19751440/site/newsweek/ (accessed August 28, 2007).

[18] It is still questionable whether brain-death is completely accepted as evidenced by the continuing debate as to its use even on the practical level of organ transplantation. See the debate surrounding non-heart- beating donors in Stuart J. Youngner, Robert M. Arnold and Renie Schapiro, ed., *The Definition of Death : Contemporary Controversies*.

[19] Freidson, *Profession of Medicine*, 137.

[20] This is the aim of including areas of human experience which were once not understood to be under the purview of medical care as essentially medical issues. For a classic statement of the issue (perhaps the first use of this trope), see also Peter Conrad and Joseph W. Schneider, *Deviance and Medicalization: From Badness to Sickness* (Philadelphia: Temple University Press, 1992). As noted above, Pernick has argued that this is merely another example of a similar medicalization which already took place in the 18th-century.

[21] Regarding this last point, I am referring to the Health Ministry's General Directive 11/86 (December 11, 1986) discussed above. It stipulated that any supervision or recording of the declarations of death be handled by the hospital director alone.

[22] See Brante, "Brain or Heart? The Controversy over the Concept of Death," 403.

[23] Ibid., 405.

[24] Ibid.

[25] Ibid., 406.

[26] For another view of ways that moral problems in the public sphere often remain unassailably difficult to resolve, see Kevin Wildes, *Moral Aquaintances: A Methodology in Bioethics* (Notre Dame, Ind.: University of Notre Dame Press, 2000). He argues that actors often remain, "moral strangers," each with his own set of values which do not seem important to the other actors in the public sphere.

# Really Dead?

27 Winston Chiong published the first article which focused primarily on the parallels between the debates over defining death and natural kinds at the end of 2005 (Winston Chiong, "Brain Death without Definitions," *The Hastings Center Report* 35, no. 6 [2005]. Many of his arguments agree with my own conclusions which I reached independently in the course of my research in 2004-5. The presentation which follows is not based upon his work, but has much in common as we both found the same similarity between the natural-kind debates and those over brain-death.

28 See Donnellan 1983, 84, 90 or Laporte 65.

29 Putnam claimed that "A discourse on paper might seem to be a perfect description of trees, but if it was produced by monkeys randomly hitting keys on a typewriter for millions of years, then the words do not refer to anything" (Hillary Putnam, *Reason, Truth and History* [Cambridge: Cambridge University Press, 1981], 4). Obviously, this is not the only view of the creation of meaning. Deconstructionists such as Stanley Fish argue that meaning is situated not in the reference of a text to something else, but rather in the reader's reaction to that text. For an excellent example of a "monkeys typing" scenario see the essay "How to Recognize a Poem when You See One" in Fish's *Is There a Text in this Class* (Cambridge: Harvard UP, 1980), 322-337. It is also from this position concerning reference that Putnam will construct his argument about linguistic "division of labor" amongst a community of speakers in order to account for an individual's discourse about objects whose identity is not fully grasped by them. Putnam also argues that a complete theory of meaning cannot stop here, but must explain how different meanings are derived from words that have the same reference (27).

30 Ibid., 129 and 133.

31 Kripke develops the notion of rigid designation as a necessary and true equivalence of different terms that refer to the same object – his by now famous Hesperus and Phosphorous. Since they both designate the same object, they are necessarily equivalent—despite the fact that each term originally was used to pick out what was *thought* to be a different object. However, I am more concerned not with correspondence between terms, but between terms and objects. See Ben S. Cordry, "Necessity and Rigidly Designating Kind Terms," *Philosophical Studies* 119 (2004): 243-64 for more on this difference and Soames *Beyond Rigidity* for an in-depth analysis of semantically logical necessity.

32 Ibid., p. 57.

33 Ibid., p. 49.

[34] Ibid. p.80.

[35] Ibid.

[36] This was Putnam's point noted at the beginning of this discussion.

[37] V. S. Quine described *kinds* as representing, in the end, groups scientifically determined as similar such that they may be considered as "interchangeable parts of the cosmic machine revealed by science" (134). So every piece of gold is a member of the kind gold in that it can be interchanged with any other piece. This of course leaves open a wide array of questions as to how such interchangeability should be understood—via function, structure or some other measure.

[38] Ibid., 119.

[39] Ibid., 127.

[40] Ibid., 128.

[41] What Kripke seems to mean by that "kind of thing" is closely related to the substance of a thing—that out of which it is composed (114). This is not a simple idea, and is also the subject of correct criticism (see Soames chap 9-11, especially page 288) but need not be explicated here.

[42] Ibid., 124-125.

[43] Ibid., 116.

[44] Leplin, 498.

[45] Thinking about kinds in this way represents a strong defense against the worries raised by the notion of Kuhnian incommensurability in terms of how theory change can affect changes in the actual meaning of a variety of scientific terms like water, gold, heat and tiger. This has been argued by many, among them Joseph LaPorte, *Natural Kinds and Conceptual Change* (Cambridge: Cambridge UP, 2004), 3, for example.

[46] Veith, et al (1978), p. 1654.

[47] Christopher Pallis, *Abc of Brain Stem Death*, 19.

[48] See, for example Alexander Morgan Capron, "Brain Death--Well Settled yet Still Unresolved," *The New England Journal of Medicine* 344, no. 16 (2001) and Calixto Machado and D. Alan Shewmon Calixto, ed., *Brain Death and Disorders of Consciousness*, Advances in Experimental Medicine and Biology (New York: Springer, 2004).

# Appendix

1) General

This protocol implements the decisions of the Hadassah Medical Center and the Medical Board regarding procedures for the determination of brain death. The diagnosis of brain-death is based upon three necessary stages.

If all of these stages are fulfilled, as outlined in this protocol, a team of doctors will be able to determine brain-death in accord with the procedure herein detailed.

2) Goal

The goal of this protocol is to establish uniform standards for the determination of brain death specifying the procedures for determining death, the constitution of the medical staff, criterion for determining brain-death and the apportioning of responsibility for implementation.

3) Definitions

3.1) Brain-death

Complete lack of brain stem function.

3.2) Severe brain trauma

Injury to brain tissue due to accident or trauma according to clinical criterion.

# Really Dead?

3.2) Intracranial hemorrhage

> Evidence of hematoma in the tissue of the brain through use of a CT scan.

3.3) Anoxic brain damage

> Damage to brain tissue, due to lack of oxygen supply, even if only temporary.

3.5) Deep Coma

> A state of unconsciousness, with no responsiveness, from which it is impossible to revive the patient. Such a patient does not open eyes, does not relate to his environment, does not respond to commands and does not move limbs in response to pain stimuli (except for spinal reflexes).

4) Criterion for Establishing Brain-Death

General

The diagnosis of brain-death will be based on three necessary stages as follows:

Stage 1: Existence of preliminary conditions.

Stage 2: Identification of factors liable to falsify establishment of death.

Stage 3: Essential tests for establishing brain-death.

For details of these three stages see sections 4.1-4.3.

4.1) Stage 1 – Preliminary conditions

> 4.1.1) A state of deep coma and lack of independent respiration (the patient is respirated).
>
> 4.1.2) Clear evidence of damage to brain tissue, which cannot be treated, with a clearly diagnosed etiology for this damage.
>
> 4.1.3) If untreatable damage to brain tissue is discovered, it is to be checked for a minimum fixed duration in accord with diagnosis. During this

minimum fixed duration, advancement to further stages will be monitored and all normal medical treatment will be given.

4.1.4) The minimum fixed duration over which advancement to further stages will be monitored, according to diagnosis:

| Diagnosis | Minimum Fixed Duration |
|---|---|
| Severe Brain Trauma | 12 hours |
| Intracranial Hemorrhaging | 12 hours |
| Anoxic Brain Damage | 24 hours |
| after heart attack | |
| or anesthesia accident | |
| or choking or drowning | |

4.2) Stage 2 – Identification of Factors Liable to Falsify Establishment of Death

4.2.1) Following are details of factors liable to cause mistakes in establishing death and whose discovery requires cessation of procedures for determining death.

A) Hypothermic state with temperature at 35 degrees Celsius or less.

B) Findings of relevant drug influence (barbituites, muscle relaxants, etc.).

C) Metabolic factors which may cause deep coma and lack of respiration.

D) Endocrinological factors which may cause deep coma and lack of respiration.

# Really Dead?

4.2.2) Upon checking all of the above, if evidence of any one or more of the above are found, no advancement to Stage 3 (as detailed in 4.3) may take place until such time as they are without doubt proven to have ceased or are disproven.

4.3) Stage 3 – Necessary Tests for determination of brain-death
It is possible to determine brain death only if all the conditions of the following tests detailed bellow are fulfilled:

4.3.1) Clinical proof of deep coma as defined in 3.5.

4.3.2) Lack of abnormal body position or face musculature as a result of:

a) decerebrate position.
b) decortical position.
c) trismus.

4.3.3) Lack of any independent muscle tension.

4.3.4) Lack of all brain stem reflexes as detailed below:

1) dolls-eyes
2) pupil light reflex
3) corneal reflex
4) vestibulo-occular reflexes

4.3.5 [lists the detailed apnea test protocol]

4.3.6 [lists the auditory nerve/brain stem responses test protocol added by the Rabbinate]

5) Procedure for determining brain-death
The diagnosis of brain-death will be determined by a three person team (each physician holding a rank of expert in his field) assembled by: the hospital director during normal working hours or by the chief duty physician after hours.

The call to the hospital director or chief duty physician will be made by the attending physician, holding a rank of expert in his field, only after he has performed all the following steps:

5.1.1) All of the three stages for determining brain-death outlined in section 4 of this protocol have been performed in full.

5.1.2) At least three hours have passed after the above stages have been completed.

5.2) After receiving the call the hospital director (during working hours) or that day's chief duty physician (when the call is made after working hours) will assemble the full team.

5.3) The team of physicians will assemble at the same time and check in an independent manner that all of the three stages outlined in section 4 have been fully carried out.

If the team has assured that all of the criterion and written instructions have been fulfilled, they will together pronounce brain-death and the three team members will sign the medical record.

5.4) The determination of brain-death must be unanimous. If there are differences of opinion—brain-death will not be determined and it is necessary to wait for the re-assembly of the team according to the procedure detailed in section 5 of this protocol.

5.5) If brain-death has been determined by all of the team members, treatment of the deceased's cadaver will be continued by the staff of the transplant department in accord with normal procedures.

6) Constitution of the Medical Staff for Brain-Death Determination

The team members will be physicians, holding expert rank in their respective fields, the duty staff of the day, in the following specialties:

1) neurology

2) anesthesiology

3) internal medicine or cardiology

# Really Dead?

7) Responsibility

The attending physician holding expert rank in his field, chief duty physician, duty physicians in the fields of neurology, anesthesiology, internal medicine and cardiology, hospital director or his assistant, and department and section heads are responsible for fulfillment of this protocol, each in accord with his field of operations.

# Bibliography

Ad-Hoc Committee of the Harvard Medical School to Examine the Definition of Death. "A Definition of Irreversible Coma." *JAMA* 205, no. 6 (1968): 337-40.

Alder, Ken. *The Lie Detectors*. New York: The Free Press, 2007.

Anonymous. "*Al Hashtalat Averim.*" *Mikhtav Lehaver* 48, no. 11 (5747).

———. "*Hashtalat Levavot.*" *Mikhtav Lehaver* Adar 10 (5728): 10-27.

———. "*Kiviat Regah Hamavet.*" *Assia* 1 (1976).

Anson, Ofra and Yehudit Shuval. *Ha'iqar Habriut*. Jerusalem: Magnes Press, 1991.

Armstrong, Thomas. "ADD: Does It Really Exist?" *Phi Betta Kappan* Feburary (1996).

Ashkenazi, H. M. "*Haqriterionim Lemot Hamoah.*" *Harefuah* 79, no. 1 (1970).

———. "*Mot Hamoah.*" *Harefuah* 76, no. 6 (1969): 252.

Ashkenazi, Tamar, Nurit Guttman and Jacob Hornik. "Signing on the Dotted Line." *Marketing Health Services* Summer (2005): 19-26.

Auerbach, Efraim. "*Samkhut Hahalakhah Beyamenu.*" In *Ben Samkhut Le'otonomiah*, edited by Ze'ev Safrai and Avi Sagi, 457-63. Tel Aviv: Kibbutz Hameuchad, 1997.

Avraham, Avraham S. "*Hashtalat Lev Beyisrael.*" *Assia* 43-44 (1987): 83.

———. *Nishmat Avraham*. Jerusalem: Machon Schlesinger, 1984.

Avraham, Michael. "*Mahi Halut.*" *Tzohar* 2, Winter (1990): 71-86.

# Really Dead?

Bar-Dah, Yitshaq. *Mishpat Vehalakhah*. Ramat Gan, 1978.

Barzilai, Gad. "Religious Fundamentalism and Law: The Jewish Ultra-Orthodox (Haredi) Community and Legal Culture." In *Communities and Law*, 209-78. Ann Arbour: University of Michigan Press, 2003.

Beecher, Henry. *Research and the Individual*. Boston: Little and Brown Publishing Co., 1970.

Belkin, Gary. "Death before Dying" PhD. Thesis, Harvard University, 2000.

Ben-David, Orit Brawer. "Ranking Deaths in Israeli Society: Premature Deaths and Organ Donation." *Mortality* 11, no. 1 (2006).

Ben-Meir, Yehoshuah. *"Re'yot Nesibatiot Bemishpat Ha'ivri."* *Dine Yisrael* 18 (5765-6): 87-143.

Berger, Peter and Thomas Luckman. *The Social Construction of Knowledge*. New York: Doubleday, 1967.

Biale, David. *Eros and the Jews*. Berkely: University of California Press, 1997.

Bleich, J. David. "New York City Water." *Tradition* 38, no. 4 (2004): 70-111.

Blidstein, R. Yaakov. *"He'arah B'inyan Qviat Hamavet Behalakhah."* *Hadarom*, no. 37 (5733).

Borman, J. "The Ultimate Cardiac Surgeon." *The Journal of Cardiovascular Surgery* 39: Suppl. 1-2 (1998): 77-82.

Brante, Thomas and Margareta Hallberg. "Brain or Heart? The Controversy over the Concept of Death." *Social Studies of Science* 21, no. 3 (1991): 389-413.

Calixto, Machado and D. Alan Shewmon, ed. *Brain Death and Disorders of Consciousness*. New York: Springer, 2004.

Canfield, John V. "Discovering Essence." In *Knowledge and Mind*, edited by Carl Ginet Sydney Shoemaker, 105-29. Oxford:

Oxford University Press, 1983.

Capron, Alexander Morgan. "Brain Death—Well Settled yet Still Unresolved." *The New England Journal of Medicine* 344, no. 16 (2001): 1244-46.

Carmi, A. *Refuah Vemishpat*. Tel Aviv: Sefriat Maariv, 1971.

Chiong, Winston. "Brain Death without Definitions." *The Hastings Center Report* 35, no. 6 (2005): 20-30.

Cohen, Asher and Baruch Zisser. *"Ben Haskemiut Shevirah Leshevirat Heheskemiut."* In *Rav-Tarbutiut Bemedinah Demoqratit Veyehudit,* edited by Menachem Mautner, Avi Sagi and Ronnen Shamir Tel Aviv: Ramot, 1998.

Cohen, Jeffery. *Dear Chief Rabbi*. Hoboken, New Jersey: Ktav Publishing House, 1995.

Cohen, Mark and Rivka Amado. *Organ Procurement and Transplantation in Israel*. Jerusalem: JDC-Brookdale Institue, 1994.

Cohen, R. Alfred. "Scientific Evidence in Jewish Law." *The Journal of Halacha and Contemporary Society* 39: 51-94.

Cohen-Almagor. *The Right to Die with Dignity*. New Brunswick, New Jersey: Rutgers University Press, 2001.

Cole, Simon. *Suspect Identities: A History of Fingerprinting and Criminal Identification*. Cambridge: Harvard UP, 2001.

Committee, Brain Death. "Report of Brain Death Committee." Jerusalem: Hadassah Medical Organisation, 1993.

Conrad, Peter and Joseph W. Schneider. *Deviance and Medicalization: From Badness to Sickness*. Philadelphia: Temple University Press, 1992.

Cordry, Ben S. "Necessity and Rigidly Designating Kind Terms." *Philosophical Studies* 119 (2004): 243-64.

D'amico, Robert. "Is Disease a Natural Kind." *Journal of Medicine and Philosophy* 20 (1995).

# Really Dead?

Depres, A. *"Efshar Vetsarih Lishtol."* *Mikhtav Lehaver* Tishre 3 (5769): 20.

Desberg, Uri. *"Haba'at De'ah Alyedei Harabanim Harashi'im Leyisrael."* *T'humin* 11 (5750): 31-40.

Deveri, A. and M. Levy. *"Shtilat Lev – Orot Vetslalim."* *Harefuah* 109, no. 10 (1985): 303-5.

Dikhovsky, R. Shlomo. *"Shililat Aba'ut Bemtsaut Bediqat HLA."* *Sefer Assia* 35 (1983): 16-31.

Dik, Yehuda. *"Trumat Averim Migoses Lehatsalat Haye Adam."* *Sefer Assia* 53-54 (5754): 48-53.

Donnellan, Keith S. "Kripke and Putnam on Natural Kind Terms." In *Knowledge and Mind*, eds. Carl Ginet and Sydney Shoemaker, 84-104. Oxford: Oxford University Press, 1983.

Dupre, John. *The Disorder of Things*. Cambridge: Harvard UP, 1993.

Eliyahu, R. Mordechai. *"Hashtalat Averim Al Pi Hahalakhah."* *Barkai* 4 (5747): 18-31.

Elon, Menachem. *Jewish Law: History, Source and Principles*. Philadelphia: JPS, 1994.

——. *The Principles of Jewish Law*. Jerusalem: Keter Publishing House, 1975.

Erlik, D., O.S. Better, A. Shramek, D. Richter-Levin, J.A. Hemli, and A. Barzilai. "Cadaveric Renal Transplantation in Man: First Report from Israel." *Israel Journal of Medical Science* 3, no. 1 (1967): 88-92.

Fattorusso, V., ed. *Heart Transplantation*. Liege, Belgium: Desoer Publishers, 1968.

Fish, Stanley. *Is There a Text in This Class*. Cambridge: Harvard UP, 1980.

Fox, R.C. and J.P. Swazey. *Spare Parts*. New York: Oxford UP, 1992.

# Bibliography

Frankel, David. *"Ha'aspeqtim Hamishpati'im shel Hashtalat Averim."* PhD. Diss., Hebrew University, 1975.

Freedman, Benjamin. *Duty and Healing.* New York: Routledge, 1999.

Freidson, Eliot. *The Profession of Medicine.* New York: Harper & Row, 1970.

Frimer, Dov. "Establishing Paternity by Means of Blood Type Testing in Jewish Law and Israeli Legislation." In *Sefer Assia*, 153-95, 1986.

Gavison, Ruth. *"Medinah Yehudit Vedemokratit."* In *Rav Tarbutiut Bemedinah Demokratit Veyehudit,* edited by Menachem Mautner, Avi Sagi and Ronen Shamir. Tel Aviv: Ramot, 1998.

Gawande, Atul. "Desperate Measures." *The New Yorker* May 5 (2003): 70-81.

Geertz, Clifford. *The Interpretation of Cultures.* New York: Basic Books, 1973.

Gervais, Karen. *Redefining Death.* New Haven: Yale University Press, 1986.

Giacomini, Mita. "A Change of Heart and a Change of Mind? Technology and the Redefinition of Death in 1968." *Social Science and Medicine* 44, no. 10 (1997): 1465-82.

Golan, Tal. *Laws of Men and Laws of Nature.* Cambridge: Harvard University Press, 2004.

Goldberg, R. Zalman Nechemiah. *"Heter Agunot Memigdal Hatuamim Benu York."* *T'humin* 23 (2003): 110-19.

Good, Byron J. *Medicine Rationality and Experience.* Cambridge: Cambridge University Press, 1990.

Goren, R. Shlomo. *"Hagderat Hamavet Behalakhah."* In *Shanah Beshanah.* Jerusalem: Chief Rabbinate of Israel, 5734.

Green, Michael B. and Wolfgang Wickler. "Brain Death and Personal Identity." *Philosophy and Public Affairs* 9 (1980): 105-33.

# Really Dead?

Hacking, Ian. *Historical Ontology*. Cambridge: Harvard University Press, 2002.

———. *The Social Construction of What?* Cambridge, Mass.: Harvard University Press, 2000.

Hakohen, Aviad. "*Harabanut Harashit Leyisrael: Hebetim Mishpati'im.*" In *Harabanut Harashit Leyisrael Shivim Shanah Leyesodah*, eds. I. Warhaftig and S. Katz. Jerusalem: *Hekhal Shlomo*.

———. "*Mishpat Verefuah Bemedinat Yehudit Vedemokratit: Ben Antonomiah Shel Hok Lepatologiah Shel Yehase Dat Vemedinah.*" *Sha'arei Mishpat* 2, no. 2 (2000): 189-221.

Hafets, Shlomo. "*Meqomo Shel Edut Bemishpat Ha'ivri.*" *Dine Yisrael* 9 (1978-1980): 51-83.

Halberstam, Chaim. "*Dr. Yaakov Levi—Kavim Ledmuto Ulemifal Hayav.*" *Sefer Assia* 3 (1983): 485-6.

Haled, Yosef. "*Qviat Moed Hamavet L'inyan Ahriut Haplilit.*" *Medah Lerofeh* 26 (1981): 30-3.

Halperin, Mordechai. "*Al Da'ato Shel Hrhgm Feinstein.*" *Assia* 47-8 (5750): 6-13.

———. "*Hashtalat Lev B'israel.*" *Assia* 42-43 (5747): 70-80.

———, Chaim Brautber and David Nelkin. "*Qviat Abahut Be'emtsaut Ma'arehet Ti'um Hariqmot Hamerkazit.*" *T'humin* 4 (1983): 431-50.

Hastillo, A., ML Hess, DW Richardson and RR Lower. "Cardiac Transplantation—1980." *South Medical Journal* 73, no. 7 (1980): 909-11.

Hawthshome, Peter. *The Transplanted Heart: The Incredible Story by Chris Barnard and His Team*. Johannesburg: Hugh Keartland, 1968.

Ilai, Alon, ed. *Harefuah Tahat Izmal Hamusar*. Tel Aviv: Papyrus, 1981.

# Bibliography

Israel Medical Association Scientific Advisory Council. *"El Sar Habriut." Mikhtav Lehaver* Adar 26 (5729): 18.

Jonas, Hans. "Against the Stream: Comments on the Definition and Redefinition of Death." In *Philosophical Essays: From Ancient Creed to Technological Man*. New Jersey: Prentice Hall, 1974.

Kahn, Susan Martha. *Reproducing Jews*. Durham: Duke University Press, 2000.

Kasher, R. Menachem. *"Bi'ayat Hashtalat Halev." Noam* 13 (5730): 10-20.

Kass, Leon. "Death as an Event: A Commentary on Robert Morrison." *Science* 173 (1971): 698-702.

Kedem-Friedrich, P. and R. Rachmani. "Israelis Willingness to Donate Organs: Result of a Survey." *Transplant Proceedings* 31, no. 4 (1999): 1910-11.

Kenigsberg, R. Gedaliah and Mordechai Rabinowitz. *"Hagdarat Hamavet Veqviat Zmano Leor Hahalakhah." Hadarom* no. 32 (5731).

Khalidi, Muhammad Ali. "Carving Nature at the Joints." *Philosophy of Science* 60 (1993): 100-13.

Kirschenbaum, Aaron. *Equity in Jewish Law*. New York: Yeshiva University Press, 1991.

Knorr-Cetina, Karin D. *The Manufacture of Knowlege*. New York: Pergamon Press, 1981.

Kogan, A., G. Sahar, B. Orlov, P. Singer, J. Cohen, G. Godovic, E. Raanani, M. Berman, B. Vidne, D. Aravot. "Organ Transplantation Statistics in Different Countries: Internet Review." *Transplantation Proceedings* 35, no. 2 (2003): 641-2.

Koppel, Moshe. *Meta-Halacha: Logic, Intuition and the Unfolding of Jewish Law*. New Jersey: Jason Aronson, 1997.

Korchin, Amos. *"Mi Shotel Lemi." Mikhtav Lehaver* Cheshvan 14 (5730): 13-14.

_____. "*Qviat Nequdat Hamavet.*" *Mikhtav Lehaver* 7 (1975).

Korein, Julius. "The Problem of Brain Death: Development and History." In *Brain Death: Interrelated Medical and Social Issues*, ed., Julius Korein, 19-38. New York: New York Academy of Sciences, 1978.

Kripke, Saul. *Naming and Necessity.* Cambridge: Harvard UP, 1980.

Kunin, J. "Brain Death: Revisiting the Rabbinic Opinions in Light of Current Medical Knowledge." *Tradition* 38, no. 4 (2004): 48-62.

Lamb, David. *Death, Brain-Death and Ethics.* Sydney: Croom Helm, 1985.

LaPorte, Joseph. "Essential Membership." *Philosophy of Science* 64, no. 1 (1997): 96-112.

——. *Natural Kinds and Conceptual Change.* Cambridge: Cambridge UP, 2004.

Lavi, S. "Letter to the Editor." *Harefuah* 76, no. 2.

Leibman, Charles and Bernard Susser. "The Forgotten Center: Traditional Jewishness in Israel." *Modern Judaism* 17 (1997): 211-20.

Lepin, Jarrett. "Is Essentialism Unscientific?" *Philosophy of Science* 55 (1988): 493-510.

LeVay, Simon. *Queer Science: The Use and Abuse of Research into Homosexuality.* Cambridge, Mass: MIT Press, 1996.

Levi, Yaaqov. "*Hashtalat Averim Ve'etiqa Refuit.*" *Mikhtav Lehaver* Adar 4 (5730).

——. "*B'inyan Hashtalat Averim Mehamet.*" *Noam* 12 (5729): 291-312.

——. "*Davar Hame'ayeu Yilsiut Hunefesh.*" *Noam* 16 (5733): 53-63.

——. "*Qviat Hamavet Al Yedei Rofim.*" *Hamaayan* 9, no. 1 (5729): 24, 64.

——. "*Me'amatie Mutar Lehotsi Ever Lehashtala.*" *Hamaayan* 10, no. 1 (1969): 3-11.

# Bibliography

Levin, Phillip D. and Charles Sprung "Cultural Differences at the End of Life." *Critical Care Medicine* 31, no. 5 (Supplement) (2003): S352-57.

Levy, Morris. *"Shtilat Lev."* *Harefuah* (1968): 145.

Lichtenstein, R. Aaron. "The Israeli Chief Rabbinate: A Current Halakhic Perspective." *Tradition* 26, no. 4 (1992): 26-38.

Lifshitz, Y.Y. "Between Authority and Autonomy." *Azure* 7 (1999).

Loberbaum, Yair. *Tzelem Elohim*. Jerusalem: Shoken Press, 2004.

Lock, Margaret. *Twice Dead*. Berkley: University of California Press 2001.

Lynch, Michael. "The Discursive Production of Uncertainty." *Social Studies of Science* 28, no. 5-6 (1998): 829-68.

Mautner, Menachem. *Yeridat Haformalism Vealiyat Ha'arkhim Bemishpat Hayisraeli*. Tel Aviv: Maagli Tzedek, 1993.

Michaeli, Dan. *"Qviat Regah Hamavet."* *Mikhtav Lehaver* 49, no. 8 (5747).

Moore, Francis. "The Doctors' Dilemmas." In *Give and Take, the Development of Tissue Transplantation*. Philadelphia: Saunders, 1964.

Mor, Eytan. "Transplant Tourism in Israel: Effect on Transplant Practice and Organ Donation." http://www.elpat.eu/CDPraag/Presentation_Mor_text.pdf.

Morrison, Robert. "Death: Process or Event." *Science* 173 (1971): 694-7.

Ne'eman, Shmuel. *"Havat Daat Al Qviat Nequdat Hamavet."* *Mikhtav Lehaver* Tevet 11 (5735): 7-9.

Naor, A. *"Qriterionim Lematan Tipul Refuie Leholeh."* *Mikhtav Lehaver* (5735): 7-10.

Novak, David. "Bioethics and the Contemporary Jewish Community." *Hastings Center Report* 20, no. 4 (1990): 14-17.

Ouaknin, G. *"Mot Hamoah."* *Harefuah* 84, no. 6 (1973): 328-30.

# Really Dead?

—— and Y. Drori. *"Pe'ulat Halev Bematsav shel Mot Hamoah."* Harefuah 86, no. 10 (1974): 489-93.

Pallis, Christopher. *ABC of Brain Stem Death.* London: The British
Medical Journal, 1989.

Parsons, Talcot. *The Social System.* Glencoe, IL: Free Press, 1951.

Patterson, Dennis. *Law and Truth.* New York: Oxford University
Press, 1996.

Pernick, Martin. "Back from the Grave: Recurring Controversies
over Defining and Diagnosing Death in History." In *Death:
Beyond Whole-Brain Criteria, Philosophy and Medicine Series,* edited by Richard M. Zaner, 16-60. Dordrecht and Boston: Kluwer
Academic Publishers, 1988.

——. "Brain Death in Cultural Context." In *The Definition of Death:
Contemporary Controversies,* edited by Arnold, Schapiro, and
Younger, 3-33. Baltimore: John Hopkins University Press, 1999.

Phillips, Benjamin. "The Concept of Futility in Medical Care."
PhD. Diss., SUNY Buffalo, 1997.

Pinhas, Shmuel. *"Qviat Regah Hamavet Vehashtalat Averim
Meyuhadot."* Mikhtav Lehaver 49, no. 8 (5747): 8-9.

Putnam, Hillary. *Reason, Truth and History.* Cambridge: Cambridge
University Press, 1981.

Qafir, Elkanah. *Sefer Hilkhot Nituhe Holim Vemetim.* Jerusalem,
1969.

Qahat, R. Baruch. *"Od B'inyan Halut."* Tzohar 6, Spring (1991).

Quine, W.V. *Ontological Relativity and Other Essays.* New York:
Columbia University Press, 1969.

Rabinowitz, R. Gedaliah and Mordechai Kenigsberg. *"Hagderat
Hamavet Veqviat Zmano Leor Hahalacha."* Hadarom 32 (5731): 59-
76.

Rakover, Nachum. *Unjust Enrichment in Jewish Law.* Jerusalem: The
Library of Jewish Law, 2000.

# Bibliography

Reichman, Edward. "Don't Pull the Plug on Brain Death Just Yet." *Tradition*. 2004 Winter; 38, no. 4: 63-9.

———. "The Halachic Definition of Death in Light of Medical History." In *The Torah and Madda Journal*, ed., J. Schacter. New York: Yeshiva University Press, 1993.

Reiser, Stanley Joel. *Medicine and the Reign of Technology*. Cambridge: Cambridge University Press, 1978.

Rich, Ben. *Strange Bedfellows: How Medical Jurisprudence Has Influenced Medical Ethics and Medical Practice*. New York: Kluwer Academic, 2001.

Rosenberg, Alexander. *American Medical Schools and the Practice of Medicine*. Oxford: Oxford University Press, 1987.

———. *The Structure of Biological Science*. Cambridge: Cambridge University Press, 1985.

Rothstein, William G. *American Medical Schools and the Practice of Medicine*. Oxford: Oxford University Press, 1987.

Sacks, Jonathan. "Creativity and Innovation." In *Halakha, Rabbinic Authority and Personal Autonomy*, edited by Moshe Sokol. New Jersey: Jason Aronson, 1992.

Sagi, Avi. "*Halakhah Veshikul Hadaat*." In *Ben Samkhut Le'otonomiah*, eds. Zeev Safrai and Avi Sagi. Tel Aviv: Kibbutz Hameuchad, 1997.

Sagi, Avi and Daniel Statman. *Ben Daat Lemusar*. Ramat Gan: Bar Ilan University Press, 1993.

Saposnik G., G. Rizzo, A. Vega, R. Sabbatiello, and J.L. Deluca. "Problems Associated with the Apnea Test in the Diagnosis of Brain Death." *Neurology India* 52, no. 3 (2004): 342-5.

Shechner, A., Y. Ovil, and M. Levy. "*Shtilat Lev-Avar Veatid*." *Harefuah* 98, no. 5 (1980): 225-7.

Schiffer, R. B. "The Concept of Death: Causes and Criteria." *The Journal of Medicine and Philosophy* 4, no. 3 (1979): 227-30.

# Really Dead?

Segal, B. *"Mabat Hadash Al Trumat Averim." Mikhtav Lehaver* 47, no. 3 (1985): 7.

Shapira, R. Avraham. *"Harabbanut Hareshit Leyisrael B'inyan Keviat Rega Hamavet Vehashatalat Lev."* Or HaMizrach 31, no. 1 (1987): 66-70.

Shewmon, D. A. "Brainstem Death, 'Brain Death' And Death: A Critical Re-Evaluation of the Purported Equivalence." *Issues in Law & Medicine* 14, no. 2 (1998): 125-45.

_____ and Elisabeth Seitz Shewmon. "The Semiotics of Death and Its Medical Implications." In *Brain Death and Disorders of Consciousness*, eds, Calixto Machado and D. Alan Shewmon, 89-114. New York: Kluwer Academic Publishers, 2004.

Shor, David. *"B'inyan Simane Mitah." Hamaor* 298 (5747): 12-19.

Shryock, Richard H. "Changing Outlooks in American Medicine over Three Centuries." In *Essays in the History of Medicine Rx Honor of David J. Davis'M.D. Ph.D.*, 182-93. Chicago: Davis Lecture Committee, 1965.

Silber, I.F. "Convergences and Cleavages in the Study of Cultural Repetoires: Theorizing the Inner-Structure of Tool-Kits, Symbolic Boundaries and Regimes of Justification." In *Annual Meeting of the American Sociological Association*. Anaheim, CA, 2001.

Silman, Yochanan. *"Hiqavuyot Hilkhatiot Ben Nominalizm Verealizm." Dine Yisrael* 12 (1984-1985): 246-66.

Singer, P. "Cadaveric Organ Donation in Israel: The Facts and the Perspectives " *Annals of Transplantation* 4, no. 1 (1999): 5-10.

Soames, Scott. *Beyond Rigidity*. Oxford: Oxford University Press, 2002.

Sohmer, Chaim. *"Habasis Hamada'i-Refui Leqviat Mot Hamoah." Assia* 42-43 (5747): 84-91.

# Bibliography

Steinberg, Avraham. *"Qviat Regah Hamavet Vehashalat Lev." Assia* 44 (5748): 56-77.

——. *"Qviat Regah Hamavet." Noam* 19 (1976): 210-38.

___ and M. Hersch. "Decapitation of a Pregnant Sheep: A Contribution to the Brain Death Controversy." *Transplant Proceedings* 27, no. 2 (1995): 1886-7.

Stern, Yedidya. *"Negishut Hilkhatit Lesugiot Mediniot."* In *Ben Samkhut Le'otonomiah*, eds. Zeev Safrai and Avi Sagi. Tel Aviv: Kibbutz Hameuchad, 1997.

Sulmasy, Daniel P. "Diseases and Natural Kinds." *Theoretical Medicine and Bioethics* 26 (2005): 487-513.

Swindler, Ann. "Culture in Action: Symbols and Strategies." *American Sociological Review* 51 (1986): 273-86.

Tendler, Moshe David. "Confusion: Brainstem, Death, Pikuach Nefesh and Halachic Integrity." *The Jewish Observer* October 1991 (1991): 12-15.

——. *"Od Al Daat Hrgrm Feinstein." Assia* 51-52 (5762): 187-8.

——. "Response to Critics of Brain-Death Criteria." *JAMA* 240, no. 2 (1978): 109.

——. "Torah and Science: Constructs and Methodology." *Torah u-Madda Journal* 5 (1994): 168-81.

—— and Frank Veith. "In Response to an Opposing Viewpoint on Braindeath." *JAMA* 243, no. 18 (1980): 1808.

—— and Fred Rosner. "Brain Death." *Tradition* 28 no. 3 (1994).

Thevenot, Laurent and Michele Lamont. *Rethinking Comparative Cultural Sociology: Politics and Repetoires of Evaluation in France and the United States.* Cambridge: Cambridge University Press, 2000.

Toulmin, Stephen and Albert Jonsen. *The Abuse of Casuistry.* Berkley: University of California Press, 1990.

Turner, Victor. *The Ritual Process: Structure and Anti-Structure*. Chicago: Aldine, 1969.

Underwood, Charles Singer and E. Ashworth. *A Short History of Medicine*. New York: Oxford University Press, 1962.

Veatch, Robert. "The Conscience Clause: How Much Individual Choice in Defining Death Can Our Society Tolerate?" in *The Definition of Death: Contemporary Controversies*, eds. Robert Arnold, Renie Schapiro and Stuart Youngner. Baltimore: John Hopkins University Press, 1999.

——. *Death, Dying and the Biological Revolution: Our Last Quest for Responsibility*. New Haven: Yale University Press, 1976.

Veith, F. J., J. M. Fein, M. D. Tendler, R. M. Veatch, M. A. Kleiman, and G. Kalkines. "Brain Death. I. A Status Report of Medical and Ethical Considerations." *JAMA* 238, no. 15 (1977): 1651-5.

Vonnegut, Kurt. *Cat's Cradle*. London: Gollancz, 1963.

Weisman, Joshua. "Organs as Assets." *Israel Law Review* 27, no. 4 (1993): 611-23.

Weistreich, Elimelech. *"Refuah Vemada'e Hateva Bep'siqat Bat'e Din Harabani'im."* *Mishpatim* 26, no. 3 (1996): 425-92.

Wijdicks, E. F. "Brain Death Worldwide: Accepted Fact but No Global Consensus in Diagnostic Criteria." *Neurology* 58, no. 1 (2002): 20-5.

Wildes, Kevin. *Moral Aquaintances: A Methodology in Bioethics*. Notre Dame, Ind.: University of Notre Dame Press, 2000.

Winch, Peter. *The Idea of a Social Science and Its Relation to Philosophy*. London: Routledge, 1999.

Wolf, Daniel. *Minhah L'aharon*. Alon Shvut: Yeshivat Har Etzion, 2005.

Wolstenholme, G. E. W. and Maeve O'Connor, ed. *Ethics in Medical Progress: With Special Attention to Transplantation 1966* (Ciba

Foundation Symposium). Boston: Little, Brown and Company, 1966.

Wozner, Beit Horaah shel Rav. "*Zihui Hilkhati Al Pi Bediqat DNA*." *T'humin* 21 (2001): 121-2.

Wozner, R. "*Al Hashtalat Lev*." *Sefer Assia* 42-43 (5747): 92-4.

Wuthnow, Robert. *Meaning and Moral Order*. Berkley: University of California Press, 1987.

Yaakov, E.T., Z. Shapira, E. Cantor, N. Bar-Nathan, G. Boner. "*Nitzul Meravi Shel Klayot Min Hamet*." *Harefuah* 90, no. 12 (1976): 552-6.

Yisraeli, R. Shaul. "*Lebirur Samkhutah Hahilhatit Shel Harabanut Harashit Leyisrael*." In *Amud Hayemini*, 51-7. Jerusalem: Eretz Chemda, 1992.

——. "*Beheter Hashtalat Haylev Kayom*." *Barkai* 4: Spring (1987): 33-40.

——. "*Hovat Hasha'ah*." In *Harabanut Vehamedinah*, edited by Avraham Israel Sarid, 38-9. Jerusalem: Erez, 1991.

——. "*Ha'ubar Umamado Hahuqi-Mishpati Vekeger*." In *Chavat Benyimin*, ed. Neriah Gutel. Part of CD-Rom, *T'humin* + (version 2.0). Place Published: Machon Zomet, 1992.

——. "*Qolah Shel Harabanut Lo Nishma*." In *Harabbinute Vehamedinah*, ed. Avraham Israel Sarid, 86. Jerusalem: Erez, 1991.

Yosef, R. Ovadiah. "*Heter Agunot Memigdal Hate'umim Benu York*." *T'humin* 23 (2003): 97-109.

Zohar, Noam. *Alternatives in Jewish Bioethics*. Albany: SUNY Press, 1997.

Zola, Irving Kenneth. "Medicine as an Institution of Social Control." *Sociological Review* 20 (1972): 487-504.

Zolod, Shaul. "*Hashtalat Levavot*." *Mikhtav Lehaver* Adar 10 (5728).

# Really Dead?

Zweibel, Chaim Dovid. "A Matter of Life and Death." *The Jewish Observer* June (1991): 11-14.

——. "A Matter of Life and Death-Revisited." *The Jewish Observer* July (1991): 11-22.


*Responsa*: accessed digitally from *The Responsa Project (Version 14+)*. Ramat Gan: Bar-Ilan University.

Auerbach, R. Shlomo Zalman. *Minhat Shlomo.*

Feinstein, R. Moshe. *Egrot Moshe.*

Risher, R. Yaaqov b. Yosef. *Shvut Yaaqov.*

Waldenburg, R. Eliezer. *Tsits Eliezer.*

Weiss, R. Yitshaq. *Minhat Yitshaq.*

## Court Cases

*Criminal Appeal: Natan Ben Yechezkial Belker Vs. Medinat Yisrael 341/82*, **Pisqe Din**, Volume 41, I, 1987 (1986).

*Criminal Case 369/78* Tel Aviv, (unpublished).

*Civil Appeal: Sharon et al. Vs. Levi 548/78*, **Pisqe Din**, Volume 35, I.

Civil *Appeal: Peloni Vs. Peloni et al. 705/79*, **Taqstir Pisqe Din**, Volume 19.

*Civil Appeal Peloni Vs. Pelonit 417/80*, **Pisqe Din**, Volume 37, III.

www.ingramcontent.com/pod-product-compliance
Lightning Source LLC
Chambersburg PA
CBHW062147080426
42734CB00010B/1593